Teacher Education for Sustainable Development and Global Citizenship

This book examines how educators internationally can better understand the role of education as a public good designed to nurture peace, tolerance, sustainable livelihoods and human fulfilment.

Bringing together empirical and theoretical perspectives, this insightful text develops new understandings of Education for Sustainable Development and Global Citizenship (ESD/GC) and illustrates how these might impact on educational research, policy and practice. The text recognises ESD/GC as pivotal to the universal ambitions of UNESCO's Sustainable Development Goals, and focuses on the role of teachers and teacher educators in delivering the appropriate educational response to promote equity and sustainability. Chapters explore factors including curriculum design, values and assessment in teacher education, and consider how each and every learner can be guaranteed an understanding of their role in promoting a just and sustainable global society.

This book will be of great interest to academics, researchers, school leaders, practitioners, policy makers and students in the fields of education, teacher education and sustainability.

Philip Bamber is Associate Professor of Education at Liverpool Hope University, UK.

Critical Global Citizenship Education
Edited by Carlos Alberto Torres
University of California Los Angeles, USA

Theoretical and Empirical Foundations of Critical Global Citizenship Education
Carlos Alberto Torres

Educating the Global Environmental Citizen
Understanding Ecopedagogy in Local and Global Contexts
Greg William Misiaszek

The Struggle for Citizenship Education in Egypt
(Re)Imagining Subjects and Citizens
Edited by Jason Nunzio Dorio, Ehaab D. Abdou, Nashwa Moheyeldine

Teacher Education for Sustainable Development and Global Citizenship
Critical Perspectives on Values, Curriculum and Assessment
Edited by Philip Bamber

Teacher Education for Sustainable Development and Global Citizenship

Critical Perspectives on Values, Curriculum and Assessment

Edited by Philip Bamber

NEW YORK AND LONDON

First published 2020
by Routledge
605 Third Avenue, New York, NY 10017

and by Routledge
2 Park Square, Milton Park, Abingdon, Oxon, OX14 4RN

First issued in paperback 2020

Routledge is an imprint of the Taylor & Francis Group, an informa business

Library of Congress Cataloging-in-Publication Data
A catalog record for this book has been requested

ISBN 13: 978-0-367-72743-7 (pbk)
ISBN 13: 978-1-138-38551-1 (hbk)

Typeset in Sabon
by Apex CoVantage, LLC

Recognising that the climate crisis is an issue of intergenerational justice, this book is dedicated to the following children, young people and future educators among the families and friends of those who have contributed to this publication:

Abass Issah Karim, Abigail Fehrenbach, Adam Franch Goodwin, Aidan O'Malley, Alexander Nasir Illich, Alex Doherty, Alex Fehrenbach, Alice Sund, Amelia Bamber, Angela Hibberd, Annie Brett, Arlo Corbishley, Arman Forghani-Arani, Cairine Lindo, Callum Allington, Charlotte Coles, Chloe Armitage, Christopher Brown, Christopher Rahim Illich, Ciaran O'Malley, Cicilia Wangui, Connor Scott, Cora Bullivant, Cora Stockdale, Daniel Brown, Darrell Pope, David Baker, Daisy Clarke, Debbie Lang, Dominic Bamber, Eddie Clarke, Edward McClelland, Elsie Simpson, Eleftheria Leontari, Elliot Bamber, Emily Fox, Emma Baker, Erin Eynon-Daly, Evan Bamber, Ewan Simpson, Fern Simpson, Fiona Wilson, Francis Guidi, Galen Bullivant, Gina Venn, Grace Brown, Grace Murphy, Harry Brown, Harry McLaughlin, Hope Simpson, Isabelle Matthews, Isobel Fenlon, Isobel Simpson, Jaime Sapsford, James Mills, Jemima Everall, Jess Wilson, Jodie Griffiths Hagan, Joe Doherty, Joey Fehrenbach, Joseph Guidi, Josh Allington, Kaitlyn Matthews, Karen Richardson, Kashi Greening, Katie Fox, Kerrin Duke, Kieran Pope, Kristen Bullivant, Lewis Fuchs, Liam McFarlane, Liam O'Malley, Lola Sinnamon-Hannafin, Lorna MacLeod, Lottie White, Luca Guidi, Lucy Bamber, Lucy Basnett, Luke Daly, Mabel Everall, Maeve Murphy, Manuela Schoffel, Megan Eynon-Daly, Mercy Macharia, Morgan Griffiths Hagan, Nadia Begum Pirbhai, Nora Duke, Oliver Fuchs, Olivia Matthews, Omar Alloush, Owen Griffiths Hagan, Pat Daly, Paul Daly, Peter Guidi, Peter McClelland, Peter Pollard, Poppy White, Raja Aloujami, Rebecca Armitage, Rebecca Martin-Wolfenden, Rhys Bamber, Robin Vernon Cardiff, Roman Lowe, Sam Ashton, Samuel MacLeod, Steph Pope, Stuart Martin, Taghd Sinnamon-Hannafin, Teddy George Bamber Readman, Tess Vernon Cardiff, Thea McFarlane, Tirej Al Joul Bek, Toby Everall, Tom Daly, Zac Mills, Zulfikar Ali Pirbhai . . .

and all tomorrow's children.

Contents

Figures and Tables

Figures

Tables

Contributors

Liz Allum has been working in global education for over fifteen years at Reading International Solidarity Centre, the core global education provider for Berkshire and Oxfordshire, supporting teachers and other educators across the South-East of England and beyond to embed social justice and sustainability in and beyond the curriculum. She has written numerous teaching resources and designs and delivers training on a wide range of subjects, for any and all educators. She also works independently as a trainer and facilitator specialising in philosophy for children and critical thinking in education, as well as in delivering global education through the creative arts.

Philip Bamber is Assistant Dean and Head of the School of Education at Liverpool Hope University. His research is concerned with transformative education, service-learning, education for citizenship and values in education. It has been published in the *British Journal of Educational Studies*, *Journal of Beliefs and Values*, *Journal of Curriculum Studies* and *Journal of Transformative Education*. Philip is Associate-Director of TEESNet, the UK Teacher Education for Equity and Sustainability Network and was awarded the International Association of University Presidents International Education Faculty Achievement Award in 2013 for leadership in research and teaching in global citizenship.

Julie Brown is head of Practical Action's education unit. Her team produces Science, Technology, Engineering and Maths (STEM) teaching resources and delivers training to UK teachers, demonstrating how they can embed global learning into their STEM teaching. Julie developed the successful European Commission funding bid for the 'Technology Challenging Poverty: Make the Link Project 2013–2016' and was responsible for overall implementation and reporting on the project.

Katie Carr is an independent trainer and facilitator of collaborative, participatory learning processes with fifteen years of experience within formal education settings, with communities, and within organisations. She has worked extensively with educators and school leaders supporting them to critically engage with development and sustainability issues, by developing and promoting approaches to learning that are based in empowerment, democracy and sustainability. Katie is studying an MA in Sustainability Leadership Development with the University of Cumbria's Institute for Leadership and Sustainability, UK.

Alison Clark is an associate of Liverpool World Centre, UK. Her current roles include educational research projects and supporting schools to develop their chosen values. She also works with start-up companies to identify their business values and to shape company culture and ethos, including awareness of the Sustainable Development Goals. Prior to this, Alison was a high school teacher for twenty-one years, and a college lecturer and a university lecturer for eleven years, gaining a PhD in 2005 focussing on *Values Formation and the Teacher*.

Helen Clarke is senior fellow of Learning and Teaching at the University of Winchester, UK, and senior fellow of the Higher Education Academy. She has particular expertise in science education in the early years and primary phases. Committed to celebrating the energy and enthusiasm that children, students and teachers bring to their learning, she has researched children's early exploration and enquiry, Rights Respecting Education, sustainability, environmental education and teacher development, both in the UK and overseas. She is currently working with a colleague to explore innovative teaching and learning ideas that connect children to environments through place attention and responsiveness (@Attention2place).

Angela Daly is senior lecturer in education studies and early childhood studies at Liverpool John Moores University, UK. Angela works alongside partners in development, combining participatory learning in action and collaborative research approaches to create formative learning spaces with practitioners from education, international and community development.

Rosalind Duke is lecturer in global citizenship education with the Development and Intercultural Education in Initial Teacher Education (DICE) Project. Based at Dublin City University, Institute of Education, she focuses on understanding and teaching issues of sustainability with student teachers, including understandings of peace and conflict. She lectures on Restorative Practice as an important foundation for good education, for authentic citizenship skills and for the development of all aspects of sustainability. She is a practising mediator and works with a Restorative Justice programme within the Irish criminal justice system.

Neda Forghani-Arani is senior lecturer and senior researcher in the Centre for Teacher Education at the University of Vienna, Austria. Her teaching and research are centred in initial teacher education, professionalisation and professional development, with a specific interest in teaching in school settings characterised by student diversity. Her publications address issues of intercultural education, global education, pedagogical tact and diversity competencies. Her current research is concerned with teachers' lived experience in the pedagogical encounter with otherness, on learning to teach in uncertainty, and being a teacher on the rough ground of social change.

Sara Franch is currently a PhD candidate at the Free University of Bolzano-Bozen, Italy. Her research focuses on how global citizenship education is conceptualised, translated into local policies and integrated in the curriculum. She teaches Global Citizenship Education and Education for Sustainable Development at the same university and has extensive experience of designing and delivering courses, seminars and workshops for teachers, non-government organisation practitioners and young people. She has worked for over fifteen years in the international development sector, managing programmes in Liberia, Sudan, Burma, Cambodia and Timor Leste, advising on the quality of civil society development programmes and developing projects and training activities on international development and global citizenship.

Charles A. Hopkins, a former school superintendent in the City of Toronto, is now the UNESCO Chair in Reorienting Education towards Sustainability at York University in Toronto, Canada, where he coordinates two research networks focussed on Education for Sustainable Development (ESD). The first network, founded in 1999, is comprised of teacher education institutions spanning seventy countries, reorienting teacher education to address the Sustainable Development Goals and the Global Education 2030 Agenda. Completing research which indicated that embedding sustainability issues in curricula in schools across eighteen countries enhanced the overall education quality led to the formation of a second research network (#IndigenousESD), covering institutions in forty countries. This current research seeks evidence of using local sustainability issues to improve the education and training of Indigenous youth. Hopkins has consulted for various institutions worldwide, including governments, universities and school systems. He is advisor to the United Nations University's global programme on Regional Centres of Expertise in ESD, UNESCO-UNEVOC on technical and vocational education and co-director of the Asia-Pacific Institute on ESD in Beijing, China. As an international speaker he has delivered lectures in over seventy countries and has numerous publications.

Mallika Kanyal is senior lecturer at Anglia Ruskin University, UK, and currently leads the Foundation Degree in Early Years, both face-to-face and online. Mallika's current research interest is around the usefulness of participatory research and its place as an alternative approach to conventional research in education. Her research focuses around the pedagogical use of participatory approaches in early years as well as in higher education. She has published this work under the strand of children's participatory rights in early years and students' voice in higher education.

Chris Keelan has several years of experience teaching in secondary schools in England and in higher education in Germany. He is currently employed as a professional tutor at Liverpool Hope University, working with both secondary and primary student teachers. He is interested in modern foreign languages, second language acquisition, EAL teaching and the impact of the refugee crisis on education.

Zoe Lavin-Miles is on the executive committee of OMEP UK (World Organisation for Early Childhood Education and Care) and with her colleagues supports Education for Sustainable Development (ESD) projects in early childhood both internationally and nationally. After her undergraduate studies in Wildlife Conservation and Environmental Policy, she became an environmental consultant, educator and forest school leader. Having worked as a bat surveyor for three years, she wrote an ESD project about bats for a preschool in Dorset. OMEP UK supports UNICEF W.A.S.H. and the United Nations Sustainable Development Goals in early years and is committed to the education and support of its members in environmental, cultural and economic sustainability.

Barbara Lowe was a founding member of Reading International Solidarity Centre (RISC) in England, where she worked for thirty-one years, providing continuing professional development to schools and student teachers at Reading, Oxford and Oxford Brookes Universities. She co-developed the Global Teachers Award for the Consortium of Development Education Centres (CoDEC), where she was a director. She has authored numerous global citizenship publications, exhibitions, chapters, articles for subject associations, and national and international conference papers. These include teaching resources published by RISC covering art and design, design and technology, history, geography and RE for teachers of early years, primary and secondary ages. She has a long-standing interest in evaluating the impact of global citizenship education on young people, teachers and school communities and has co-authored three widely respected works on this subject. Barbara's passion for development education remains undiminished.

Paulette Luff is principal lecturer in the School of Education and Social Care at Anglia Ruskin University, UK. She currently leads the MA in Early Childhood Education and convenes the Early Childhood

Research Group. Paulette has worked in education throughout her career. Her specialist areas of teaching, doctoral supervision, writing and research are: observation for learning and research; professional enquiry; education for sustainability; and creative and cultural learning. Paulette is an active member of OMEP (World Organisation for Early Childhood) and president of the OMEP UK executive committee. With OMEP colleagues, she campaigns for early childhood Education for Sustainable Development.

Fran Martin, a white Western, gay, middle-class scholar, has lived all her life in England. She brings a critical lens to global and intercultural learning in postcolonial contexts. Her work focuses on the nature of the 'inter', or location between cultures, as a space for intercultural learning. Bringing spatial understandings from geography, and dialogic understandings from education, her research contests policies that reduce successful intercultural communication to the acquisition of a set of skills and competencies, arguing that knowledge of the histories (socio-cultural, political) and the power dynamics behind the relationship of those in conversation is a crucial factor influencing what is 'heard', how it is 'translated' and therefore what it is possible to learn from each other.

Jacqueline Neve has over fifteen years of experience in teaching across a range of primary schools within Merseyside, England. She is currently working at Liverpool Hope University as a professional tutor, with primary responsibility for initial teacher education provision in teaching English as an Additional Language (EAL). Her interest in this project comes from a culmination of community-based projects alongside working predominantly in primary schools with a high percentage of EAL pupils.

Zoi Nikiforidou is senior lecturer in early childhood at Liverpool Hope University, UK, teaching undergraduate and postgraduate courses. Her research interests relate to methodological and theoretical issues on teaching and learning in early childhood, with an emphasis on the role of cognition, pedagogy and technology. Zoi is a co-convenor of the Holistic Wellbeing SIG of EECERA and a member of the OMEP UK Executive Committee, where, with colleagues, she advocates for Education for Sustainable Development.

Opeyemi Osadiya is a doctoral researcher with Anglia Ruskin University, UK. She was previously a lecturer of early years education in a college of further and higher education in the UK. Opeyemi's current research interest is in Education for Sustainable Development in the early years. Her research focuses on how teaching and learning can be shaped to promote Education for Sustainable Development in the early years using participatory approaches.

Karen Pashby is reader at Manchester Metropolitan University, UK. An experienced secondary, tertiary and teacher educator (in Toronto, Northern Quebec, suburban Brazil and northern Finland), she engages theoretical and empirical research supporting new ways of relating within and across differences through ethical global issues pedagogy. Her recent work, supported by a British Academy grant, brought together critical literacy work informed by postcolonial theory in both environmental and sustainability education and global citizenship education to co-produce a resource for supporting a complex and ethical approach to global issues in secondary classrooms with teachers in England, Finland and Sweden.

Fatima Pirbhai-Illich, a brown, feminist and transnational educational researcher of South Asian descent, was born in Tanganyika (Tanzania after independence) and immigrated to Canada at the age of sixteen. She brings a critical lens to language and literacy education, specifically to the intercultural space between white mainstream Canadian pre-service teachers and the minoritised and marginalised students they work with, including those from First Nations communities. Her praxis focuses on creating innovative approaches to language and literacy education using culturally responsive pedagogies within a decolonising framework. Her research deepens understandings of the beliefs systems and the historical, cultural, political, social and economic contexts that affect how diverse cultural groups learn with and alongside each other in the specific postcolonial context that the province of Saskatchewan in western Canada offers.

Stephen Scoffham is visiting reader in sustainability and education at Canterbury Christ Church University, UK, where he has worked for many years as a teacher educator. A long-term member of the Canterbury Development Education Centre, he is currently chair of Education4Diverstiy, a local group dedicated to working with refugees and education. Stephen has written widely on environmental education and primary school geography and is the author/consultant for the *Collins Junior World Atlas* and the Collins *'In Maps'* atlas series. His research interests focus on sustainability, creativity, cartography and international understanding, and his latest books include *Teaching Primary Geography* and *Leadership for Sustainability in Higher Education*. Stephen has been involved with the Geographical Association for many years and is currently its president (2018–2019).

Jen Simpson qualified as a primary teacher, later joining Cheshire Development Education Centre in the UK as an Education Officer. In 2014, she was appointed as a local advisor for the Global Learning Programme (GLP) for Cheshire and Merseyside. She completed an MA module with University College London on global development, followed by two research projects for the GLP Innovation Fund. She is also trained to Level 3, Advanced Facilitator in Philosophy for Children (P4C), a passion which she has developed over many years and led to a new role in 2017 as Assistant National Training Manager for SAPERE, the Society for the Advancement of Philosophical Enquiry and Reflection in Education. Her research interests centre around pedagogy, student participation, social justice and considering methods for influencing teachers' practice and enjoyment in teaching.

Louise Sund is an experienced secondary school teacher, a teacher educator at Mälardalen University's School of Education, and a researcher in education at Örebro University's School of Humanities, all in Sweden. She is a member of the research group SMED (Studies of Meaning-Making in Educational Discourses), a cross-university research group in the field of didactics and educational science at Örebro University. Louise has an interest in environmental and sustainability education and citizenship education. Her research interests include philosophical perspectives and approaches to education and sustainable development. Louise is a member of the network Environmental and Sustainability Education Research for the European Conference on Educational Research.

Victoria W. Thoresen holds the UNESCO Chair for Education about Sustainable Lifestyles at the Collaborative Learning Centre for Sustainable Development at Inland Norway University of Applied Sciences. Thoresen has specialised in curriculum development, global education, peace education, value-based education and consumer education. In addition to many years of experience as a teacher and teacher trainer, Thoresen has written articles and textbooks and functioned as an international educational consultant. As leader of PERL, the Partnership for Education and Research about Responsible Living, she has worked closely with UNEP, UNESCO and other international agencies, in particular on the 10-Year Framework of Programmes on Sustainable Lifestyles and Education and the U.N. Decade on Education for Sustainable Development and Global Action Plan for ESD. Thoresen has been an invited speaker at many conferences on sustainable human development, education and behaviour change, citizenship and social responsibility, economic growth and well-being.

Carlos Alberto Torres is Distinguished Professor of Education, UNESCO Chair in Global Learning and Global Citizenship Education, and Director of the Paulo Freire Institute at the University of California, Los Angeles (UCLA), USA. He is President of the World Council of Comparative Education Societies, Founding Director of the Paulo Freire Institutes in Sao Paulo, Buenos Aires and at UCLA, and Past President of the Comparative International Education Society.

David Vernon has over fifteen years of teaching experience in primary schools, working in a wide range of different settings but with a particular expertise working with children aged seven to eleven. He currently leads the final year of primary undergraduate initial teacher education at Liverpool Hope University, UK. He has senior leadership experience in the primary sector with specific responsibilities for assessment, pupil progress and attainment. David is also interested in the social and emotional aspects of learning and how schools can ensure effective provision to support and develop children holistically as well as academically. Added to this, he is keen to promote the wider significance of education and the potential it has in creating a fairer, more equitable society, particularly in 'bridging the gap' for the most vulnerable.

Sharon Witt is senior lecturer at the University of Winchester, UK, and senior fellow of the Higher Education Academy. Sharon is passionate about educational place encounters and playful pedagogies. She loves to work with primary-aged children, student teachers and educators in local areas, woodlands, coasts and wild landscapes. Sharon's doctorate is a post- qualitative experiment in which she explores posthumanist/new materialist perspectives to consider an expanded notion of fieldwork that places relational thinking and understanding at the heart of geography. She is currently working with a colleague to explore innovative teaching and learning ideas that connect children to environments through place attention and responsiveness (@Attention2place).

Series Editor Foreword

This book, edited by Philip Bamber, emerges from work connected to the United Kingdom Teacher Education Network for Education for Sustainable Development/Global Citizenship, formed in 2007 and renamed in 2012 as the UK Teacher Education for Equity and Sustainability Network (TEESNet). The Network aims to integrate issues of social and environmental justice, poverty eradication and ecological conservation and social and biological diversity. It also was formed with the commitment to work on teacher education and how curriculum and instruction could bring these critical issues into the classrooms. Yet, though situated in the UK, the work is by no means restricted to the UK or Western themes but reflect multiple international experiences trying to understand the role of educators as agents of change.

This book is divided in three parts. A focus on values as a framework to the conversation articulates part 1. Part 2, in turn, discusses curriculum and instruction, with intriguing suggestions for teachers and teaching. Finally, part 3 focuses on assessment. With the digital culture, millennials may not be accustomed to reading extensively. Perhaps that is one of the reasons each chapter, in addition to being clear and concise, is mercifully brief. Focussing on the holistic, critical and transformative dimensions of Education for Sustainable Development and Global Citizenship, many of the chapters discuss the multilayered tensions among and within spaces, the different agendas that may collide in the context of implementing the SDG and Global Citizenship, but also the richness of options and possibilities in what Giddens properly defined as 'utopian realism'.[1]

The conversation about these topics needs to be reframed politically and theoretically. There is enough discussion on this subject to argue that Global Citizenship Education (GCE) and sustainability may represent the culmination of democratic global cosmopolitanism and cosmopolitan democracy in the twenty-first century. As such, both projects in their conjunction could be rhetorically defined as the civic education for the twenty-first century. However, these two models are not without their problems and push-backs.

There are two different strands of pushback against GCE. One is associated to populist, nationalist, ethnocentric and authoritarian models aiming to undermine liberal democracy. Proponents react against the globalisation 'pedigree' adjudicated to GCE and, by implication, against any model of cosmopolitanism which they perceive with suspicion as a foreign intervention of the world's elites.

Is it possible to dissociate globalisation from GCE and, at the same time, challenge the populist, ethnocentric, authoritarian models reaffirming the validity of GCE? Keep in mind that authoritarian populism seems to be losing steam in 2019 judging from the failure of Donald Trump and the Republican Party administration in the mid-term USA elections and similar electoral events in Western and Eastern Europe.

A second pushback against GCE comes from local or regional concepts, such as Ubuntu (Africa) or El Buen Vivir (Latin America), to cite just two. There is a tension between these local concepts and the concept of democratic cosmopolitanism that has been articulated since the eighteenth century by Kant and other modern Western philosophers. This model of democratic cosmopolitanism to some extent rests on the concept of the common good but on world scale. So, what type of democratic cosmopolitanism, if any at all, will be acceptable to practitioners of Ubuntu, El Buen Vivir or similar local or regional models?

The concept of common good is central for a model of cosmopolitan democratic citizenship, including Global Citizenship Education. Without a reference to the common good at a global level, GCE as an emerging concept may not have resonance and operational value. The challenge is to contrast common good as a cosmopolitan concept sustaining the goals of GCE with regional concepts like Ubuntu or El Buen Vivir, which may serve similar purposes but may not be fully cosmopolitan in the traditional sense of the expression. How to articulate both set of concepts, local and global, constitutes a real challenge both in terms of policy and in terms of theory defining exactly, as UNESCO has hinted, that GCE is a framework for implementation.[2]

Making the situation more conflictive indeed, GCE and sustainability are interrelated concepts but emerging from different policy and research programmes, perhaps even responding to somewhat different agendas, audiences and narratives. How to reconcile these audiences and agendas is a complex task. How do they intersect with each other? How does one help the goals of the other? What are the conditions for both of them being simultaneously implemented with mutual beneficial outcomes in their intersections? It seems that a majority of people, facing the global warming crisis, tend to agree with the need for sustainability, but it is not that clear that there is the same generic agreement for GCE. So, what difference does GCE make to the project of sustainability?

The importance of this book resides in the importance of education and its role on teaching values. We should be unambiguous. There is a tumultuous set of values at play in schooling, informal and non-formal education, well captured in this sentence by António Teodoro:

> national educational systems were used to assimilate immigrant cultures, to encourage patriotic values, to promote established religious doctrines, to disseminate the standardized norm of the national language, to generalize new patterns and rational forms of thought, to inculcate moral discipline, and, especially, to indoctrinate according to the creeds and economic policies of the ruling classes.[3]

How to make sense of these values as they pertain to moving forward the agendas of Global Citizenship Education and sustainability is a worthy endeavour, but the job is fraught with perils and challenges, as this book tries to make it clear in all its examples, analyses and theories.

What the readers have in their hands is a number of insightful and practical experiences of how to bring GCE and sustainability into classrooms and make them count. TEESNet thrives on three dimensions that are highlighted throughout the book: holistic, critical and transformative dimensions of ESD/GC (Education for Sustainable Development and Global Citizenship). The authors hope these three dimensions permeate the work in their three areas of concern: values, teaching and curriculum, and assessment. Perhaps the best way to define this book is with the term 'transdisciplinary research': knowledge emerging from this type of research may nurture both global sustainability and global citizenship. It is up to the reader to judge the different experiences, analyses and knowledge produced in this book.

Carlos Alberto Torres

Notes

1. Anthony Giddens, Preface to Benno Werlen, Editor. *Global Sustainability. Cultural Perspectives and Challenges for Transdisciplinary Integrated Research.* London, Springer, 2015, vii.
2. UNESCO. *Accountability in education: Meeting our commitments.* A review of Education for Sustainable Development and Global Citizenship Education in Teacher Education. Paper commissioned for the 2017/18 Global Education Monitoring Report, *Accountability in education: Meeting our commitments.*
3. António Teodoro "The Political Construction of European Education Space", in Robert Arnove, Carlos Alberto Torres, and Stephen Franz, *Comparative Education: The Dialectics of the Global and the Local.* Lanham, MD, United States, Rowman & Littlefield, 2012, fourth edition, page 447.

Foreword

What is a 'global citizen'? What makes a citizen a global one? Are we all global citizens in today's interconnected word? What does global citizenship as a concept entail for us, both individually and collectively? What is involved in becoming a global citizen? Are we referring to a cessation of nation states or creating one worldwide government? What are the rights of such a citizen? How does this pursuit align with the United Nations' overarching development framework of the 2030 Agenda for Sustainable Development?

In September of 2012, Ban Ki-Moon, then Secretary-General of the United Nations (UN), launched his Global Education First Initiative, including the concept of Global Citizenship Education (GCE) amongst the three priorities. Rather than defining the concept strictly, it was meant to provide a framework to address the sense of belonging and identity within society, rising to a global responsibility to address the existing inequalities in the world. Using the power of education, GCE was thought to provide guidance in how we are dealing with the world's existing injustices, changing values and disparities, and addressing the challenges of the digital transformation. Member states responded in different ways: some introduced GCE as an additional discipline or a new goal; others looked for what they were already doing in their education systems. Yet, even if formal inclusion of GCE into curricula has taken place, to many of the world's almost 90 million teachers at all levels of education, this concept is still unknown or perplexing. With 69 million additional teachers needed in order to achieve the education goals of the 2030 Agenda for Sustainable Development, GCE is one of the most crucial concepts to understand and to apply in the classroom in order to deliver quality education for students.

The alignment of GCE with sustainable development and lifelong quality education for all has now emerged as a global priority for all ministries of education. Embedded in the UN Sustainable Development Goals (SDGs) within the 2030 Agenda for Sustainable Development, and highlighted as aspects of the Global Education 2030 Agenda in SDG 4.7, there is a new need for teacher educators to embed both GCE and

Education for Sustainable Development (ESD) into both their pre- and in-service programming. Since the launch of the Global Education Monitoring Report in 2015, nations are being monitored annually regarding their progress in implementing not only SDG 4.7, which includes both GCED and ESD, but all of SDG 4.

While the conceptual framework for Education for Sustainable Development and Global Citizenship (ESD/GC) is continually developing, many consider ESD/GC as a state of mindfulness and caring for the planet, all human beings and all other living entities with whom we share the globe. It is concerned more with global responsibilities than rights and fosters opportunity for empowerment applied both to the individual and to the collective actions of society as a whole. In this expanded sense, nation states, corporations and other institutions can also be deemed global citizens and hence should adhere to the underlying principles of GCE.

Written around the three core education elements of values, curriculum and assessment, this book provides guidance to educators, those who prepare future teachers and those who develop curricula in order to address issues relating to the active role of citizens in advocating for sustainable development. Covering perspectives from a number of regions of the world, the authors unravel the complexities and challenges to address the concepts underpinning ESD/GC and underline the major potential contribution necessary to achieve quality education in light of SDG 4 for effective education systems today and in the future.

The first section draws on a number of examples to mindfully engage educators in exploring their own values and ethics. This is a critical step in helping student teachers and teacher educators to prepare for future changes and decisions, yet unknown, that they will encounter in the future. The individual's own construction of an internal learning guidance system that will shape their future choices and decision making is an important aspect of quality education and distinguishes the pursuit of ESD/GC from either simple training or mere indoctrination. Forming this personal value dimension that will impact how the next generations will treat the planet and 'others', be they known or unknown, living nearby or in some remote region, human or simply another being on the planet, are all aspects of both GCE and ESD.

The book progresses from this important discussion of values to use the research and experience of educators from around the world to show practical cases of curriculum approaches and activities that meaningfully engage students from preschool to higher education. Examples shared range from place-based learning activities to exploration in thoughtful dialogue. All exemplars offer perspectives on ESD/GC that encourage us, and those we teach, to live our lives in a manner that will not preclude future generations from living a full life, embellished by well-being.

Fortunately, this book does not shy away from the usual complications of monitoring and assessment. Educators have long understood and acknowledged that not all that can be counted actually counts and much of what counts cannot be counted immediately. As a result of this understanding, educators realise they must go on planting the seeds of ideas they will not personally see harvested in the future. We must assess what we can but cannot exclude topics from the curriculum that we have not learnt to assess (yet). Assigning a numerical indicator for compassion or concern is difficult, but as with developing and nurturing most human qualities, educators should not abstain to focus on other more easily measured attributes. They need to let these new concepts grow in their own time while constantly developing better frameworks of appropriate assessment.

In the search for a sustainable future, preparing a citizenry with a knowledgeable, thoughtful and inclusive human world view must find a central place in all societies as advocated by this book. This will begin in the education systems of the world and be nourished in the other institutions that shape our future perspectives.

Charles A. Hopkins

Acknowledgements

This book is an outcome of the UK Teacher Education for Equity and Sustainability Network (TEESNet) annual conferences held at Liverpool Hope University from 2013 to 2017. I would like to thank all those from across the UK and beyond who attended and contributed to the success of these events, including the TEESNet steering committee that comprises representatives from schools, universities and civil society organisations, from each of the four nations of the UK. In particular, TEESNet Director Andrea Bullivant has been pivotal in sustaining and energising this dynamic community of practice. The wider Liverpool World Centre team have also been instrumental in publicising the work of TEESNet and ensuring a 'sell-out' at the 2017 and 2018 conferences.

It is appropriate at this point to recognise the contribution of those who, in 2007, founded the UK Initial Teacher Education Network for Education for Sustainable Development and Global Citizenship that was to become TEESNet; most notably, the founding director, Professor Sally Inman, who, alongside Professor Ros Wade and Maggie Rogers, co-organised the network between 2007 and 2012. Since then, Pablo Guidi, Director of Liverpool World Centre, and Professor Kenneth Newport, Dean of Education and Pro-Vice Chancellor at Liverpool Hope University, have provided invaluable support and ongoing commitment to the work of the network. This activity has also been supported by the Centre for Education and Policy Analysis at Liverpool Hope University, UK.

The contributors to this volume would like to acknowledge all individuals and partner organisations who enabled the research that is reported upon here. This includes research participants, universities and civil society organisations in Austria, Canada, Cyprus, Czech Republic, England, Ethiopia, Finland, Germany, Italy, Kenya, Northern Ireland, Poland, Republic of Ireland, Scotland, Slovakia, Sweden and Wales, as detailed in the individual chapters.

Finally, I would like to thank J'annine Jobling and Amy Scott for their patient and efficient support in the editorial process.

Abbreviations

CDA	Critical Discourse Analysis
CSO	Civil Society Organisation
DEC	Development Education Centre
EAL	English as an Additional Language
EC	European Commission
ECS	Early Childhood Studies
ERS-SDEC	Education Rating Scale for Sustainable Development in Early Childhood
ESD	Education for Sustainable Development
ESD/GC	Education for Sustainable Development and Global Citizenship
ESE	Environmental Sustainability Education
EU	European Union
EYFS	Early Years Foundation Stage
GCE	Global Citizenship Education
GLP	Global Learning Programme
HEI	Higher Education Institute
IPCC	Intergovernmental Panel on Climate Change
ITE	Initial Teacher Education
LHU	Liverpool Hope University
LWC	Liverpool World Centre
MEL	Monitoring, Evaluation and Learning
NGO	Non-Government Organisation
OECD	Organisation for Economic Co-operation and Development
OMEP	World Organisation for Early Childhood Education
PISA	Programme of International Student Assessment
PSHE	Personal, Social and Health Education
RISC	Reading International Solidarity Centre
SDGs	Sustainable Development Goals
SKE	Subject Knowledge Enhancement
SMSC	Spiritual, Moral, Social and Cultural Education

STEM	Science, Technology, Engineering and Mathematics
TEESNet	United Kingdom Teacher Education for Equity and Sustainability Network
UK	United Kingdom
UN	United Nations

Introduction

Reconnecting Research, Policy and Practice in Education for Sustainable Development and Global Citizenship

Philip Bamber

Introduction

> One of the tasks of the progressive educator, through a serious, correct political analysis, is to unveil opportunities for hope, no matter what the obstacles may be.
>
> (Freire, 1992, p. 3)

We have witnessed, in the first two decades of the twenty-first century, a series of interconnected economic, environmental, social and political crises affecting individuals and communities across the planet: the global war on terror, the financial crash, worldwide migration from violence and climate change, the rise of populism, assertions of nationality, and the moral panic surrounding religious fundamentalism. The fragility of hope in our world is exposed by a news cycle that distresses and overwhelms, provoking paralysis and a sense of fatalism. Most recently, the alarming report from the Intergovernmental Panel on Climate Change (IPCC) outlined how the impact of climate change could be reduced in important ways by limiting global warming to 1.5°C (IPCC, 2018). This would save parts of the arctic and coral reefs and expose 10 million fewer people to the risks of rising seas. Nevertheless, the latest scientific evidence indicates we will exceed the 1.5°C temperature rise by 2030, "dicing with the planet's liveability" (McGrath, 2018). The 'bigger-than-self' challenges facing society demand 'bigger-than-self' solutions that we struggle to both envision and enact. This book focuses on the role of teacher education in delivering a response that promotes equity and sustainability, bringing together research, policy and practice from the emergent fields of Education for Sustainable Development and Global Citizenship Education (ESD/GC).

Resisting naive idealism, this book recognises that education as it is currently structured and practised may exacerbate the challenges we face. Indeed, "the truth is that without significant precautions, education can equip people merely to be more effective vandals of the earth" (Orr, 2004, p. 5). Instead, this book seeks to open up spaces to support teachers and teacher educators in developing independent, confident and critical voices in the wider ethical and political conversation about the ultimate moral and social purposes of education. Drawing upon examples from research and practice, it considers overarching questions such as: what are the knowledge, skills, values and capabilities required of teachers and teacher educators in facilitating a meaningful curriculum for a just and sustainable world? How does ESD/GC develop our understanding of what it means to be an educator? How can values, curriculum and assessment support the challenge of changing climates and shifting policy contexts? Bringing together empirical and theoretical perspectives, this book develops new understandings of ESD/GC that reconnect research, policy and practice.

Global policy discourse has renewed attention on the role of teacher education in general and the nature of teacher Education for Sustainable Development and Global Citizenship in particular. The Organisation for Economic Co-operation and Development (OECD) has developed a framework (OECD, 2018) to make international comparisons of 'global competency' in the Programme for International Student Assessment (PISA). ESD/GC has also emerged as pivotal to the universal ambitions of the Sustainable Development Goals (SDGs) (UNESCO, 2016a, p. 287). SDG 4.7, aiming for all learners to acquire the knowledge and skills needed to promote sustainable development, arguably constitutes "the very heart of the sustainability agenda in education" (King, 2017, p. 808). More specifically, and particularly pertinent to the focus of this book, the global indicator for measuring progress towards meeting Target 4.7 is the extent to which ESD/GC is mainstreamed at all levels in "national education policies, curricula, teacher education and student assessment" (United Nations Statistical Commission, 2018, p. 5). Furthermore, the latest report on progress towards meeting Target 4.7 (UNESCO, 2018) concluded that "insufficient teacher training remains a stumbling block" (p. 1).

The recent global policy focus connecting Education for Sustainable Development (ESD) and Global Citizenship Education (GCE) is not the only evidence of integration: since the 1992 Earth Summit on sustainable development in Rio de Janeiro there has been "consensus that the only way to protect the environment is to face the challenges from a global perspective" (Scheunpflug and Asbrand, 2006, p. 39). Moreover, 40% of research reviewed in a recent mapping exercise of global citizenship education in teacher education (Yemini et al., 2019) included reference to environmental education. While ESD and GCE may have developed in parallel, they are both rooted in overlapping conceptual and pedagogical approaches emanating from fields such as development education, critical pedagogy, environmental education, citizenship education and inquiry based-learning that all feature prominently in this volume.

The focus here is primarily on the role and nature of initial (or pre-service) and in-service continuing professional development within compulsory schooling, whilst also explicating the implications for educators more broadly. It includes contributions from teacher educators in universities and schools, educators in civil society organisations, researchers, policymakers, classroom practitioners and those engaged in informal educational settings across a diverse range of different countries. This approach is particularly timely as analysis of curricula and policy, rather than practice, currently predominate ESD/GC research (see Andreotti, 2006; Mannion et al., 2011). For instance, Oxley and Morris's (2013) influential global citizenship typology analyses the intended transactions and outcomes of curricula without considering policy enactment. Furthermore, it has recently been identified that the 'implementation' of SDG 4.7 is "generally lower than the high level of policy commitment would lead one to expect" (UNESCO, 2018, p. 12): reform at the policy level is not necessarily reaching the classroom (Evans et al., 2017). Moreover, the guiding principles of participative and values-based ESD/GC runs counter to dominant approaches to the training and education of teachers (Bourn et al., 2017; Yemini et al., 2019). This book therefore provides much-needed empirical evidence of how such ESD/GC is experienced in teacher education.

The Holistic, Critical and Transformative Dimensions of ESD/GC

The United Kingdom Teacher Education Network for Education for Sustainable Development/Global Citizenship (ESD/GC) was formed in 2007 to "integrate issues of social and environmental justice, poverty eradication and ecological conservation, and social and biological diversity, and develop a teacher education curriculum that enables new teachers to explore these critical issues within their classrooms" (Inman et al., 2011, p. 150). Through a series of annual conferences and regional seminars between 2008 and 2012, this community of practice developed a "radical" (Inman, 2011, p. 155) approach integrating ESD and GCE. 'Holistic', 'critical' and 'transformative' aspects of ESD/GC emerged as pivotal to this discourse and associated practices, as summarised in Table 0.1.

This book seeks to deepen understanding of these 'holistic', 'critical' and 'transformative' dimensions of ESD/GC in research, policy and practice. Holistic approaches that seek to cultivate values and dispositions have become pivotal to contemporary frameworks for the delivery and evaluation of ESD/GC (Fricke and Gathercole, 2015; UNESCO, 2014) but remain deeply under-theorised and pay limited attention to implications for practice (Bamber et al., 2013; Goren and Yemini, 2017). At the same time, limited evidence exists of what critical ESD/GC looks like in

Table 0.1 Holistic, critical and transformative dimensions of ESD/GC

Dimensions of ESD/GC	*Description*	*Addressed through*
Holistic approaches through co-operation with others	As an inclusive practice, ESD/GC recognises the learners' different starting points, engaging not only their own preferred perspectives but also the different views of others. Both within and across subject disciplines, ESD/GC engages not only with the cognitive but also with the emotional, not only with ecological perspectives but also with broader ethical, social, economic, cultural and spiritual perspectives. It encompasses not only the present but also the future, not only the human world but also the world of all other living organisms, not only the self in a state of change but also local and global society in states of change.	Developing enquiries across subject boundaries Linking the local and global Holistic approaches to ESD/GC including the dimensions of well-being, the spiritual, the emotional, the cognitive and action
Criticality through cognitive and affective dissonance	ESD/GC draws on multiple perspectives and encourages a contested view of both knowledge and pedagogical choices. It raises critical questions about such ideas as continuous economic growth on a finite planet, about the challenges to health and well-being that come from our consumerism and associated lifestyles, about forms of justice at local and global levels, and about pedagogical approaches that can be developed in response. It problematises frameworks such as militarism and peace, the conditions of the world's poor, the production of food, population growth and control, biodiversity, the use of genetically modified crops, the creation of biofuels, economic dependency on oil products, the impact of different energy sources, the relationship between social justice and ecological justice, and the relative power of social and ecological actions.	Developing criticality in learners Engaging with controversial and difficult issues Pedagogy that encourages participation, engagement, collaboration and critical enquiry
Transformative activity and creativity	ESD/GC provides insights into the feasibility of alternative lifestyles, alternative value systems and breaks with the dominant economic paradigms. It explores new environmental and ecological relationships and encourages innovative educational partnerships. It prioritises personal and professional development and growth that arises from engaging with diversity and dissonance. It supports teacher educators in navigating the changing educational and political context in the cause of equity and sustainability.	ESD/GC as a pedagogy of hope, enabling innovation and creativity Navigating the changing educational and political context Educators as agents of change

Source: Adapted from Belgeonne et al., 2014, p. 5.

practice: the overwhelming demands from theoretical research for more critical GCE contrast starkly with minimal discussion of criticality found within a meta-analysis of empirical research (Goren and Yemini, 2017). Finally, despite a groundswell of evidence of the need for 'transformative approaches' to education (UNESCO, 2015), proponents of transformative pedagogy for ESD/GC (see, for example, UNESCO, 2014; Fricke and Gathercole, 2015) only provide cursory analysis of the theoretical foundations that substantiate and stimulate such pedagogy.

Influenced by the traditions of critical pedagogy and post-colonialism, critical GCE aims to unmask processes that hide difference, exacerbate inequality and marginalise. It does so by supporting learners to examine the sources of their deeply held assumptions and expose contemporary manifestations of power embedded in practice, leading towards responsible and ethical action. However, researchers and practitioners risk using 'criticality' as a floating signifier, devoid of meaning, reifying overtly rational approaches (Brookfield, 2009). Johnson and Morris (2010) argue the role of affect differentiates critical pedagogy from notions of critical thinking. This refocuses attention on lived experience: in particular, "how notions of consciousness, ideology, and power enter into the way human beings constitute their day-to-day realities" (Giroux, 1980, p. 348).

From this view, critical ESD/GC should not simply be concerned with developing 'critical thinking' among teachers but also critical being, "which embraces critical reason, critical action and critical self-reflection" (Barnett, 1997, p. 105). This challenges the assumption that learners are capable of engaging in abstract critical reflection in which they are disconnected from their own experiences. Indeed, such reflective, constructivist approaches serve to separate the subject from the environment, viewing the individual as the central actor in the processes of meaning-making. Learning is thereby perceived to be independent and autonomous rather than connected and relational.

Similarly, the transformative aspects of ESD/GC discussed in this book elucidate 'how' we know rather than 'what' we know, with a particular focus on tacit, aesthetic and relational ways of knowing. For transformative learning conceived holistically in this way (Bamber, 2016), knowing emerges from a way of being, not vice versa, and is redolent of the suggestion that "we don't think our way into a new kind of living; rather we live our way into a new kind of thinking" (Palmer, 1980, p. 57). From this view, education must be concerned less with knowledge acquisition and more with supporting individuals as they move into alternative modes of being, elevating the importance of existential change for the learner, as regards both their way of being in the world and ways of knowing that world (Bamber, 2016).

A particular focus for the UK Teacher Education Network for ESD/GC, renamed in 2012 as the UK Teacher Education for Equity and Sustainability Network (TEESNet), has been to embed ESD/GC in the ethos, curriculum and assessment of teacher education (Inman et al., 2011, p. 151). Drawing upon the work of TEESNet between 2013 and 2018, this volume takes the overarching themes of values, curriculum and assessment in turn, and explores how each of these is being reconceptualised and revisioned in the context of holistic, critical and transformative approaches to ESD/GC across a range of settings. The cultivation of a range of international partnerships, as recommended by a report on the network's activity (Hunt et al., 2011, p. 5), has enhanced this activity and is reflected in the breadth of contributions to this volume. A number of chapters could have been located in any of the parts, and, indeed, many threads run across all three; this serves to highlight pragmatic and profound issues relating to teacher education for ESD/GC and the implications for the educator sector more broadly. This chapter will now briefly introduce each of the three parts of this book including synopses of the individual contributions.

Values for ESD/GC

International efforts to improve education have recently moved beyond 'values-neutral' goals such as universal 'access to education'. The 2015 World Education Forum concluded that 'quality education' is characterised by "the skills, values and attitudes that enable citizens to lead healthy and fulfilled lives, make informed decisions, and respond to local and global challenges" (UNESCO, 2015). At the same time, UNESCO has established a vision for GCE emphasising holistic aspects of learning, acknowledging education must move "beyond the development of knowledge and cognitive skills to build values, soft skills and attitudes among learners that can facilitate international cooperation and promote social transformation" (UNESCO, 2014, p. 9). Values have also been invoked to address challenges of social cohesion, radicalisation and citizenship internationally (UNESCO, 2016b), in Europe (EC, 2015) and across a range of national settings, including US, Canada, Germany and Australia (Peterson and Bentley, 2016). Statutory requirements to promote explicit values open up spaces for critical democratic engagement, creating possibilities for nurturing criticality (Bamber et al., 2018). Despite this interest in values education, a recent call for developing a research-based approach to teacher education for ESD/GC highlighted how little is known about teachers' values within ESD/GC (Scheunpflug, 2011, p. 37). This is particularly surprising since teachers having "the value base to be able to interpret the impact of the global society on the learner" (Bourn, 2008, p. 11) has been identified as an established strength of pedagogy for global social justice.

Interestingly, values-based themes did not emerge as important in a recent mapping of global citizenship research in teacher education (Yemini, 2019). This may result from a reluctance to confront controversial issues in the classroom (ibid, p. 87). Certainly, evidence exists that beginning teachers lack the required subject knowledge and confidence to teach such topics effectively (Bamber et al., 2018). At the same time, some object to the idea that the educator's role is to mould 'certain kinds of people' according to certain values and attitudes. Education in general, and ESD/GC in particular, is deeply value-laden and, whether consciously or unconsciously, values underpin practice. Confronted with challenging situations or controversial issues in the classroom, student teachers draw upon complex professional knowledge, much of which is tacit, bound up with one's own goals, beliefs and values. As Stephen Scoffham reminds us in this volume: "values underpin all aspects of education at both an explicit and implicit level". While educators may wish to avoid being accused of dogmatism or bias, "the sobering reality is that all teachers are indoctrinators for a 'doctrine' is a 'teaching' and to 'indoctrinate' is to lead others into that 'teaching'" (Pike, 2011, p. 184). Nevertheless, the imposition of values can clearly fail to inspire commitment to those values (Bamber et al., 2018). International attempts to mainstream ESD/GC will expose further the gap between the values-driven orientation of ESD/GC and how this is enacted in practice.

This book therefore seeks to better understand the role of educators as agents of change. A strong discourse within GCE in particular postulates the existence of a continuum of participation from awareness of issues to action that challenges injustice (Bourn, 2015). This perspective is reinforced in the new OECD framework for measuring global competency. Particular knowledge, skills and attitudes are predefined as central to global competency and will be measured through young people self-reporting on their involvement in a set of particular and predetermined activities (OECD, 2016, p. 32). The understanding of ESD/GC developed in this publication refocuses attention on the learners' being alongside their agency. This discussion interrogates the role of teacher education in cultivating values and virtues, moving beyond developing awareness of issues and values transmission towards ensuring critical engagement and action.

Part 1 therefore investigates the role of teacher education in nurturing the values of educators for a just and sustainable world. This includes examination of the values underpinning education policy and practice for ESD/GC at the local, national and international level. Chapters 1 and 2, from Stephen Scoffham and Alison Clark respectively, pursue the formation of teachers and teacher educators with respect to particular values. Stephen Scoffham investigates how teacher educators in a university setting foreground values and deeply held principles in their everyday work. Through a participatory methodology, notions of "community, respect, knowledge, evidence and innovation" emerged as being particularly important to teacher education in this setting. These core values are shown to provide the foundations for ESD, enabling ESD to be considered beyond "a narrower set of considerations". A recent systematic literature review of approaches to embedding sustainability in teacher education (Evans et al., 2017) found only 1 of 151 studies that investigated the implementation of ESD across an institution of teacher education. Scoffham's work therefore provides an important and much-needed illustration of a systemic approach to 'institutionalise' ESD.

Alison Clark also highlights the complexity of the process whereby particular values are explored and lived out in educational settings. Her case study of a school whose ethos is underpinned by the Five Core Values of "Respect, Co-Operation, Compassion, Honorable Purpose and Stewardship" illustrates the importance of 'acting out' these values in the governance, systems and relationships of school life. Whilst emphasising that meaningful curriculum must move from the cognitive to affective, she concludes that educators need the time and space to reflect upon and identify the values which are meaningful to them. Clark echoes Scoffham in concluding that values provide an essential moral compass for ESD that must be continually re-assessed and re-affirmed.

In chapter 3, Jen Simpson's school-based action research study investigates a particular aspect of this ongoing learning process. Examining the role of personal and professional critical reflection during in-service teacher education, her chapter focuses on how to nurture moves from a charitable to a social justice orientation amongst educators. This research suggests teachers must continuously 'learn to unlearn', to 'see beyond our colonial psyche', in order to support the development of a more equal global society. In chapter 4, Fatima Pirbhai-Illich and Fran Martin also explore decolonising pedagogies for teachers to open up inviting spaces for interaction and learning. Their particular backgrounds and perspectives regarding intercultural learning inform this fascinating research with pre- and in-service teachers in Canada. Drawing upon postcolonial theory and relational pedagogies, they present data that explicates the important notions of invitation and hospitality pertinent to teacher education for ESD/GC. They argue that such critical intercultural dialogue cultivates the plurality of ways of knowing and being required to address the political, environmental and economic challenges facing society.

Understanding how we can learn to live together with a shared commitment to the recognition of difference is a central concern of transformative GCE (Bamber, 2016). Chapter 5 also highlights the importance of acknowledging the differences and conflicts that inevitably emerge in a diverse and complex society. Rosalind Duke investigates the potential of restorative practice, a pedagogical approach used in schools to build relationships, to manage conflict and nurture peaceful living. Drawing upon work in Ireland, this chapter highlights the importance of curriculum and pedagogy that nurture the values and skills of listening, empathy, respect and responsibility for one's own actions and behaviours. Again, a 'whole-school' approach is advocated to ensure culture and relationships that teach us 'how to live together sustainably'.

In the final chapter of this part, Helen Clarke and Sharon Witt illustrate the potential for 'eco-playful pedagogy' and 'small-world play' to develop the knowledge, skills and values of pre-service teachers. Providing a bridge into thinking about 'curriculum for ESD/GC' in part 2 of this book, they use the metaphor of the curriculum as a 'vortex' to represent the dynamic processes involved in planning holistic learning for children. They identify the centrality of values such as curiosity, creativity, openness, imagination and responsiveness alongside care and love for the subject. Their conclusion, that nurturing the relationship between children and their environment empowers them to act for that environment, is equally applicable to the pre-service teachers and teacher educators involved in this work.

Curriculum for ESD/GC

In the context of recent curriculum changes across the UK (Bamber et al., 2016) and beyond (Bourn et al., 2017), part 2 explores the contribution of ESD/GC scholarship and practice to meaningful curriculum in teacher education and schools. It explores critical perspectives on curriculum as we seek to address societal challenges such as inequality, migration, climate change and the rise of nationalism. It also includes evidence of ESD/GC research and practice informing curriculum innovation in diverse settings internationally.

The conceptual and practical challenges of developing curricula that cultivate the holistic, critical and transformative dimensions of ESD/GC are extensive and run deep. For instance, attempts to educate global citizens and internationalise the curriculum have become ubiquitous across a range of countries, as institutions of formal education seek to enhance both the learning experience and student employability. Marketisation in higher education has encouraged transactional approaches that, arguably, cultivate global workers rather than global citizens (Hammond and Keating, 2018). Initiatives that demand international travel and which seek to nurture intercultural learning, such as study abroad and International Service-Learning, are increasingly the subject of scholarly scrutiny (Bamber, 2016). Distinctions have been made between liberal and transformative interpretations of resultant curricula, and how they are enacted (Clifford and Montgomery, 2015). However, to illustrate the lack of clarity and theoretical limitations of work in this area, Clifford and Montgomery's definition of the global citizen as the "personification of a transformative internationalised curriculum" (2015, p. 47) is not related to discourses of (global) citizenship and invokes a colonising and exclusive notion of global citizenship.

At the heart of approaches to ESD/GC explored in this publication are processes such as shared reflection, immersion, deliberation and exchange which are inimical to pedagogies and curriculum which pre-specify learning outcomes (Bamber, 2016). For example, the curriculum objective of encountering the other may predispose the learner to simply confirm previously held suppositions. The first part of this book provided numerous examples of how values and virtues emerge through lived experience: transformative learning that occurs when it is least expected. From this view, 'not looking' for learning becomes a strength, and informal, marginal or liminal spaces and times can become the priority. This places demands upon educators who must be able to identify this learning as it becomes manifest. Educators must therefore become accustomed to living alongside and sharing experiences with their students in order to fully understand them.

Part 2 therefore purposefully begins by bringing lived experiences "from the edge to the centre". Neda Forghani-Arani interrogates the experience of teaching in diverse classrooms given the context of migration and transnational population movement. Her chapter draws upon a fascinating vignette that challenges us to rethink how we prepare teachers to teach in "multi-layered spaces of collision, tension and possibility". Her attention to the role of practical wisdom, judgment and tact in such situations complicates understandings of teacher efficacy, raising the important question of how 'transcultural pedagogical tact' can be taught. Teacher education curricula that fail to do so may indeed "undermine the very education teaching should seek to make possible" (Biesta, 2012, p. 45).

Chapter 8 also draws upon day-to-day classroom experiences to expose, rather than gloss over, complex ethical issues. The universal applicability of the SDGs, ensuring ESD/GC must be embedded in all countries, brings particular challenges to teacher education in the 'developed' world. Karen Pashby and Louise Sund interrogate how educators in the Global North can be resourced to ethically engage in teaching about global issues, including those relating to the environment, that directly address the systemic nature of inequalities at the root of such issues. Synthesising the growing body of critical scholarship in ESD/GC they expose the (often unintentional) reproduction of colonial systems of power through mainstream curriculum and pedagogical approaches. This reiterates concerns raised in chapters 3, 4 and 13 that substantiate a growing critique of GCE's Western focus (Yemini et al., 2019). Drawing upon participatory research with secondary teachers in England, Finland and Sweden, they illustrate how the HEADSUP analytical tool can unveil ethnocentrism, power and contradictory perspectives in the classroom. They conclude that the aim of GCE to support learners to "revisit assumptions, world views and power relations in mainstream discourses and consider people/groups that are systematically underrepresented/

marginalized" (UNESCO, 2014, p. 12) should be a bridging aim for SDG 4.7, inclusive of ESD. Nevertheless, that nearly all empirical studies detailed in this book were conducted in Western, 'developed' countries is a notable limitation of this publication.

This volume reminds us of the importance of tackling complex and controversial issues such as climate change with the youngest learners. A number of chapters consider curricula and pedagogy that is age-appropriate and sensitive, preparing children for an uncertain but more hope-full future. The Bat Conservation Project outlined in chapter 9 linked young children in England and Kenya to provide an innovative model of professional development for teachers and practitioners in early childhood. Zoi Nikiforidou et al. argue this approach supported educators committed to the principles of sustainable development to gain the knowledge and confidence to incorporate ESD/GC within their work.

Chapter 10 seeks to complicate the simplistic distinctions between liberal and transformative curricula (Clifford and Montgomery, 2015) outlined earlier. Mallika Kanyal et al. argue that ESD/GC should attempt to reconcile some of the implicit questions that divide education into two dichotomous discourses: on the one hand consumerism, performativity and managerialism, and, on the other, inclusion, reciprocity and potential for social transformation. They use two case studies to explore the role of experience, enquiry, critical reflection and dialogue to encourage creative, participatory and collaborative approaches in early childhood and higher education. Their advocacy for democratic approaches to learning opens up a debate regarding the forms of curriculum, pedagogy and assessment that can be both orderly and dynamic, and that pay attention to the subjective nature of children's, students' and educators' experiences.

Helen Clarke and Sharon Witt also focus upon the role of experiential and aesthetic education in their study of imaginative and storied encounters with places and the natural world in chapter 11. For them, meaningful learning is unsettling and, echoing Kanyal et al. in the previous chapter, demands a creative approach to the curriculum. This penultimate chapter of part 2 includes compelling illustrations of sensory and immersive experiences that enable young people and student teachers to (re)imagine new relationships with places through play, imaginative exploration and discovery.

Finally, Sara Franch explores the tensions between ESD/GC and citizenship education focussed on promoting national goals. Her chapter investigates how GCE is conceptualised by educators in a province of northern Italy that has recently introduced education policy reference to the global dimension of citizenship. Drawing upon a review of curriculum guidelines and extended interviews with teachers and policymakers, three broad approaches to the enactment GCE are identified: avoidance, pioneering and building communities of peers. In the context of a failure to adopt a systematic approach to GCE, this research identifies a lack of differentiation between citizenship education and GCE and the development of a de-politicised conception of the former. These findings highlight the risk that simply re-orientating citizenship education towards the global (Bamber et al., 2018) can result in a conflation of global citizenship with global competences, to the detriment of the political and critical objectives of (global) citizenship education as expounded by the book series of which this volume is part.

Assessment for ESD/GC

A preoccupation with easily measured short-term outcomes, rather than longer-term changes in behaviour, values, attitudes and practices, presents a threat to education in general and to ESD/GC in particular. Part 3 challenges educators to rethink what they value as outcomes from education and consider that "measurable outcomes may be the least significant results of learning" (McNeil, 1986, p. xviii). Building upon the analysis in parts 1 and 2, this section examines the assessment of values and curriculum, providing an important contribution to growing interest in the research and evaluation of ESD/GC (Bourn et al., 2017). Given that values and attitudes play a significant role in translating aspirations for ESD/GC into practice, they must necessarily become a focus for monitoring and evaluation in this field.

This analysis is timely given the judgement on global competence included in PISA 2018, assessing fifteen-year-olds' awareness of our interconnected world and their ability to deal effectively with the resulting demands. This new international measure may seduce ESD/GC advocates wishing to raise the profile of the field: attention and resources worldwide will be directed towards improving performance. Nevertheless, the complexity of approaches to global issues, and the associated values required of young people, indicate that such global metrics oversimplify. It is similarly problematic that progress towards SDG target 4.7 is being measured through blunt proxy indicators such as whether particular concepts, for example human rights and gender equality, have been mainstreamed in the curriculum (UNESCO, 2016a, p. 287). Not only does this approach fail to account for how such curricula are taught in practice, but focus upon universal human values, such as human rights, gender equality, cultural diversity, tolerance and environmental sustainability, can fail to recognise the liquidity, historicity and evolution of difference (Bamber et al., 2018).

The drive to secure international data for comparison perpetuates the use of quantitative measures, generated by Western multilateral agencies (King, 2017) through studying the Western context (Salzer and Roczen, 2018), antithetical to the principles of ESD/GC. Well-chosen indicators from national, and even international, surveys can of course be compelling drivers for change. It is important, however, to anticipate the unintended consequences of deploying particular measures. For instance, the forensic focus on outcomes in numeracy and literacy that seek to 'level the playing field' has led to the narrowing of curricula, particularly in schools 'catching up' in the core areas. Attempts to make educational phenomena and processes explicit can easily become overdetermined by metrics that become perverse ends in themselves. Indeed, Hannah Arendt called upon educators not to predict the needs of the future and inhibit what cannot be foreseen. Educators should instead prepare their students "in advance for the task of renewing a common world" (1977, p. 177):

> Our hope always hangs on the new which every generation brings; but precisely because we can base our hope only on this, we destroy everything if we so try to control the new that we, the old, can dictate how it will look.
>
> (Arendt, 1977, p. 192)

The OECD has already stated that exploring "new methods to improve the measurement of the value dimension of global competence" (OECD, 2018, p. 38) is a priority for PISA 2021. This book makes a contribution to this debate. Teacher education for equity and sustainability does not require students, teachers or researchers to seek correct answers. It involves a spectrum of possibility rather than a search for one particular thing. The scenarios for measuring global competence in PISA 2018 have therefore been criticised for suggesting "socially desirable reactions (according to Western standards)" (Salzer and Roczen, 2018, p. 13). As put forward in parts 1 and 2 of this book, ESD/GC must find a space for the unexpected and the tacit, aesthetic and relational aspects of learning. This is a significant challenge within current educational structures that resist change and prevent the envisioning of alternatives. Amidst a culture of accountability and measurability in formal education, this understanding of education has implications for assessment of learning that demands radical solutions. A particular challenge is to ensure monitoring and evaluation of ESD/GC interventions consistent with the values of ESD/GC itself.

Part 3 therefore seeks to illustrate creative and innovative strategies to overcome the constraints of institutional assessment mechanisms and move beyond individual assessment. It interrogates attempts to facilitate and assess cooperative learning and forms of knowing, being and doing that emerge through working collaboratively, demonstrating the role of assessment in nurturing the learners' ongoing becoming. It also suggests, as argued by Jen Simpson in chapter 3, that educators should consider whether they require professional (un)development in structuring and facilitating tasks such as these with which they are unlikely to be familiar.

Historically, Civil Society Organisations (CSOs) working in the areas of environmental, development, sustainable development, human rights, peace and other adjectival educations have played a critical role in promoting teacher Education for Sustainable Development and Global Citizenship, in the UK (Bamber et al., 2016) and internationally (Bourn et al., 2017; Tarozzi and Inguaggiato, 2018). The work of CSOs is a significant feature of part 3, with four of the five chapters authored by members of CSOs and all chapters drawing upon empirical findings from CSO-led international projects.

The opening chapter problematises the pursuit of 'what works' in educational contexts, introducing critical discourse analysis as a methodology to challenge the predominance of quantitative measures. For Katie Carr and Leander Bindewald, 'critical' ESD/GC is required that unveils power relations, domination and resistance. Drawing upon a diverse range of sources, including the novella *The Little Prince*, they argue that measures conveying objectivity and quantifiability undermine ESD/GC founded upon values. For them, critical thinking and dialogic learning must underpin ESD/GC research and practice in order to resist and subvert the dominant discourse. Where evaluation is imposed, for instance by external funders, they advocate for clarity and transparency to capture detrimental unintended consequences. The four chapters that follow draw upon empirical evidence to substantiate different aspects of this argument, reiterating the importance of adopting a critical scholarly approach to assessment for ESD/GC.

In chapter 14, Zoi Nikiforidou et al. examine the assessment of value formation early in life. Drawing upon evidence from cross-cultural ESD projects in Kenya and England, they review the Environmental Rating Scale for Sustainable Development in Early Childhood (ERS-SDEC) as a research/self-assessment tool for practitioners. The authors, all members of the World Organisation for Early Childhood Education (OMEP), highlight ways in which the scale provides a shared language for rating and celebrating ESD work in early childhood settings. Different orientations towards elephant conservation in Kenya and England exemplify the problematic nature of adopting Western-centric metrics on an international scale. Exemplifying concerns raised in the previous chapter, the authors strike a note of caution regarding the use of assessment mechanisms within a culture of managerialism. At the same time, they acknowledge the role of such tools in cultivating a 'discursive community' of international stakeholders.

The formative potential of assessment to guide discussion is reiterated in chapter 15. In an international collaboration across higher education institutions and CSOs, Angela Daly and Julie Brown report upon monitoring and evaluation in a three-year EU-funded project, 'Technology Challenging Poverty', on global learning in Science, Technology, Engineering and Mathematics (STEM) curriculum. Working with non-state development actors from across the UK, Cyprus, Italy and Poland, they identify important "spaces for learning, both planned and serendipitous", within monitoring and evaluation processes. Given significant pressure to demonstrate effectiveness, efficiency and impact within time-bound activity, their research highlights the imperative of capturing unexpected outcomes and ensuring a central role for participatory learning spaces throughout such a project. The mixed evaluation methods, participatory action research and public engagement that they describe here may serve to cultivate more meaningful relationships between monitoring and evaluation, research, policy and practice in ESD/GC.

The evaluation of teacher education that sought to address the consequences of the refugee crisis by Chris Keelan et al. in chapter 16 offers an innovative case study of international partnership for ESD/GC. The two-phase study in Germany and England, supported by Liverpool World Centre, highlights the possibilities when integrating international and local experience across an ESD/GC intervention. The student teacher accounts richly capture how beginning teachers engaged with global issues whilst enhancing their confidence, ability and motivation to teach. More importantly, given the invocation in chapter 13 for ESD/GC practitioners to interrogate hidden assumptions and drivers determining educational interventions, the student teachers were enabled to critically reflect on their own moral purpose as educators. Reflecting upon their values in this way enables future educators to subsequently support their students to consider their own value development.

In the concluding chapter of this part, Barbara Lowe and Liz Allum reflect on the implementation of their toolkits 'How do we know it's working?' (Allum et al., 2008) and 'Are we nearly there yet? A self-evaluation framework for Global Citizenship' (Allum et al., 2010) within a large EU-funded project in the UK, Ethiopia, Czech Republic, Slovakia and Ireland. Demonstrating the significance of local values and ideologies in the mediation and enactment of ESD/GC (Bamber et al., 2016), the authors outline how their methodologies were adapted to suit different international contexts through a 'discursive community' of stakeholders as advocated in chapter 14. This research reveals scepticism amongst pre-service teachers regarding their role in influencing student attitudes including a fear of being accused of political indoctrination. They conclude that ensuring evaluation tools remain open to critique distinguishes assessment for ESD/GC from mainstream approaches.

Conclusion

This book takes forward understanding of the 'holistic', 'critical' and 'transformative' dimensions of ESD/GC as they relate to the role of values, curriculum and assessment within teacher education. It draws upon current and ongoing research in ESD/GC, engages with broader theoretical and methodological perspectives, and provides focussed studies that propose recommendations for policy and practice. The final concluding chapter by Victoria W. Thoresen revisits the fundamental principles of sustainable development to elucidate the centrality of empathy, adaptability, moderation and sharing for teacher education for ESD/GC. She reflects on the methodologies, content and assessment models described in the various chapters to consider the processes of fostering these values. Drawing upon the work of authors across this volume, her conclusion argues that critical thinking, caring collaboration and creativity nurture the transformative learning necessary to convert past knowledge into constructive new insights.

Whilst the scope for implementing teacher education for equity and sustainability in ways that promote transformational rather than transactional forms of education appears to be narrowing, this book highlights tensions that pull against these current trends. These include the naming of values within policy to address challenges facing society and the development of innovative holistic and relational methodologies. Furthermore, a willingness to pursue systemic approaches that embed ESD/GC across institutions and sectors addresses concerns that ESD/GC in teacher education is an emerging area of curricular activity driven by individual academics (Evans et al., 2017; Bourn et al., 2017). Finally, networks (be they national, regional or international) clearly have a pivotal role in sharing expertise, developing and applying theory, influencing policymakers and monitoring progress in this field.

This book, resulting from the work of one such network, TEESNet, details important empirical evidence of ESD/GC in practice including case studies that demonstrate impact on teacher educators, teachers and their students. In doing so, it is a timely contribution that "makes hope possible rather than despair convincing" (Williams, quoted in Inman et al., 2011, p. 156), enhancing our understanding of how educators internationally can better understand the role of education as a public good to more effectively nurture peace, tolerance, sustainable livelihoods and human fulfilment for all.

References

Allum, E., Lowe, B. and Robinson, L. (2008). *How Do We Know It's Working? A Toolkit for Measuring Attitudinal Change*. Reading: RISC.

Allum, E., Lowe, B. and Robinson, L. (2010). *Are We Nearly There? A Self-Evaluation Framework for Global Citizenship*. Reading: RISC.

Andreotti, V. (2006). Soft versus critical global citizenship education: Policy and practice, *Development Education Review*, 3(1), pp. 40–51.

Arendt, H. (1977). *Between Past and Future*. New York: Penguin.

Bamber, P. (2016). *Transformative Education Through International Service-Learning: Realising an Ethical Ecology of Learning*. London: Routledge.

Bamber, P., Bullivant, A., Clark, A. and Lundie, D. (2018). Global Britain? Promoting 'national' values through teacher education for global citizenship. *British Journal of Educational Studies*, 66(4), pp. 433–453.

Bamber, P., Bullivant, A. and Stead, D. (2013). Measuring attitudes towards global learning among future educators in England. *International Journal of Development Education and Global Learning*, 5(3), pp. 5–27.

Bamber, P., Lewin, D. and White, M. (2018). (Dis-) Locating the transformative dimension of global citizenship education. *Journal of Curriculum Studies*, 50(2), pp. 204–230.

Bamber, P., Sullivan, A., Glover, A., King, B. and McCann, G. (2016). A comparative review of policy and practice for education for sustainable development/education for global citizenship (ESD/GC) in teacher education across the four nations of the UK. *Management in Education*, 30(3), pp. 112–120.

Barnett, R. (1997). *Higher Education: A Critical Business*. Buckingham: Open University Press/SRHE.

Belgeonne, C., Clough, N., Inman, S., Rogers, M. and Warwick, P. (2014). *Education for Sustainable Development and Global Citizenship: Good Practice Case Studies in Teacher Education*. Available at: <www.heacademy.ac.uk/system/files/resources/esdgc_casestudiesinteachereducation.pdf>

Biesta, G. (2012). Giving Teaching Back to Education: Responding to the Disappearance of the Teacher. *Phenomenology & Practice*, 6(2), pp. 35–49.

Bourn, D. (2008). Introduction. In: D. Bourn (ed.), *Development Education: Debates and Dialogues*, 1–17. London: Institute of Education.

Bourn, D. (2015). *The Theory and Practice of Development Education: A Pedagogy for Global Social Justice*. Abingdon: Routledge.

Bourn, D., Hunt, F. and Bamber, P. (2017). *A Review of Education for Sustainable Development and Global Citizenship Education in Teacher Education*. Paris: UNESCO. Available at: <http://unesdoc.unesco.org/images/0025/002595/259566e.pdf>. Accessed 27 January 2018.

Brookfield, S. (2009). Engaging critical reflection in corporate America. In: J. Mezirow and E. Taylor (eds.), *Transformative Learning in Practice: Insights from Community Workplace and Higher Education*, 125–135. San-Francisco: Jossey-Bass.

Clifford, V. and Montgomery, C. (2015). Transformative learning through internationalization of the curriculum in higher education. *Journal of Transformative Education*, 13(1), pp. 46–64.

European Commission. (2015). *Promoting Citizenship and the Common Values of Freedom, Tolerance and Non-Discrimination Through Education*. Paris: European Commission.

Evans, N., Stevenson, R., Lasen, M., Ferreira, J. and Davis, J. (2017). Approaches to embedding sustainability in teacher education: A synthesis of the literature. *Teaching and Teacher Education*, 63, pp. 405–417.

Freire, P. (1992). *Pedagogy of Hope*. London: Continuum.

Fricke, H. J. and Gathercole, C. (2015). *Monitoring Education for Global Citizenship*. Brussels: DEEEP.

Giroux, H. (1980). Critical theory and rationality in citizenship education. *Curriculum Inquiry*, 10(4), pp. 329–366.

Goren, H. and Yemini, M. (2017). Global citizenship education redefined—A systematic review of empirical studies on global citizenship education. *International Journal of Educational Research*, 82, pp. 170–183.

Hammond, C. and Keating, A. (2018). Global citizens of global workers? Comparing university programmes for global citizenship education in Japan and the

UK. *Compare: A Journal of Comparative and International Education*, 48(6), pp. 915–934.

Hunt, F., Li Ting Chung, H., Rogers, M., et al. (2011). *Taking Stock: A Report from the UK Teacher Education Network for Sustainable Development (ESD)/ Global Citizenship (GC)—Survey on Provision for ESD/GC in Initial Teacher Education in the UK*. London: London South Bank University.

Inman, S., Mackay, S. and Rogers, M. (2011). Developing values and purposes in teachers for a better world: The experience of the United Kingdom teacher education network for education for sustainable development/global citizenship. *Citizenship, Social and Economics Education*, 10(2&3), pp. 147–157.

Intergovernmental Panel on Climate Change. (2018). *Global Warming of 1.5°C*. Switzerland: IPCC. Available at: <www.ipcc.ch/site/assets/uploads/sites/2/2018/07/SR15_SPM_High_Res.pdf>

Johnson, L. and Morris, P. (2010). Towards a framework for critical citizenship education. *The Curriculum Journal*, 21(1), pp. 77–96.

King, K. (2017). Lost in translation? The challenge of translating the global education goal and targets into global indicators. *Compare: A Journal of Comparative and International Education*, 47(6), pp. 801–817.

Mannion, G., Biesta, G., Priestley, J. and Ross, H. (2011). The global dimension in education and education for global citizenship: Genealogy and critique. *Globalisation, Societies and Education*, 9(3–4), pp. 443–456.

McGrath, M. (2018). *Final Call to Save the World from 'Climate Catastrophe'*. BBC News, 8 October. Available at: <www.bbc.co.uk/news/science-environment-45775309>

McNeil, L. (1986). *Contradictions of Control: School Structure and School Knowledge*. New York: Routledge & Kegan.

OECD. (2016). *Global Competency for An Inclusive World*. Paris: OECD. Available at: <www.oecd.org/pisa/aboutpisa/Global-competency-for-an-inclusive-world.pdf>

OECD. (2018). *Preparing our Youth for An Inclusive and Sustainable World: The OECD Global Competence Framework*. Paris: OECD.

Orr, D. (2004). *Earth in Mind: On Education, Environment, and the Human Prospect. Tenth Anniversary Edition*. Washington, DC: Island Press.

Oxley, L. and Morris, P. (2013). Global citizenship: A typology for distinguishing its multiple conceptions. *British Journal of Educational Studies*, 61(3), pp. 301–325.

Palmer, P. (1980). *The Promise of Paradox*. San Francisco: Jossey-Bass.

Peterson, A. and Bentley, B. (2016). Securitisation and/or Westernisation: Dominant discourses of Australian values and the implications for teacher education. *Journal of Education for Teaching*, 42(2), pp. 239–251.

Pike, M. A. (2011). Ethics and citizenship education. In: J. Arthur (ed.), *Debates in Citizenship Education*, 181–193. London: Routledge.

Salzer, C. and Roczen, N. (2018). Assessing global competence in PISA 2018: Challenges and approaches to capturing a complex construct. *International Journal of Development Education and Global Learning*, 10(1), pp. 5–20.

Scheunpflug, A. (2011). Global education and cross-cultural learning: A challenge for a research-based approach to international teacher education. *International Journal of Development Education and Global Learning*, 3(3), pp. 29–44. Available at: <https://unstats.un.org/sdgs/indicators/Global%20 Indicator%20Framework%20after%20refinement_Eng.pdf>

Scheunpflug, A. and Asbrand, B. (2006). Global education and education for sustainability. *Environmental Education Research*, 12(1), pp. 33–46.

Tarozzi, M. and Inguaggiato, C. (2018). Implementing global citizenship education in EU primary schools: The role of government ministries. *International Journal of Development Education and Global Learning*, 10(1), pp. 21–38.

UNESCO. (2014). *Global Citizenship Education: Preparing Learners for the Challenges of the 21st Century*. Paris: UNESCO.

UNESCO. (2015). *Incheon Declaration*. Paris: UNESCO. Available at: <https://en.unesco.org/world-education-forum-2015/incheon-declaration>

UNESCO. (2016a). *Global Education Monitoring Report. Education for People and Planet: Creating Sustainable Futures for All*. Paris: UNESCO.

UNESCO. (2016b). *A Teacher's Guide on the Prevention of Violent Extremism*. Paris: UNESCO.

UNESCO. (2018). *Progress on Education for Sustainable Development and Global Citizenship Education*. Paris: UNESCO.

United Nations Statistical Commission. (2018). *Global Indicator Framework for the Sustainable Development Goals and Targets of the 2030 Agenda for Sustainable Development*. New York: United Nations. Available at: <https://unstats.un.org/sdgs/indicators/Global%20Indicator%20Framework%20after%20refinement_Eng.pdf>

Yemini, M., Tibbitts, F. and Goren, H. (2019). Trends and caveats: Review of literature on global citizenship education in teacher training. *Teaching and Teacher Education*, pp. 77–89.

Part 1
Values

1 In Search of Core Values

Stephen Scoffham

Introduction

It is widely acknowledged that effective Education for Sustainable Development (ESD) needs to be underpinned by personal values and conviction. A concern for social justice and equity is an integral component of sustainability thinking and a sense that we are doing the 'right thing' contributes to the notion that engaging with sustainability really matters. ESD is much more than simply learning specific knowledge and skills. To use a much quoted mantra, it involves the 'head, hands and heart'.

Such perspectives play out in different ways in educational contexts. Hicks (2014) acknowledges his personal commitment to exploring just and sustainable futures, Booth and Ainscow (2010) focus on inclusion and our responsibility to future generations, while Parkin (2010) points out that a sustainability literate world view involves equity in international relations as well as in the use of resources. These various approaches all imply a moral dimension and are referenced to values.

This chapter explores how tutors in a Faculty of Education at one UK University are attempting to foreground values and deeply held principles in their everyday work. As part of a staff development day, colleagues working in the primary phase met together to try to articulate the ethos which permeates their work. Five main themes emerged—community, respect, knowledge, evidence and innovation. These values have the potential to underpin many different types of work and to support ESD at a deep and lasting level. They also provide a moral compass against which to make judgements and strategic decisions.

The debate around sustainability and the environment raises fundamental questions about what we value, what we think is important and the way that we live our lives. It calls into question the purpose of schooling and the nature of the society we want to create both now and in the future. These are overarching issues which are not just confined to ESD. They are legitimate concerns for all academic disciplines, and they impact directly on economics, politics, religion, literature, the arts, architecture, engineering and many other areas. Building the capacity of educators is vital if we are to develop an informed response to current ecological challenges.

Why Do Values Matter?

Put simply, values provide us with a sense of direction and help us to make choices and decisions in both our professional and personal lives. Booth and Ainscow (2011) see values as "fundamental guides and prompts to action" which spur us forward (p. 21). How we derive our values and whether they are absolute or subjective are questions which have exercised moral philosophers and spiritual leaders from at least the time of the Ancient Greeks. Some people opt for theological interpretations—values are God-given and are part of a set of religious beliefs. Others favour social and cultural explanations which highlight the needs and welfare of groups. But values also operate on an individual and personal level. Altruism and self-sacrifice, for example, describe the way a single person behaves rather than the response of a whole group or nation.

Without trespassing further into this debate, it is interesting to note that modern neurological research is beginning to suggest that some socio-moral norms may be 'hard wired' and thus culturally universal (Goswami, 2015). Even very young babies, for example, appear to have a sense of fairness and preference for helping rather than hindering others. Although further evidence is needed, such findings begin to suggest that the beliefs and principles which are central to ESD could be based on innate human propensities.

There is a sense in which values need to be contextualised and applied in practice. It is easy to say that we believe in certain things, but it is much harder to live by our ideals as conflicts often arise. For example, our loyalty to our friends and family may be at odds with our respect for authority. Or the people that we love may not always turn out to be the people that we trust. Furthermore, what we believe matters most in our private life may not always align with the ethos of our working or professional environment. Children too are liable to experience differences between the values that they experience at home and how they are expected to behave at school. It is important to recognise these tensions. Talking about what is most meaningful and important in our lives builds our understanding of ourselves and enhances our sense of identity, even if it doesn't result in agreement. It also helps to stop us feeling unhappy, misunderstood or compromised.

Such dilemmas open up a debate about whether there is a hierarchy of values. Is love or loyalty, for example, more important than honesty or trust? Rather than seeking to establish an order or sequence, Booth and Ainscow (2011) provide an alternative model which illustrates how values interconnect with each other. Using the metaphor of a flower, they

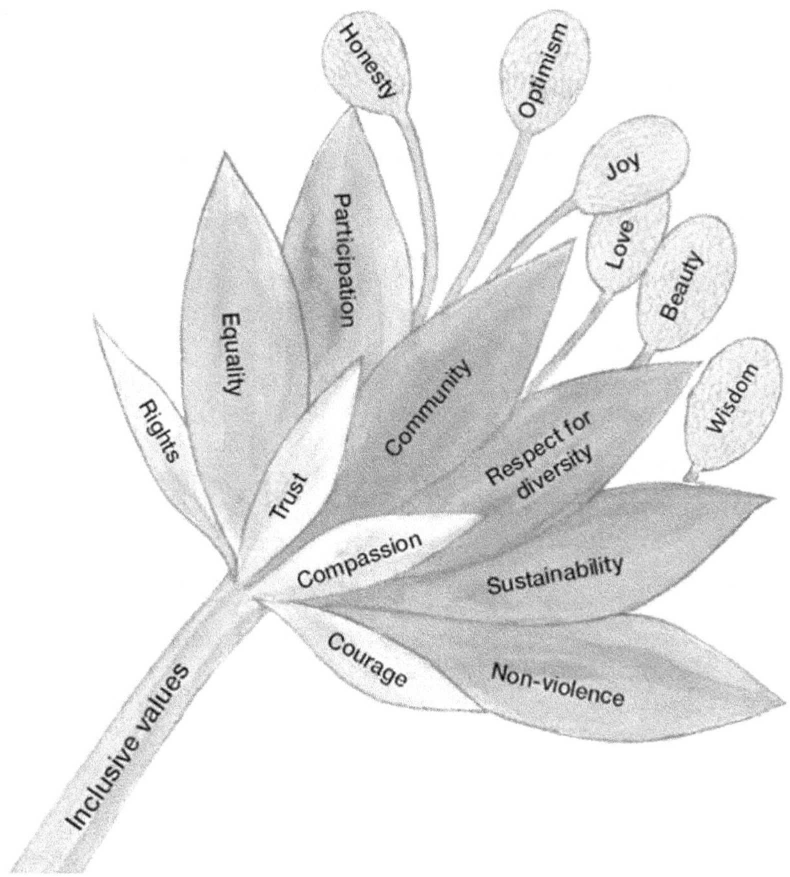

Figure 1.1 Values are overlapping and interrelated

Source: Booth and Ainscow, 2011, reproduced with permission.

portray inclusion as the 'stalk' which, together with courage, compassion, trust and rights, provides the support for other values. The 'petals' are formed of a number of mutually reinforcing values such as community, equality, non-violence and sustainability. Wisdom, love, joy, honesty and other positive qualities appear at the centre of the flower (Figure 1.1). For Booth and Ainscow, the role of inclusion as a core principle is fundamental. If it is replaced by its opposite value, exclusion, all the other values change too. For example, courage is replaced by compliance, trust is replaced by competition and sustainability is replaced by exploitation. There would, of course, also be fundamental implications in terms of our behaviour and sense of priorities.

Opening Up a Debate

How then can educators, both individually and collectively, build their understanding of the values which underpin their work and develop common understandings? The cycle of strategic planning which schools and universities undertake provides a key opportunity to open up such discussions as a wide range of stakeholders are usually involved. At Canterbury Christ Church University, for example, managers, staff, students and governors have all contributed to a debate which has seen a steady shift towards sustainability perspectives. Ten years ago environmental issues hardly gained a mention. Now the latest strategic framework acknowledges the importance of building a sustainable future in both the mission and values statements. Furthermore, sustainability is explicitly identified as one of "six cross-cutting themes" and it is implied in several of the others, especially internationalisation and employability (Canterbury Christ Church University, 2015). In due course, the university's achievements and progress will be evaluated against these criteria.

The restructuring of the Faculty of Education which was undertaken in 2014 provided a further chance for a fundamental review at a more specific level. This process involved a fundamental evaluation of roles and responsibilities and led staff to reflect on their practice in both private and public conversations. As they considered their fundamental beliefs, many colleagues referred to the distinctive ethos which they believed was widely shared across the faculty. Features which stood out as particularly significant included a deep commitment to understanding learning and a concern for children and their various needs, coupled with a strong sense of collegiality. Such values, although implicit, are vulnerable unless publicly affirmed and are liable to become eroded by external pressures. It is for this reason that staff working in the primary phase met together for an in-service development event to try to further articulate their shared values and beliefs.

Building a Consensus

Colleagues from the School of Teacher Education and Development began by exploring the terrain and entering into an open discussion about their values, visions and dreams. They then divided into groups where they could share and develop ideas in greater detail and begin to collaborate on building a consensus. Although there were no official convenors, one member of each group agreed to take notes to share with others and to compile a summary. There was tacit agreement that discussions should be positive and forward looking—this was not the forum for making complaints or sharing grievances.

After a lengthy and animated dialogue, each group reported back to the others to share ideas. The main points were written down as bullet points on a flip chart by the group spokesperson, together with any immediate observations or comments from other staff. Colleagues were also invited to provide individual feedback using sticky notes to capture wider, and possibly divergent, views. The format of the day and the spirit in which it was conducted was both affirmative and collegial. Amin and Roberts (2008) build on Wenger's notion of a 'community of practice' (Wenger, 1998) to recognise how impromptu networks can develop in situations where professionals come together to experiment and create new ideas. The way that colleagues engaged with the values discussion showed many of the features which Amin and Roberts identify—including the untidiness that surrounds creative endeavour and the difficulties surrounding dissemination.

In order to identify an agreed statement of values, three colleagues with research experience agreed to undertake a more detailed analysis of the day's discussions. The flip-charts, sticky notes and other notes were carefully scrutinised and categorised into emerging themes using a grounded theory approach (Glaser and Strauss, 1967). Each statement was examined in turn, and all three researchers had to agree that it had been correctly categorised and was genuinely rooted in what staff had written, both in spirit and in detail. After much discussion, a set of statements emerged as succinct summaries which encapsulated the original notes and which articulated the ethos of the school in a meaningful way (Figure 1.2). There were five themes, each imbued with values:

Community: We learn from each other, through co-operation, collaboration and the building of quality relationships.

Respect: All learners need to be in environments where they are trusted, nurtured, loved and supported in becoming autonomous.

Knowledge: We believe in the importance of developing the expertise of all learners in all disciplines.

Evidence: We recognise that the education profession must be underpinned by research, debate and the opportunity for critical reflection.

Innovation: We support each other to move beyond compliance by taking risks, being creative and thinking globally.

The next step was to report back to the school on what had been achieved and to discuss how the summary statements might best be used. In the ensuing discussions, questions were raised about how the values could be disseminated to students, whether they should be published and if they might be used for judgment or assessment. The values statements were also seen as important for informing all aspects of practice, including school partnerships, and as a base for programme and course development. Some colleagues challenged the extent to which the values reflected their personal views. Others affirmed that the process of discussion had

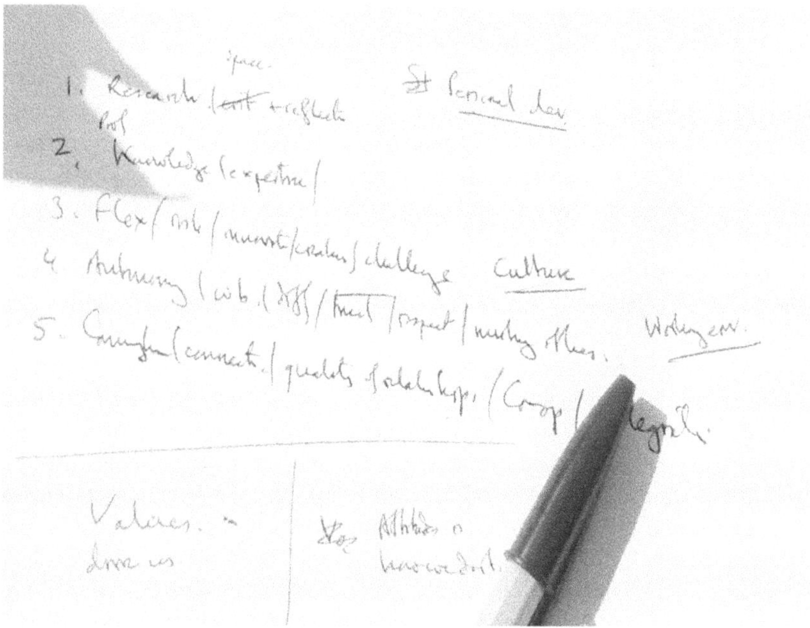

Figure 1.2 Five main themes emerged from the data

itself reinforced the ethos of the school which had been the stimulus for the whole exercise. The debate continued.

Reflection and Analysis

It would be an exaggeration to claim that discussing and agreeing values has transformed the practice of the faculty or school. It has, however, had a significant impact. As well as being affirmative, the process has served to raise the profile of values and reinforced their important in underpinning practice. An article about the process has been posted on the university blog (Barnes and Scoffham, 2014). Colleagues are also clearer about the values that they share and better placed to talk about values in their work with students. Finding commonalities and affirming the deeper purpose of educational practice also seems to have been particularly helpful at a time of unsettling organisational change.

There are also signs that the values debate will have a more lasting impact. Candidates applying to work in the School of Teacher Education and Development are now made aware of its ethos when they come to be interviewed. The values which underpin the Christ Church approach to primary education are also included in marketing material. Interestingly, there has been an impact in other academic areas too. The new framework for sustainability which will be applied across the university now identifies a similar set of values as its ethical underpinning and has clearly been informed (and inspired) by the developments in the faculty of education.

How then do the general principles and values of primary educators relate to sustainability which is a much more specific area of study? At first glance, there might seem to be little congruence. The term 'sustainability' does not appear directly in any statements the educators devised, and terms such as social justice and global equity—two key values which are integral to ESD—are not identified either. However, a closer reading reveals that the foundations for sustainability education are embedded within all the statements. Taking each in turn:

1. *Community:* Building and working with communities at both a local and global scale are part of inclusive practice and lead directly to considerations of equality and justice.
2. *Respect:* Learning to understand yourself, honouring the wisdom and experience of others and working collaboratively are key features of a sustainability mindset.
3. *Knowledge:* Being sufficiently well informed about environmental issues is a basic requisite for wise decision making.
4. *Evidence:* Recognising research evidence that sustainability education involves overcoming hidden barriers and psychological resistance is essential if it is be effective.
5. *Innovation:* Being creative and adopting new approaches to environmental problems is essential if we are to address global warming and other global issues.

This overlap should not come as a surprise. The ethos which underpins sound educational practice is necessarily universal. What is much more interesting, however, is that ESD is not normally considered in such a wide context and is usually underpinned and supported by a narrower set of considerations. Concepts such as conservation, stewardship and resource management, whilst important, have limited application outside the world of ESD. Taking a different starting point has led to a much broader perspective.

Conclusion

Generic values such as the ones developed by teacher educators at Christ Church need unpacking if they are to be applied to sustainability education. However, they have wide appeal and are relevant to many different contexts. The way they have been generated in an inclusive manner and the meaningful involvement of a significant number of colleagues is also important. Such an approach offers a model which could be reinterpreted in different settings.

Recent guidance for higher education providers from the Qualifications and Assessment Authority (QAA) now formally recognises the role of values in ESD. The guidance declares that "all graduates will share responsibility as stewards not only of the environment but also of social justice" (p. 6). The guidance goes on to note that "the development of personal values is increasingly seen as important for professions where ethics and moral behaviour are a hallmark of good practice" (2014, p. 6). This guidance is not unproblematic. There is deep-seated unease in both schools and universities about promoting particular orthodoxies and ways of behaving. Bias and indoctrination stand in stark opposition to critical thinking and academic freedom. However, giving greater prominence to values and recognising them more explicitly might be one of the hallmarks of an increasingly confident and mature approach to ESD.

Whether we acknowledge it or not, values underpin all aspects of education at both an explicit and an implicit level. Basic decisions about learning and the selection of curriculum content are necessarily based on a set of beliefs and principles about the things which we believe really matter. But it is also important to acknowledge that the values dimension to education is much more prominent in some subject areas than others. In mathematics, for example, the subject matter is very often either abstract or neutral, and there is a particularly strong emphasis on skills. ESD stands at the other end of the spectrum. Here a commitment to the welfare and well-being of others at an individual, local and global level is a fundamental pre-requisite. So too is a deep concern for the natural world and the health of the planet that sustains us. It is important to acknowledge this ethical basis, to find ways in which colleagues can develop shared values, and to incorporate them appropriately in teaching programmes. Recognising the way that values interconnect and overlap is an important part of this process and exploring these complexities could be one way to develop an increasingly mature understanding of the role of sustainability perspectives in all aspects of education.

Acknowledgement

The author would like to thank Jonathan Barnes for his support and involvement in writing this chapter.

References

Amin, A. and Roberts, J. (2008). Knowing in action: Beyond communities of practice. *Research Policy*, 37(2), pp. 353–369.

Barnes, J. and Scoffham, S. (2014). Values Matter. *Considered—The Faculty of Education Blog at Canterbury Christ Church University*. Available at: <www.consider-ed.org.uk/values-matter/>. Accessed 8 September 2015.

Booth, T. and Ainscow, M. (2011). *Index for Inclusion: Developing Learning and Participation in Schools*. Bristol: Centre for Studies on Inclusive Education.

Canterbury Christ Church University. (2015). *Strategic Framework 2015–2020*. Available at: <https://cccu.canterbury.ac.uk/strategic-framework/strategic-framework.aspx>. Accessed 11 May 2015.

Glaser, B. and Strauss, A. (1967, 2012). *The Discovery of Grounded Theory: Strategies for Qualitative Research*. London: Aldine.

Goswami, U. (2015). *Children's Cognitive Development and Learning*. York: Cambridge Primary Review Trust.

Hicks, D. (2014). *Education for Hope in Troubled Times*. Stoke on Trent: Trentham.

Parkin, S. (2010). *The Positive Deviant*. London: Routledge.

Quality Assurance Agency. (2014). *Education for Sustainable Development: Guidance for UK Higher Education Providers*. Gloucester: QAA.

Wenger, E. (1998). *Communities of Practice: Learning, Meaning, and Identity*. Cambridge: Cambridge University Press.

2 How Do Teachers Engage With School Values and Ethos?

Alison Clark

Introduction

The question 'How do teachers engage with school values and ethos?' has implications for Education for Sustainable Development and Global Citizenship (ESD/GC). Drawing on a case study in a Catholic high school, this chapter will suggest that teachers who take a stance on values can have a powerful impact in the classroom. However, the process of exploring and living out that stance is a complex one for teachers, and deserves more consideration and support. This chapter draws upon a research project conducted with twenty-one teachers in a Catholic high school. The study examined how these teachers perceived and implemented the expectation that they engaged with school ethos, which had a focus on Five Core Values. While the research was not specifically on how teachers managed a curriculum for ESD/GC (although that was part of the school's curriculum), I believe the process teachers used for values presentation and ESD/GC to be similar, precisely because these aspects of a school are more than simply functional. Values in a school ethos and curriculum for ESD/GC relate to more than academic content—they cause us to ask: *What does this mean for me, and how I choose to live my life?*

The Research Context

The research took place in a Catholic 11–18 high school in England during the school year 2012–2013. There were school students from a wide range of socio-economic backgrounds, and 62% were identified as baptised Catholics (Diocesan Inspection Report, 2011). An Ofsted Inspection in 2011 referred to the school as "characterised by a palpable ethos" and an "inclusive, harmonious community", where "students have a well-developed moral sense" (Ofsted, 2011).

Values were a prominent part of the expressed ethos of the school, and had been established as such since the appointment of the headteacher, in 2006. However, the values had not been a strong focus in the school prior to his arrival, despite its Catholic foundation; while always 'a great school', the headteacher commented that when he arrived, "teamwork, and culture and ethos . . . needed renewing" (HT, 2012b, p. 8). The Five Core Values were developed by a process of discussion and negotiation, finalised by the senior management team and adopted as the aspirational ethos of the school. They were: Respect, Co-operation, Compassion, Honourable Purpose and Stewardship. The headteacher stated, "Values are at the core of what I think is the main motivational driver in terms of leading a good church school" (HT, 2012a, p. 6). Along with this set of core values, there were themes such as 'Pay it Forward' relating to acts of kindness, and the strap line 'Aspire not to have more, but to be more', attributed to Archbishop Oscar Romero (1917–1980) of El Salvador (Gearon, 1998).

The main data collection for the case study took place during the academic year, with a minimum of five days in each of the six half-term blocks. There were three stages of interviews with volunteer teachers, and the interviews were recorded and fully transcribed. The volunteer sample consisted of twenty-one teachers, which was about a third of the teaching staff; twelve were female, and nine were male. Five of the teachers were newly qualified teachers (NQTs), and another two were experienced teachers, although new to the school. Through these subgroups I gained fresh impressions of the school. Seven of the sample had been in the school for ten years or more, so were able to speak about the changes brought about since 2006 when the headteacher had introduced the Five Core Values and a new approach to school ethos. Three of the sample held senior responsibility, and a further three had pastoral middle management roles while six were academic department leads. All curriculum subject areas were represented in the sample. Five of the teachers had training or mentoring roles with other schools.

This group of teachers formed the core of the data collection and analysis, but many other staff at the school had general discussions with the researcher. The longitudinal nature of the data collection meant that there was time to reflect on data, and then return to the school with new questions, or to revisit previous topics in order to triangulate data and to test emerging themes. The two key research questions were:

- How do the Five Core Values influence the day-to-day activities, choices and behaviours in the school?
- How do the Five Core Values impact upon the roles and work of teachers?

The relevance of these questions in relation to ESD/GC resides in the following areas. Firstly, this research sought to identify a perspective that was being imparted in the school and find out how teachers interpreted and communicated that perspective. Secondly, the research sought to understand what made the perspective meaningful.

Theoretical Framework

The study focussed on the school's aspirational ethos and how this was interpreted. Ethos as a term is used in the literature a variety of ways, of which two dominate: one is to refer to the aspirations of a school and its educational purposes, and the other to the mood or atmosphere that is experienced (Allder, 1993; Donnelly, 2000; Hogan, 1984; McLaughlin, 2005). Ethos may be aspirational as the intention is that "A mission statement should frame, inspire, give purpose to, drive and guide the daily work of an educational community" (Sullivan and McKinney, 2013, p. 216). Therefore, the ethos of an institution may be evident in its policies, activity, decisions and relationships (Donnelly, 2000, p. 150) and promoted visually in displays and on the website. However, experience of school life may or may not live up to or match the public message (Donnelly, 2000; McLaughlin, 2005). I used Donnelly's terminology to frame the layers of ethos, as shown in Figure 2.1.

Within this framework, the content of the aspirational ethos was examined and the outward manifestations of it identified. Teachers' perceptions of how the ethos should be expressed in action and relationships were sought. Through analysis of the data an aim was to identify evidence of inward attachment to the school's values and ethos and what that might mean to the teachers and for the school community's future action and development.

Findings and Discussion

The values terms were evident in a variety of contexts. There were visuals such as posters in corridors and headings on school documentation. The

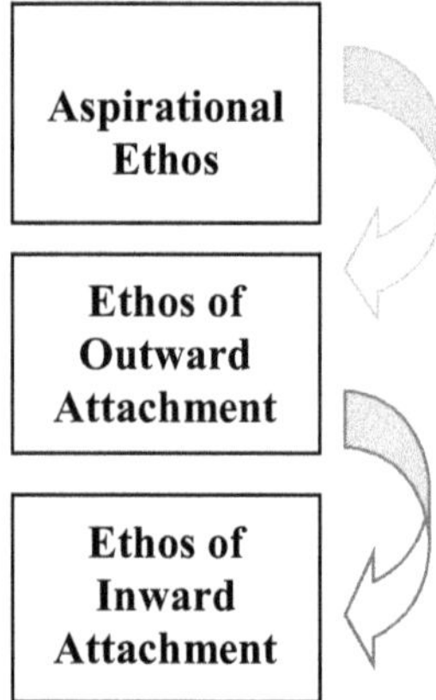

Figure 2.1 Structure of school ethos

Source: Adapted from Donnelly (2000).

values were reflected upon in assemblies, both those taken by teachers and those by the students. The use of space and time during the school day to make them evident indicated that the school's ethos, as a message, was important to senior management. In observations around school and in the classroom, it was noted that teachers referred to the Five Core Values, especially when talking about how the students should work together, and often linking to the content of the lesson.

In order to understand how the Five Core Values "influenced the day-to-day activities, choices and behaviours in the school", I used word-cards of the values terms on a table during the interviews, and encouraged teachers to arrange them in a way that was meaningful to them. Questions focussed on the meaning of the terms to each teacher, and how, in their experience, the values were experienced. On occasion, values terms were prioritised. An example of this is shown in Figure 2.2.

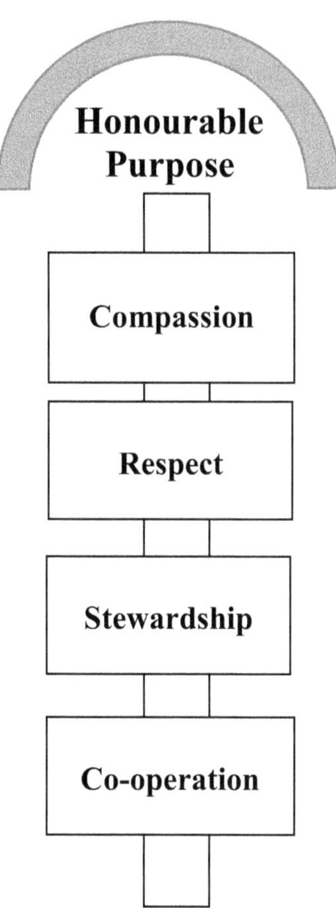

Figure 2.2 Pattern of the Five Core Values cards: Teacher Y

For Teacher Y, the concept of Honourable Purpose was the umbrella that brought all the meaning of the Five Core Values together, and acceptance of it could be life changing, as he explained:

> Honourable Purpose is the one that . . . sits up there separately at the moment, it says that "If you do it, you are the pupil that we're looking for. You are the individual human being that could *make a difference*".
>
> (Teacher Y.71, researcher's emphasis)

The variety of the patterns given to the Five Core Values word-cards and the different priorities given to terms by teachers were striking. There was no uniformity and no evidence that certain values terms would be emphasised by a particular teacher, for example, by subject taught, or faith perspective, or time in the school. There was, however, an indication that Heads of Year, who have a pastoral role in the school, found 'Compassion' particularly meaningful. This term was used frequently by them in the context of understanding the difficulties many students faced in their home lives and the world today.

Cooling argues that a shared anthropology is fundamental for genuinely shared values (Cooling, 2013, p. 110). There was evidence of values underpinning the relationships with students: for example, seeing each student as an individual deserving of Respect. It meant teachers were subject to the same expectations as students—an example being, saying sorry. All the teachers in the study identified that they had a responsibility to be a role model, and the term 'lived-out values' was used by the teachers to express this obligation: as Hill states, "[requiring] commitment of the whole self" (Hill, 2013, p. 29; see also Pring, 2010, p. xxi). Another example of living-out values was the link made between 'Stewardship' and management of resources in the classroom, the use of Fair Trade products in the canteen and action on recycling. 'Stewardship' extended into the curriculum, as in Art, where murals were created of found objects (litter) in the school grounds. Indeed, the term 'Stewardship' appeared even more personally meaningful for two teachers. One spoke of stewardship in terms of the futures of the students, linking it to how she taught her subject and the commitment she had to the students. The values term had moved beyond simply relating to external behaviour to providing internal meaning. Another teacher used the term to define what being a teacher was all about for him, particularly in care for them as people: "I think it's stewardship of the kids . . . you are stewarding their life in some way" (Teacher H.48).

This diversity of interpretation and emphasis indicated three aspects of engaging with an aspirational ethos. The first was that all teachers in the study did indeed connect with the values of the school, accepting their importance, and these values were in varying degrees and with different emphases significant in their role and work. The second related to the teachers themselves: they assimilated the terms into a pre-existing personal ethos, as shown by stories and key moments they described to illustrate the importance of a values term. The third aspect was the sense of freedom that teachers had in relation to the school's very specific message. The headteacher spoke of the school's aspirational ethos as supporting a 'personal journey'. The assurance with which teachers described that journey in their individual interpretations showed that this was an enabling factor in engaging with the ethos of the school.

Implications for ESD

The focus of this chapter is on the 'knowledge, skills, values and capabilities' which teachers need to facilitate a meaningful curriculum. The knowledge that teachers needed for values education concerned not just content but also the visible application of it, and they interpreted how they as teachers would live them out. Equally, they identified the need to provide opportunities to students to live out the values as well. The skills and capabilities teachers stated as most helpful in supporting the ethos of the school were dialogue and negotiation. Thiessen's term 'critical openness' is a useful concept and descriptor for the way that dialogue operated. It encourages frank questioning, conducted with respect (Thiessen, 1993). This, I would argue, allowed for genuine engagement with the values and ethos and would also help to make a curriculum meaningful.

Given that the aspirational ethos and values of the school were presented as a meaningful, relevant and important message, the same would need to be said of the curriculum related to ESD/GC. This research indicated that for a curriculum to be made meaningful it needs to move from cognitive to affective. The values in this school were not just talked about, they were acted out. Teachers explained in the research interviews and ad hoc conversations how they made the school's values relevant in the classroom and around school. Furthermore, there was evidence of how values influenced the systems of the school—through policy decisions, timetabling and budgets; how they were integrated into the life of the school outwardly through assemblies and inwardly in relationships. However, teachers also discussed how an ethos (or curriculum) may lack meaning when it is perceived to be hypocritical (Hill, 2008). The same can be true for ESD/GC: if it is just words, without commitment, then it will not be meaningful and it is likely that the message will be dismissed or even ridiculed.

Conclusion

The teachers in the study had been presented with Five Core Values that they were to promote, in the same way that teachers may be asked to deliver ESD/GC. All teachers in the study stated that the values were important and sought to apply them in their teaching role and relationships, albeit in diverse ways. This willing attitude towards the aspirational ethos is linked to Donnelly's idea of outward attachment and might be seen as simply compliance. However, it became clear that, by having time to reflect on and consider the implications of the school ethos, there was evidence of a values cycle, where the values engagement became part of the individual's perception of what it meant to be a teacher and promoted attitudes relating to the values. It was at this level that the ethos moved towards inward attachment and, through this values cycle, further enhanced the meaning of the aspirational ethos.

As a result of this case study, I would suggest that the ESD/GC curriculum needs to involve several features. The most important is the clarity of the aspirational ethos that underpins it—that is, the educational purpose of ESD/GC and also the values connected with it. Having identified this starting point, there needs to be a commitment to cultivating an ethos of outward attachment at every level of school life, including governance, systems and relationships. ESD/GC must be lived out, and in order for this to be meaningful, and not hypocritical, all members of the community need time and space to reflect on and identify how the purpose and values of ESD/GC are shown in the school and the areas for which they are responsible. Finally, there needs to be support for teachers to develop the 'knowledge, skills, values and capabilities' that will empower and sustain them in this role.

References

Allder, M. (1993). The Meaning of 'School Ethos'. *Westminster Studies in Education*, 16, pp. 59–69.

Cooling, T. (2013). Teachers and Christian religious values. In: J. Arthur and T. Lovat (eds.), *The Routledge International Handbook of Education, Religion and Values*, 100–113. Abingdon: Routledge.

Diocesan Inspection Report. (2011). [Reference Anonymised].

Donnelly, C. (2000). In Pursuit of School Ethos. *British Journal of Educational Studies*, 48(2), pp. 134–154.

Gearon, L. (1998). *A Modern Martyr*. Norwich: Chansitor Publications Ltd.

Hill, B. V. (2008). How learners respond to the teaching of beliefs and values. *Journal of Education and Christian Belief*, 12(2), pp. 101–113.

Hill, B. V. (2013). Do values depend on religion? would it be best if they didn't? In: J. Arthur and T. Lovat (eds.), *The Routledge International Handbook of Education, Religion and Values*, 28–41. Abingdon: Routledge.

Hogan, P. (1984). The Question of Ethos in Schools. *The Furrow*, 35(11), pp. 693–703.

HT. (2012a, 2012b, 2013). *Interviews with the Headteacher*.

McLaughlin, T. (2005). The Educative Importance of Ethos. *British Journal of Educational Studies*, 53(3), pp. 306–325.

Office for Standards in Education (OFSTED). (2011). *Inspection Report.* Manchester: Ofsted. [Reference anonymised].

Pring, R. (2010). Preface and introduction. In: T. Lovat, R. Toomey and N. Clement (eds.), *International Research Handbook on Values Education and Student Wellbeing*, xix–xxiv. Dordrecht: Springer.

Sullivan, J. and McKinney, S. J. (eds.). (2013). Exploring practical implications. In: S. J. McKinney and J. Sullivan (eds.), *Education in a Catholic Perspective*, 209–225. Farnham, Surrey: Ashgate.

Thiessen, E. J. (1993). *Teaching for Commitment: Liberal Education, Indoctrination, and Christian Nurture.* Montreal and Kingston, Canada: McGill-Queen's University Press.

3 Learning to Unlearn

Moving Educators From a Charity Mentality Towards a Social Justice Mentality

Jen Simpson

Introduction

Educators hold a potentially pivotal role in promoting a just and sustainable world for current and future generations. However, in reality, for many schools and educators, global learning begins with charity and fundraising or what Andreotti (2006) likens to 'soft global citizenship'. This 'charity mentality' can distort people's perceptions of other countries or peoples, particularly of those in the 'South'. This chapter discusses the possible negative outcomes of a 'charity mentality' and how, by engaging in critical reflections into local and global injustices, especially from the perspectives of others, educators can begin to disrupt the 'myths' about our relationship with the global 'South' and ensure a more equitable educational response to global issues based on social justice.

This chapter endeavours to explore the possibilities for educators to move from a 'charity mentality' towards a 'social justice mentality' and how we, as educators, can engender this 'social justice mentality' in ourselves and our pupils. Drawing upon research and qualitative evidence from my school-based action research study funded by the Global Learning Programme (GLP) Innovation Funding in the UK, this chapter examines interventions used in a professional development scenario designed around the 'learning to unlearn' ideology to encourage a process of critical and reflective learning to produce a transformative move towards a social justice mentality.

Learning to Unlearn

> The mind is not a vessel to be filled but a fire to be lit.
>
> Plutarch

Learning is, essentially, about moving the learner forward, whether it is their knowledge, skills, behaviour, understanding of or initiation of change. Our education systems for both children and adults generally reflect the constructivist theory of learning which throws up a number of issues, especially for trainers of Development Education or Global Learning. Our learners do not arrive in our classrooms ready to have their minds 'filled', but are individuals with their own construct of their immediate world and their 'global' world. The 'landscape' of their minds, as suggested by Piaget (2001), has been continuously built upon (assimilated or constructed) and moulded (accommodated) as the individual has tried to make meaning from the world around them. The 'constructed world' of the learner can significantly hinder real or deep learning as it relies on building on previous ideas to develop new understanding. These previous ideas may be distorted, shaped by various education initiatives, or overly impacted by influences such as media, family, social groups and the internet.

Spivak argues that active unlearning is an essential part of the process of deep learning (Andreotti, 2007). Through embracing a practice of deconstruction and reconstruction of knowledge (Campbell and Baikie, 2013), teachers can encourage critical and reflective learning or learning to unlearn which has the potential to result in a "major shift in perspective" (Hoggan, Simpson and Stuckey, 2009, p. 8).

Charity Mentality vs Social Justice Mentality

> Philanthropy is commendable, but it must not cause the philanthropist to overlook the circumstances of economic injustice which make philanthropy necessary.
>
> Martin Luther King, Jr.

Commentary and debate on charity is not new; philosopher J. S. Mill, writing in the late 1860s, criticised the lack or type of education of those providing charity. He argued that when philanthropists focus on the "education of sentiments rather than understanding" and "looking to immediate effects on persons and not to remote effects on classes of persons" (cited in Saunders-Hastings, 2014, p. 246), it is ultimately detrimental to those they wish to aid.

Moving to the twenty-first century, this critique of charity still holds true in the context of education; there is still too much emphasis on the helplessness of those in 'need' and the emphasis on 'our' role in solving the problem which, as Andreotti argues, just perpetuates an unequal relationship and continues a "colonial framing of the world" (Tallon, 2012, p. 7). This focus on the West's responsibility for the South places those in the North in a position of power, creating a seemingly kind and benevolent master but a master nonetheless.

The charity mentality may have more recently been re-packaged into more palatable forms, such as Band Aid, Comic Relief in the UK, or through education initiatives such as active global citizenship, but essentially the message remains the same: "we learn about you, and then we help you" (Tallon, 2012, p .8). This sentiment reinforces that sense of responsibility without questioning why. This standard message promoting a charity mentality as the norm has the potential to distort people's perceptions of other countries or peoples, and it can become a smokescreen behind which hide complicated issues and historical prejudices which allow the continuation of unfair practices and promote unbalanced societies. Andreotti likens it to a "sanctioned ignorance" (2006, p. 44) for societies of the West, preventing critical engagement whilst perpetuating the 'myth' of the West as the 'good guys' on a civilising mission.

If we consider a social justice mentality in relation to a charity mentality, the main difference is that we remove the smokescreen of 'sanctioned ignorance'; by engaging in critical reflections into local and global injustices, especially from the perspectives of others, we begin to disrupt those 'myths' about our relationship with the global 'South'.

It is suggested by Andreotti that education policies relating to the global dimension in England have provided a continuation of imperialistic thinking and encouraged educators towards a soft global citizenship (GC) approach to teaching and learning about the world. The tokenistic attempts at promoting the 'Other' through dance, art and music along with the images of poverty-stricken countries have unintentionally undermined educators' attempts to engage their pupils with issues and possibly reinforced stereotypes and prejudices. I would suggest that much of what Andreotti calls soft GC can be compared to charity mentality with similar negative outcomes such as "cultural supremacy", "reinforcement of colonial assumptions" and "uncritical action" (Andreotti, 2006, p. 48). It must be recognised, however, that charity or soft GC is often the starting point into learning about global issues and development (Bourn, 2014), especially within schools, and therefore unlearning this bias is essential for educators in order to move forward towards a social justice or critical GC mentality.

Research Methodology

The Participants—Context

This research involved a group of six primary school teachers from a primary school participating in the GLP in England. The range of teaching experience varied from 1 to 5 years (2), 5 to 10 years (2), 10 to 20 years (1) and one of over 20 years' experience. Initially, all participants were requested to complete a Learning Needs Analysis (LNA) baseline on their understanding of the terms 'charity mentality' and 'social justice mentality' and to discover what forms of global learning currently occur in school.

The training session was recorded, transcribed and analysed, and a final report for the GLP Innovation Fund has been published on their website (Simpson, 2016). This chapter will provide an overview of the intervention and focus on the key findings regarding moves from a charity to social justice mentality.

The Training Session—Interventions

Employing the 'learning to unlearn' ideology, I designed the training session around the following critical reflection process proposed by Fook (2006) and which is used to structure my reflections here:

1. Unsettling or unearthing of fundamental assumptions;
2. Potential for further reflection on assumptions;
3. Breakthrough connections are made/recognising the origins of assumptions;
4. Evaluating assumptions against current experience/experiences of others;
5. Old assumptions are reframed;
6. Changes within practice based on new/reconstructed understanding.

Intervention 1: Framing (Part 1)—Unearthing of Fundamental Assumptions

Taking Andreotti's (2006) suggestion of a 'colonial framing of the world', I adapted a 'spectacles' activity used in GLP professional development, using instead a frame to surround a world map (Simpson, 2016, p. 22), and asked the participants to write elements of their identity which might influence their world view. The activity highlights how our influences, experiences and personalities can affect our perception of the world around us and draws attention to the fact that we 'construct' our world view based on those elements:

> D—"You could write some of these down".
> A—"I wouldn't think of those. . . . I am not middle-aged, married or a parent".
> D—"I wonder if we see the world different, you and me".

This activity set the scene for the 'unlearning' to begin.

Intervention 2: Why Are We Changing the Maps?—Unsettling and Further Reflection of Fundamental Assumptions

The 'unlearning' or 'deconstructing' process was initiated using a clip from 'The West Wing' (2001), as used by Campbell and Baikie (2013) as a means of challenging assumptions and the notion of a 'world view'. This proved a surprisingly 'unsettling' experience for the participants:

> B—"You never think about it that way".
> C—"Do you not just assume North is up?"
> D—"You've freaked us out a bit".

It was also a liberating experience as it opened up new possibilities and avenues of thinking or questioning and was referred to throughout the session. The participants themselves rated this intervention highest in terms of impact.

Intervention 3: Framing (Part 2)—Breakthrough Connections Are Made/Recognising the Origins of Assumptions

This intervention was designed to mimic the 'colonial framing' of the world by introducing a 'hidden' frame of influences such as colonialism, Empire, media, to further challenge the participants' assumptions and their origins.

> C—"We should have a balanced view".
> D—"But we don't have a balanced view do we? Because of the way we have been brought up and the way we've been taught these countries are portrayed".

Intervention 4: Box o' Poverty Cartoon—Evaluating Assumptions against Current Experience/Experiences of Others

In Intervention 4, the focus moved to considering social justice itself through Andreotti's (2006) 'Soft versus Critical Global Citizenship' grid (pp. 46–48). The intervention used the Box o' Poverty cartoon (Sorensen, 2014) as a stimulus for thinking about our role within a socially unjust world and to work through Andreotti's grid. The teachers found this challenging due to the complexity of the text and contentious stimulus.

Intervention 5: Soft GC vs Critical GC—Old Assumptions Are Reframed

This provided an opportunity for the participants to begin to reconstruct or reframe their new understanding around critical GC, thereby encouraging their future educational practice around a social justice approach. The teachers were asked to further explore the 'soft vs critical global citizenship' grid created by Andreotti (2006) by sorting school initiatives such as Fairtrade and Foodbanks into either 'soft' or 'critical' categories.

The grid (Andreotti, 2006) has been subsequently redesigned (Simpson, 2016, p. 28) after the initial research project and made more accessible for teachers (represented as Figure 3.1).

The general agreement was that much of school practice focuses, as expected, on the 'soft' GC and, as participant D is quoted, "I think most schools would say that wouldn't you?".

	Soft global learning/charity mindset	*Critical global learning/social justice mindset*
Approach *(What?)*	One-off campaigns, assemblies, theme days, food tasting Charity or fundraising linked to local, and global events/ needs Moral/emotive focus (caring value) Focus on poverty (reduction of), helplessness or lack of rights	Global Learning approaches within lessons/topics/ campaigns as well as one-off events/days Consider and explore local and global issues Knowledge and understanding focus (educational value) Focus on inequality, social justice and rights
Reason *(Why?)*	'Impulse to help', moral, being 'good' Responsibility FOR the other (or to teach them) Caring for poor people	'Impulse to understand', equity and ethical Responsibility TOWARDS the other (to learn/decide with the other) Solidarity with people without rights or opportunities and challenge this where possible
Action *(How?)*	Help people to survive poverty—raising money for poor countries overseas Sharing our wealth	Participate in structural change for elimination of poverty and inequality Critiquing how we got wealthy
Learning *(Message)*	Reduce poverty through charitable work, campaigning and fundraising	Challenge inequality and injustice and support rights for all
Outcomes *(Positive)*	Feel-good Greater awareness of some of the problems Motivation to help/do something	Sustained engagement Independent/critical thinking and more informed, responsible and ethical action Encourage pupil voice and advocacy Encourages self-reliance and self-determination for poor countries

Figure 3.1 Comparing the charity and social justice mindsets

	Soft global learning/charity mindset	*Critical global learning/social justice mindset*
Outcomes *(Negative)*	Can encourage or sustain a sense of cultural superiority or privilege Sustains dependency for poor countries Reinforces prejudice and stereotypes Uncritical action	Sometimes uncomfortable and can bring about guilt and shame Can feel overwhelming, leading to a feeling of helplessness
Ultimate goal *(of education?)*	Empower individuals *to act* (or become active citizens) according to *what has been defined for them* as a good life or ideal world	Empower individuals *to reflect critically* on their understandings and perceptions, *to imagine different futures and to take responsibility* for their decisions and actions
Pupil participation *(Where does change happen?)*	From the outside inside *(imposed change)*	From the inside to the outside *(negotiated change)*

Figure 3.1 (Continued)

Various reasons for this were discussed, such as their own confidence in teaching about the complex issues involved because "you shy away from stuff you don't know" (Participant D) and that soft GC presented "easier solutions" (Participant B) for primary age children. The idea that primary age children, especially at Key Stage 1, were not able to learn or understand the concept of injustice or inequality ran throughout the session and within the questionnaires. However, studies such as Oberman (2013) illustrate that young children have the capacity to approach these concepts and issues. Fundamentally, I feel that the main barrier or challenge is teacher confidence in this instance: "unsure as many of the issues seem too complex to discuss in sufficient detail with such young children" (Participant E). Wider research in this area concurs with this observation (Hunt, 2012) that confidence and skills in approaching complex global themes can be an inhibitor for teachers as well as time within the curriculum and opportunity for training. There seems to be an assumption that global issues are a subject to be taught and therefore teachers must have expert knowledge of these complex issues. This is more of an insight into the current educational climate where all knowledge is tested and the focus is on subjects being taught rather than a focus on the learning itself.

Initial Evaluation: Changes within Practice Based on New/Reconstructed Understanding

In order to analyse whether the intervention produced a transformative move towards social justice mentality the follow-up questionnaire was focussed on impact in terms of the participants' personal and professional perspectives and their educational practice. It also provided opportunity to review their understanding of social justice, providing comparisons with the LNA.

The initial analysis of the qualitative data from the questionnaire showed promising results in most areas.

Impacts on personal perspectives, for some, were profound:

D—"It has made me question my own life, my family life and my perspective on my teaching of geography and global issues".

F—"I have been inspired to do some more research into the issues raised, reading chapters and listening to talks to gain a deeper insight into some of the issues, particularly the issue of tackling poverty and providing education for all".

While others revealed changes in attitudes and behaviour:

B—"I will now question and have a more critical view of things seen in the media and what I am being told".

A—"I am going to question everything".

In relation to teaching practice, the participants reported some changes in their approach to teaching and learning, especially in terms of facilitating questioning and encouraging open dialogue:

D—"In the future I will be a lot more careful about giving a balanced view of things and making sure that the information I give the children is correct. Or if I don't know—putting it out there for discussion".

One participant demonstrates a 'shift' from the charity mentality or focus to a more critical/Social Justice approach:

F—"When discussing the 'send my friend to school' campaign with my class, I ensured that I guided the discussion beyond the idealistic idea of building schools in villages in Africa by discussing the issues of safety, resources, expertise, etc. I also asked the children to think about possible reasons why some countries do not have the same opportunities for everybody".

When asked about whole-school impact, the participants reported some potential changes:

> F—"I think that as a school we will look into more detail about the subjects that we deliver making sure that we are providing the children with a non-biased up to date education".
>
> B—"I think we may be less willing to join in with the loudest shouting charities and instead focus on something that we have really looked into and researched".

Follow-Up Review: Changes within Practice Based on New/Reconstructed Understanding

One of my initial concerns with the project was the potential for a loss in 'transformation' once the participants returned to the classroom and usual pressures came into play. Therefore, a second questionnaire, conducted three months later, was quite important in terms of gauging the longer-term impacts of the interventions, especially as there was also a six week summer break in-between (three out of six participants completed the anonymised questionnaire).

All three respondents concurred that teaching and learning about social justice was important with one explaining: "*so they understand that everybody needs to be equal and deserves the right to be equal*".

In terms of engendering and maintaining a move from charity mentality towards a social justice mentality the responses are very encouraging:

> I think it's important for all children (and adults) to realise that charity is a temporary short-term solution.
>
> I never really agreed with charity anyway but it just emphasised my thinking that if we want to make a change or impact we need to look deeper into the issue instead of giving money to charity.

Part of the reason the interventions were so successful might be that they were designed to personally challenge as well as professionally challenge the participants. Those initial interventions which shook the foundations of their own assumptions or constructed knowledge had a subsequent significant impact on their personal perspective and openness to 'new' ideas or concepts:

> Thinking carefully about the charities I support and how they work.
>
> It raised my awareness of global issues and the way we could change our perceptions of charity.

Although this seems very positive in terms of a move from charity mentality, I do have some concerns about the success of their understanding or interpretation of social justice. For instance, it seemed that the giving of money was being replaced: "instead of us giving money we should be giving the knowledge" (Participant A). This also came out within the second questionnaire:

> We have skills and resources which would, if shared, have a bigger impact on world issues than our 'charity'.
>
> Long-term social justice teaches us to help others to help themselves through generations.

I would suggest the danger here is that the giving of 'knowledge' has the potential to be creating another form of 'little developers' (Biccum, 2010). This idea that the West has the universal knowledge that others need still has the potential to distort perceptions of other people and places. The use of the term 'charity' is unhelpful as it is so closely connected to money, and therefore moves away from giving funds may provide the illusion of moving away from a charity mentality. An additional concern is highlighted within the varied responses to impact on teaching practice:

> It has changed the way I think about teaching geography, citizenship and global learning. It makes me want to make the children more aware of our impact on the world both by doing nothing and by supposedly giving support.
>
> I don't feel it has impacted my teaching practice as much because we still have to follow the curriculum but I try to show the children the wider picture instead of the stereotypes.

These opposing comments illustrate very clearly one of the great challenges for this research and for the Global Learning as a whole. Teachers can feel limited by the curriculum and demands on their practice. One responder explains simply that:

> if changes were to be made it would have to go through the head teacher, because it was done with a small group of us we can't enforce the changes as much as the head teacher would be able to.

This may not be strictly true, as teachers do have some flexibility within their own practice and classroom provision, and if these interventions had significant impact on their personal perceptions one would hope that would 'filter' into their practice. However, the hierarchy structures within schools can feel quite restrictive for teachers, and some require the 'sanction' from Senior Leadership Team (SLT) to engage in this area of learning. As mentioned previously, this could be attributed to an assumption that global learning sits on the periphery of the curriculum and the perception from teachers that they need the SLT to engage and actively endorse teachers to bring it to the core. One participant suggested that this professional development should be offered "to management so they can enforce any changes". Engaging SLT is essential if we are looking for whole-school change; at the same time, unless we also engage and alter the perceptions of teachers in the classrooms there is the potential for a 'top-down' approach whereby teachers find they have been given yet another task or target to meet. This could result in the dual negatives of disengagement and resentment and could ultimately result in short-lived changes. Instead, for this mind-shift to be successful in the long term, teachers need to be personally engaged and involved from the beginning. In fact, there is growing evidence that teachers themselves are the drivers for global learning within schools (Hunt, 2012).

Conclusion

First impressions from the dialogue and qualitative data show a promising trend or a significant shift in perspectives and practice by many of the participants. Realistically, in the scope of this small research study, I would suggest that full transformation might not be the goal and it is difficult to qualify; as Bourn (2014) argues, simply judging success based on participants' changes in views or actions is too simplistic. That being said, the findings presented here suggest that promoting the skill of critical reflection or learning to unlearn amongst teachers is invaluable for their practice. I would argue it should be recognised as a core pedagogical skill. The ability to engage in critical thinking with their peers and their pupils as an approach to learning has the potential to engender a culture of transformative learning. The evidence shows that the participants' personal perceptions and, to some extent, their professional practice have been impacted through the interventions, both in the short term and long term.

Moving away from a charity mentality was, for some, essentially about moving away from fundraising, or more specifically, fundraising without question or consideration of impact or perceptions. For these participants, their 'move' involved only a few 'steps' from handing over money to handing over knowledge or skills for development, which is essentially still rooted in what I consider a form of the charity mentality. This is not wholly negative for those participants, and they did still show understanding of a need to move away from fundraising and the importance of questioning and becoming critical thinkers.

Nevertheless, it would seem that these interventions have engendered a perception change about charity and how schools in particular approach charity and the potentially negative consequences such an approach can have. Instead of the knee-jerk reaction or 'impulse to help' as Bryan (2013) describes it, the teachers indicated that they might approach charity or fundraising with a more critical eye and consider adopting a more critical educational approach which might have a more lasting impact than previously thought.

In terms of educators and a social justice mentality, Bryan et al. (2009) suggest that its importance has been amplified with modern globalisation and the realisation that many issues are indeed global ones which "transcend national borders" (2009, p. 21). If this is the case, the role of educators in encouraging young people to develop a social justice mentality is more significant than ever, as is the need to overcome a charity mentality and see beyond our colonial psyche to engender a truly equal global society.

References

Andreotti, V. (2006). Soft versus critical global citizenship education. *Policy & Practice: A Development Education Review*, 3(Autumn), pp. 40–51. Available at: <www.developmenteducationreview.com/issue/issue-3/soft-versus-criticalglobal-citizenship-education>

Andreotti, V. (2007). An ethical engagement with the other: Spivak's ideas on education. *Critical Literacy: Theories and Practices*, 1(1), pp. 69–79.

Biccum, A. (2010). *Global Citizenship and the Legacy of Empire: Marketing Development*. New York: Routledge.

Bourn, D. (2014). *The Theory and Practice of Global Learning. DERC Research Chapter No.11 for the Global Learning Programme*. London: Institute of Education.

Bryan, A., Clarke, M. and Drudy, S. (2009). *A Study of Student Teachers' Social Justice and Development Education*. Available at: <www.ubuntu.ie/media/bryan-clarke-drudy-2009.pdf>. Accessed 14 December 2018.

Bryan, A. (2013). 'The impulse to help': (Post) humanitarianism in an era of the 'new' development advocacy. *International Journal of Development Education and Global Learning*, 5(2), pp. 5–29.

Campbell, C. and Baikie, G. (2013). Teaching critically reflective analysis in the context of a social justice course. *Reflective Practice: International and Multidisciplinary Perspectives*, 14(4), pp. 452–464.

Fook, J. (2006). Beyond reflective practice: Reworking the critical in critical reflection. Keynote Lecture Presented at Professional Lifelong Learning: Beyond Reflective Practice, Trinity and All Saints College, Leeds, 3 July.

Hoggan, C., Simpson, S. and Stuckey, H. (2009). Transformative learning, multiple ways of knowing, and creativity theory in progress. In: C. Hoggan, S. Simpson and H. Stuckey (eds.), *Creative Expression in Transforming Learning: Tools and Techniques for Educational Adults*, 5–19. Malabar, Florida: Krieger.

Hunt, F. (2012). *Global Learning in Primary Schools: Practices and Impacts. DERC Research Chapter No. 9*. London: Institute of Education.

Oberman, R. (2013). From research to resource: Critical literacy and global citizenship education in middle primary school. In: *Proceedings of the Irish Association for Social, Scientific and Environmental Education (IASSEE) Annual Conference 2013*. IASSEE, Centre of Human Rights and Citizenship Education, 29–39. Drumcondra: St. Patrick's College.

Piaget, J. (2001). *The Psychology of Intelligence*. London and New York: Routledge.

Saunders-Hastings, E. (2014). No better to give than to receive: Charity and women's subjection in J S Mill. *Polity*, 6(2), pp. 233–254.

Simpson, J. (2016). *A Study to Investigate, Explore and Identify Successful 'Interventions' to Support Teachers in a Transformative Move from Charity Mentality to a Social Justice Mentality*. London: Global Learning Programme England and Development Education Research Centre. Available at: <https://drive.globaldimension.org.uk/wp-content/uploads/glp/GLP_pdfs/Research/Jen_Simpson_study.pdf>. Accessed 18 December 2018.

Sorensen, J. (2014). *Big Box o' Poverty*. Available at: <https://thenib.com/big-box-o-poverty-b7339419c9e5>. Accessed 16 December 2018.

Tallon, R. (2012). Emotion and agency within NGO development education: What is at work and what is at stake in the classroom? *International Journal of Development Education and Global Learning*, 4(2), pp. 5–22.

West Wing. (2001). *Why Are We Changing Maps?* YouTube clip. Available at: <www.youtube.com/watch?v=eLqC3FNNOaI>. Accessed 2 December 2014.

4 Understanding Hospitality and Invitation as Dimensions of Decolonising Pedagogies When Working Interculturally

Fatima Pirbhai-Illich and Fran Martin

Introduction

As academics working in teacher education, our different socio-cultural histories and subject disciplines mean that we bring different personal and professional lenses to our social justice work. Fatima, a scholar of colour, was born in Tanzania and immigrated to Canada at the age of sixteen. She brings a critical lens to language and literacy education, specifically to the intercultural space between white mainstream Canadian pre-service teachers and the minoritised and marginalised students they work with, including those from First Nations communities. Her praxis focuses on creating innovative approaches to language and literacy education using culturally responsive pedagogies within a decolonising framework. Her research deepens understandings of the beliefs systems and the historical, cultural, political, social and economic contexts that affect how diverse cultural groups learn with and alongside each other in the specific postcolonial context that the province of Saskatchewan in western Canada offers.

Fran, a white, Western, middle-class scholar, brings a critical lens to global and intercultural learning in postcolonial contexts. Her work focuses on the nature of the '*inter*', or location between cultures, as a space for *inter*cultural learning. Bringing spatial understandings from geography, and dialogic understandings from education, her research contests policies that reduce successful intercultural communication to the acquisition of a set of skills and competencies, arguing that knowledge of the histories (socio-cultural, political) and the power dynamics behind the relationship of those in conversation is a crucial factor influencing what is 'heard', how it is 'translated', and therefore what it is possible to learn from each other.

Our interests converge in developing relational understandings of how, through intercultural interactions, it is possible to establish a form of critical intercultural literacy that is supportive of education for just and sustainable futures. In so doing, we aim to make explicit the powerful forces at work in education that, we argue, *reproduce* inequalities rather than challenging them. For the purposes of this chapter, we discuss the ideas behind a pilot project that we commenced in 2015. The pilot builds on Fatima's research, conducted between 2007 and 2014, the key findings of which indicated the need to develop pre-service teachers' understandings of the importance and relevance of invitation and hospitality when using culturally responsive pedagogies of relation.

Fatima runs a yearly course, ERDG 425, on Culturally Responsive Literacy Education. It is a thirteen-week course that has a service-learning element in which pre-service teachers tutor a student from a minoritised, marginalised community for one hour a week on the university campus.

The majority of the students are from First Nations communities, while the pre-service teachers are predominantly from white settler communities; in this regard, the relationship between them is therefore influenced by colonialism (Martin and Pirbhai-Illich, 2015) and, as such, throws up many of the issues of global intercultural encounters discussed by Pashby and Sund in chapter 8. The ERDG 425 course is therefore designed to decolonise pre-service teachers' minds as part of their preparation for working with the students.

In the sections that follow, we first provide a brief description of culturally responsive pedagogy, followed by an overview of the research on ERDG 425 conducted between 2007 and 2014, the findings of which informed the pilot study reported here. We then provide an overview of the theory behind the concepts of invitation and hospitality and how they might be used by the pre-service teachers as part of a decolonial approach to developing non-coercive relationships with the students. In the final sections, we report on the initial findings and consider the implications for education for sustainable and just futures.

Culturally Responsive Pedagogy

Gloria Ladson-Billings (1995), acknowledged to be the founder of culturally responsive pedagogy (CRP), developed the theory and associated pedagogical approaches in the USA during the 1990s. Concerned about the significant educational underachievement of African-Americans, she drew on Critical Race Theory (CRT) (Ladson-Billings and Tate, 1995) to inform her work. CRT examines the appearance of race and racism across dominant cultural modes of expression. CRP has a dual focus on revealing how institutional inequalities based on race pervade the experiences of people of colour in every aspect of their lives, and on giving a voice to those whose experiences have been silenced by using story-telling and other narrative forms to "heal the wounds of pain caused by racial oppression" (Ladson-Billings and Tate, 1995, p. 57).

Ladson-Billings showed that culturally responsive teachers have five key characteristics in common: they believe that all students are capable of academic success; they view pedagogy as an art; they see themselves as members of the community; they see teaching as a way to give back to the community; and they hold the belief that teaching is pulling knowledge out, and that the curriculum is therefore created and shared by teacher and students (Ladson-Billings, 1995). CRP works from the assumptions that much of mainstream education is framed on the cultural, historical and social norms of the dominant group; the approach unpacks these norms through the development of critical consciousness and, rather than positioning minoritised students as deficient, teachers working within a culturally relevant framework encourage them to utilise their 'funds of knowledge' (Moll et al., 1992) in the process of developing a "community of learners" (Ladson-Billings, 1995, p. 163) that includes the teacher 'self' in the equation. In this way, CRP serves to disrupt the dominant idea of the white teacher as racially neutral, while at the same time to challenge the assumption of the white teacher as the knower imparting wisdom upon racially diverse learners.

Previous Research

Between 2007 and 2014, Fatima conducted a longitudinal, ethnographic study into pre-service teachers' ability to use culturally responsive pedagogy (CRP) when working with minoritised and marginalised adolescent students in the Regina school district of Saskatchewan who have been failed by the education system (Pirbhai-Illich et al., 2009, 2010, 2011; Pirbhai-Illich, 2013; Austin et al., 2014). The findings are summarised under four key areas, from which flow a number of implications that have informed the next phase of research and which are the focus of the second part of this chapter.

Constructions of Culture

Understandings of how culture is conceptualised in education need to be broadened, moving away from essentialist, surface level manifestations (skin colour, dress, food, customs etc.), to fluid, deep level understandings (the meanings and significances that underpin dress, food, customs etc.) that include home/family cultures or 'funds of knowledge' (Moll et al., 1992). This enables teachers to envision culture as integral to people's individual and communitarian identities, and as situated within specific domains that are historically, politically, spatially and socially contextualised. The findings suggest that pedagogical practices need to be based on the premise that these situated, contextualised domains contribute to the production of cultural litera*cies*—literacies are expressed in the plural because the form that literacy takes will differ according to the specific nature of the influencing factors and domains. In turn this requires recognition on the part of the teachers that their conceptualisation of culture and literacy is just *one* conceptualisation and that other conceptualisations are just as legitimate. Developing deep understanding of the funds of knowledge of the minoritised and marginalised youth they work with is one step towards this, but the findings of the 2007–2014 studies demonstrated that on its own this is not sufficient.

Funds of Knowledge

The concept of 'funds of knowledge' is based on a simple premise: people are competent and have knowledge, and their life experiences have given them that knowledge (Moll et al., 1992). The findings of the 2007–2014 studies showed that when the pre-service teachers built on the students' funds of knowledge and connected them to the formal curriculum, this empowered the school students because they felt they had agency in determining their curriculum. This led to high levels of student engagement, which helped the teachers to push the students to stretch themselves and have higher expectations of what they were able to achieve. In order to successfully use funds of knowledge, the pre-service teachers had to learn how to work with multiliteracies, since these were the forms in which the students shared their funds of knowledge.

However, some pre-service teachers struggled to work with these approaches because they confused funds of knowledge (which stem from family culture and are enduring) with 'interests' (which stem from any cultural context and can be temporary), and they continued to focus on surface level features of culture. The students of these pre-service teachers showed absenteeism, disengagement and low levels of achievement. Data suggest that one of the key reasons for teacher candidates apparently rejecting the multiliteracies, CRP and funds of knowledge approach is that in ERDG 425, the module that is scheduled at the end of their degree, they learn that the accepted pedagogical models that predominate in mainstream classrooms are best suited to, and reflect, the cultural norms of, the mainstream students. If the pre-service teachers wish to be truly inclusive, they need to take a risk in using a new approach (CRP) that, in many ways, turns everything they have learnt up to that point on its head. Some were prepared to take the risk on, but others stayed within their comfort zone.

Pedagogies of Relation

Another finding that emerged is that learning cannot take place without relation, and it is the nature of this educational relationship that requires more explicit examination by the pre-service teachers. This became clear during the early iterations of the ethnographic studies, and in later iterations of ERDG 425, an explicit focus on relationality was incorporated into the course (Pirbhai-Illich, 2013). However, teacher candidates struggled with the concept of relationality, confusing it with relationships and, within the relationships that they built with their students, often confusing professional relationships (being enabling and supportive) with personal relationships (being a confidant and friend). This is explored in more detail below.

Culturally Responsive Pedagogy of Relations and Intercultural Learning

In our work both separately and together (Pirbhai-Illich, 2013; Martin and Griffiths, 2014) we argue that educational relationships are, by their very nature, intercultural. That is, what is learned through the relationship is in part the result of how the differences between those in the educational relationship are engaged with (see Martin and Pirbhai-Illich, 2016, for further detail). Intercultural learning entails intercultural communication, and much of the research and educational policy in this area argues that effective intercultural dialogue is achieved through the development of communicative competence. However, our findings show that while communicative competence is important, how people relate interculturally is strongly influenced by the socio-historical and political contexts of those engaging in dialogue. Our findings also indicate that while a focus on commonalities is important for creating a sense of connection between people, on its own it avoids the more challenging work of learning about and from differences. We argue that a deeper understanding of the concept of difference, informed by a relational ontology and epistemology, enhances understanding of one's own *and* others' cultures and identities (Martin and Griffiths, 2014). If culture is conceptualised in the way we described above, then *critical* intercultural learning might take place between individuals and/or groups on a variety of levels, where the dimensions of difference to be explored might include gender, ethnicity, language, religion, sexuality, discipline, organisational affiliation, nationality and so on. Pedagogies that aim for deeper understandings of self and other in the educational venture therefore need to focus not only on object-based outcomes but also relational outcomes.

Implications for the Next Phase of Investigation

The findings from our research have demonstrated that cultural responsiveness is not, on its own, sufficient. CRP is not just a technical know-how; it also requires a shift in a state of mind from one that is object-focused to one that is relational (Pirbhai-Illich, 2013; Martin, 2012). In this, the work of Nel Noddings and, in particular, Martin Buber, provide a means of theorising what we have found to be the case empirically. Relationality includes but is not limited to teacher–pupil relationships. Bigger (2011) argues that in order to develop successful teacher-pupil relationships it is necessary to understand the relationship between self and identity (Buber's I–It) before one can develop an understanding of the spiritual/existential nature of 'I' in relation to others (Buber's I–Thou). Buber believed that "the relation in [genuine] education is one of pure dialogue" (Buber, 1947, p. 98). In order to help the realisation of the best potentialities in the student's life, the teacher must learn to see the student "in his potentiality and his actuality", and to do so through awareness of "him as a whole being and affirm him in this wholeness" (Buber, 1958, pp. 164–165). For Buber, ethical education therefore entails educators engaging with others with their whole being through direct relations and dialogue.

There are parallels with Noddings' work on care ethics in education:

> Those of us who work from an ethic of care regard moral life as thoroughly relational. From this perspective, even the self is relational. . . . our selves are constructed through encounters with other bodies, objects, selves, conditions, ideas, and reflective moments with our previous selves.
>
> (Noddings, 2003, p. 158)

Where Buber uses the term 'affirmation', Noddings talks about 'confirmation': "when we confirm someone we identify a better self and encourage its development. To do this we must know the other reasonably well. Otherwise we cannot see what the other is really striving for . . . formulas and slogans have no place in confirmation" (Noddings, 1998, p. 192). In this regard Noddings disagrees with universal ideals and goals in education; rather, "we recognize something admirable, or at least acceptable, struggling to emerge in each person we encounter. The goal or attribute must be seen as worthy both by the person trying to achieve it and by us. We do not confirm people in ways we judge to be wrong" (Noddings, 1998, p. 192).

The challenge, and one that we investigated in the ERDG 425 pre-service course in 2015, is how to provide pre-service teachers with the knowledge and skills to enter into a professional relationship with marginalised and minoritised students that enables this to happen. Fisher (2013) argues that this requires humility on both the part of the teacher educators and the pre-service teachers. Everyone has a journey to make, and teacher educators should use their power to "guide, promote, encourage, challenge, pursue and hold accountable . . . but not to shame, ridicule, embarrass, humiliate or punish" (Fisher, 2013). We need to model "authentic, loving, and humble human interactions that [are] transformational and affirming" (Fisher, 2013) in order that our teacher candidates can do the same—this is called by some a pedagogy of unconditional love (Andreotti, 2011).

Drawing on postcolonial theory and decolonising pedagogy, Andreotti has referred to the conditions needed for such a relation as being "before will" (2011), in the sense that to enter into the encounter without objective, without seeking in relation to any agenda, requires a suspension of the ego and the historical-cultural influences on this—a stepping outside of the socialised self—into a space between (what Bhabha, 1994, refers to as third space, or the intercultural space). However, in order to do this and to avoid 'translating' the encounter through a socialised lens, one has to learn how to do it. Power relations are so implicit that (as Spivak, 1991, notes) there is a need to learn to unlearn before one can learn to listen and be open to what the Other has to teach us, a process discussed more fully by Jen Simpson in chapter 3 of this volume. Knowledge of self and the processes that have formed that self are therefore crucial first steps to stepping outside that self and learning how to encounter before will. This is what Buber refers to as the I–Thou.

Pilot Project: Using the Concepts of Invitation and Hospitality in a Service-Learning Course

The pilot project conducted in 2015 investigated the application of these concepts in ERDG 425 with pre-service teachers during their final semester before qualifying. In this project we took a collaborative, action research approach to: trialling interventions that have developed from our findings; gathering data on the impact of these on pre-service teachers' epistemological and pedagogical conceptions; and monitoring the effect this had on the young minoritised and marginalised youth they worked with during the service-learning element of the course. Having developed a relational approach to culturally responsive pedagogy, we found that questions remained as to the extent to which pre-service teachers were able to put this into practice.

The questions guiding our study were: what approaches can pre-service teachers use to open up an inviting space for interaction and learning? Once open, how can teacher candidates work with their students to maintain that engagement over a period of time? These questions provided the focus for the pilot project and were informed by invitational theory (Purkey and Novak, 1996; Schmidt, 2004) and the concept of hospitality as proposed by Derrida (2000).

Invitational theory has been developed within a counselling context and applied to education—particularly where learner populations are diverse (Schmidt, 2004). Professionals who apply the principles of invitational theory and practice adhere to four fundamental beliefs:

1. Every person wants to be accepted and affirmed as valuable, capable, and responsible, and wants to be treated accordingly.
2. Every person has the power to create beneficial messages for themselves and others, and because they have this power, they have the responsibility.

3. Every person possesses relatively untapped potential in all areas of learning and human development.
4. Human potential is best realised by creating places, programs, policies and processes intentionally designed to invite optimal development and encourage people to realise this potential in themselves and others.

(Purkey and Novak, 1996)

Currently invitational education theory focuses on how the teacher invites students to work with them; our research extended this by focussing on the interaction between teacher and student, conceptualising it as a dialogic, rather than monologic, space.

Hospitality, according to Derrida (2000), has an inherent tension between ownership of a bounded space and unconditional opening of this space to an unknown 'Other'. In order to be hospitable, there is an assumption of ownership that gives the power to host. It follows from this that the host will have control over the people being hosted—where they can have access to, what they might be able to do in the host's space. On the other hand, genuine hospitality requires the host to relinquish judgement and control in regard to those receiving the hospitality, abandoning all claims to property—Derrida refers to this as unconditional, or impossible, hospitality. Welcoming someone on one's own terms is therefore a hollow form of hospitality. Oden (2001, cited in Burwell and Huyser, 2013, p. 10) takes this further, to suggest that "hospitality is not so much a singular act of welcome as it is a way, an orientation that attends to otherness, listening and learning, valuing and honoring" (p. 14). Regarding the purpose of providing hospitality, Oden goes on to say, "The host identifies with the stranger/guest and chooses not to live out of any privilege those resources offer, but rather to understand himself or herself as a recipient, too" (p. 26). This dialogic conceptualisation of hospitality is central to our study.

Tentative Findings

Data were gathered from the course using pre-service teachers' online discussion board entries and their course assessments. In this chapter we present the initial analysis conducted for the UK Teacher Education for Equity and Sustainability Network (TEESNet) conference in 2015, at which this chapter was given as a paper (Pirbhai-Illich and Martin, 2015). The extracts below indicate how three pre-service teachers (pseudonyms are used) understood and applied the concepts of invitation and hospitality during their one-to-one tutoring during the course. These have been taken from their final assessment portfolio. Each extract is presented as raw data, followed by a short commentary.

Melissa, female, mid-twenties, white Canadian, Christian with degree in anthropology and religious studies, middle class. Tutored a male student age twelve.

> Invitation is about recognizing people's boundaries and trying to see the situation through the eyes of the other person, so thinking about how they might react to situations. It is about examining your own actions with an eye to being respectful. It is also about being aware of greeting and conversation conventions that are common within your own community and examining whether they are acceptable to everyone. This self-awareness is important with working with students from communities who have historically had negative relationships with mainstream communities because it means that you aren't taking the interaction for granted. When working with H I need to be keenly aware of the messages I'm sending to him. I need to think about whether I am supportive, reassuring, and receptive. Taken together this creates a space that Schmidt refers to as intentionally inviting. Being intentionally inviting means showing an interest in H's background and experiences, but I think it is equally important to realise that this can't be forced. I can open a window to H to share this with me but I can't push him through it [so] you are also giving this student the opportunity to reject your offer. It also welcomes the whole individual to the interaction, giving them the space to be present and make whatever contributions they wish to. It is not about the teacher directing conversation or content; by agreeing to participate in the interaction the students is also agreeing to contribute and share. It makes the interaction less one-sided.

Melissa emphasises the importance of being aware of her own positionality and subjectivity, and that her own ways of being and doing are not universal, as a pre-cursor to being inviting. This awareness enables her to decentre and to create a space of invitation into which the student has the choice to enter or not. Melissa's focus on intentionality suggests that she is aware of the work she needs to do on herself if she is to start to be and do 'otherwise' as a teacher—in doing so she begins to disrupt the dominant westernised teacher ontology into which she has been socialised.

Evie, female, twenty-two years, white Canadian final year of elementary education degree. Tutored a female student age thirteen.

> When critically analysing our tutoring sessions, I found that when there was choice and power given to student C, she was much more

> willing to participate. Cultural responsiveness focuses on the ability to learn from, and relate respectively to others, and I found at the beginning I was not prepared to allow student C to play an active role. When I took on the teacher role and led the activity she would disengage and I was not prepared for this reaction. . . . When student C had a say and was given the opportunity to interact on an equal level she did great. It was then that I realized that I need to be more hospitable and let student C show me what she knows and how she wants to demonstrate her knowledge.

Evie shows some of the tension (Derrida's aporia) between wanting to be inviting but, when it came to working with the student, not knowing how to do this. At a theoretical level she understood the rationale for being culturally responsive, but at a practice level her socialised teacher ontology was too strong and she initially seemed unable to find ways to equalise power in the relationship. Evie indicates that hospitality was a concept that enabled her to begin to relinquish some of her control and to invite the 'other' in.

Kevin, male, thirty-one years, Canadian with mixed European and Cherokee heritage, final year of middle school education degree. Tutored a male student age ten.

> Students struggle in educational settings that they are not represented in and that do not reflect their ways of knowing. Students who are a part of the dominant culture of a society are more likely to be successful in that society's educational institutions. Indigenous peoples in colonized regions rarely if ever represent the dominant culture but are often described as marginalized. Invitation and hospitality are part of creating a comfortable learning environment and most importantly building relationships with students. These concepts challenge negative historical educational relationships where students were expected to conform to what the dominant culture decided was the right way of knowing. Our schools in Canada are far from the residential schools that closed in the 1990s, but there still are some lingering oppressive qualities that need to be addressed.

Kevin focuses more on institutional power and the importance of understanding how educational relationships today are deeply connected to those of the past. He views the concepts of invitation and hospitality as useful in offering a non-dominating approach to working with students and as a challenge to curricula that are presented as neutral and therefore as universally relevant.

It is too early to draw any conclusions from the project. However, we think there is enough evidence to suggest that a focus on invitation and hospitality has enabled pre-service teachers to develop deeper understandings of culturally responsive pedagogies that are based on relational ways of being and knowing (see Pirbhai-Illich et al., 2017 for our more recent work in this area).

Conclusion: Interculturality and Sustainability

We argue that a plurality of knowledges and ways of being is needed to address socio-cultural, political, environmental and economic challenges, and we further argue that critical intercultural dialogue is an essential part of this process. Yet in Education for Sustainable Development policies, although they acknowledge the relevance of intercultural dialogue, it is rarely explicitly promoted. Indeed, culture is often presented as a "challenge rather than an opportunity to move closer to sustainability" (Tilbury and Mulà, 2009, p. 16).

It is important to emphasise that sustainable development is an open concept which embraces different understandings. This plurality in understandings needs to become an invitation for dialogue to contextualise (culturally and regionally) the definitions. This pluralism should not be understood as a limitation or disqualification among the different opinions and views (SEMARNAT, 2006, p. 32, cited in Tilbury and Mulà, 2009, p. 16).

A focus on multiple ways of being and knowing, including those of diaspora and indigenous communities, is crucial for teachers and learners if we are to develop future citizens who are able to work towards a just and sustainable world. This is a project which explicitly seeks to centre other ways of knowing and doing, and to decentre the dominant ways that continue to divide the world in inequitable ways. Our teaching and research is a contribution to that goal.

References

Andreotti, V. (2011). *Actionable Postcolonial Theory in Education*. New York: Palgrave Macmillan.

Austin, T., Pirbhai-Illich, F., Grant, R., Tinker Sachs, G., Wong, S. Nasser, I. and Kumagai, Y. (2014). From research to transformative action: Interpreting research critically. In: K. Bhopal and R. Deuchar (eds.), *Researching Marginalized Groups*, 183–195. New York and London: Routledge.

Bhabha, H. (1994). *The Location of Culture*. London: Routledge.

Bigger, S. (2011). *Self and Others: Relational Pedagogy for Critical Pupil Engagement*. Unpublished Talk for the Swindon Philosophical Society, 14 January.

Buber, M. (1947). *Between Man and Man*. Translated by R. G. Smith. London: Kegan Paul.

Buber, M. (1958). *I and Thou*. 2nd edition. Translated by R. G. Smith, T. Edinburgh and T. Clark.

Burwell, R. and Huyser, M. (2013). Practicing hospitality in the classroom. *Journal of Education and Christian Belief*, 17(1), pp. 9–24.

Derrida, J. (2000). Hostipitality. *Angelaki: Journal of the Theoretical Humanities*, 5(3), pp. 3–18.

Fisher, R. (2013). *A Case for Humility*. Commission for Social Justice Educators' Blog. Available at: <https://acpacsje.wordpress.com/2013/05/28/a-case-for-humility-by-roger-fisher/. Accessed 16 December 2018.

Ladson-Billings, G. (1995). But that's just good teaching! The case for culturally relevant pedagogy. *Theory into Practice*, 34(3), pp. 159–165.

Ladson-Billings, G. and Tate, W. F. (1995). Toward a critical race theory of education. *Teachers College Record*, 97(1), pp. 47–68.

Martin, F. (2012). The geographies of difference. *Geography*, 92(3), pp. 116–122.

Martin, F. and Griffiths, H. (2014). Relating to the 'Other': Transformative, intercultural learning in post-colonial contexts. *Compare: A Journal of Comparative and International Education*, 44(6), pp. 938–959.

Martin, F. and Pirbhai-Illich, F. (2015). Service learning as postcolonial discourse: Active global citizenship. In: R. Reynolds, D. Bradbery, J. Brown, K. Carroll, D. Donnelly, K. Ferguson-Patrick and S. Macqueen (eds.), *Contesting and Constructing International Perspectives in Global Education*, 135–150. Rotterdam: Sense Publishers.

Moll, L., Amanti, C., Neff, D. and Gonzalez, N. (1992). Funds of knowledge for teaching: Using a qualitative approach to connect homes and classrooms. *Theory into Practice*, 31(2), pp. 32–141.

Noddings, N. (1998). *Philosophy of Education*. Boulder, CO: Westview Press.

Noddings, N. (2003). *Happiness and Education*. Cambridge: Cambridge University Press.

Pirbhai-Illich, F. (2010). Aboriginal students' engagement and struggles with critical multi-literacies. *Journal of Adolescent and Adult Literacy*, 54(4), pp. 257–266.

Pirbhai-Illich, F. (2013). Crossing borders: At the nexus of critical service learning, literacy, and social justice. *Waikato Journal of Education*, 18(2), pp. 79–96.

Pirbhai-Illich, F., Austin, T., Paugh, P. and Farrino, Y. (2011). Responding to 'innocent' racism: Educating teachers in politically reflexive and dialogic engagement in local communities. *Journal of Urban Learning, Teaching and Research (JULTR)*, 7, pp. 27–40.

Pirbhai-Illich, F. and Martin, F. (2015). Understanding hospitality and invitation as dimensions of decolonizing pedagogies when working interculturally. In: Phil Bamber and Andrea Bullivant (eds.), *TEESNet Conference Proceedings 2015. From Curriculum Makers to World Shapers: Building Capacities of Educators for a Just and Sustainable World*, 89–101.

Pirbhai-Illich, F., Pete, S. and Martin, F. (2017). *Culturally Responsive Pedagogy: Working towards Decolonization, Indigeneity and Interculturalism*. London: Palgrave Macmillan.

Pirbhai-Illich, F., Turner, N. and Austin, T. (2009). Using digital technologies to address Aboriginal adolescents' education: An alternative school intervention. *Journal of Multicultural Education and Technology*, 3(2), pp. 144–162.

Purkey, W. W. and Novak, J. M. (1996). *Inviting School Success*. 3rd edition. Belmont, CA: Wadsworth.

Schmidt, J. J. (2004). Diversity and invitational theory and practice. *Journal of Invitational Theory and Practice*, 10, pp. 27–46.

Spivak, G. (1991). *The Post-Colonial Critic: Interviews, Strategies, Dialogues*. London: Routledge.

Tilbury, D. and Mulà, I. (2009). *A Review of Education for Sustainable Development Policies: From a Cultural Diversity and Intercultural Dialogue Perspective*. Paris: UNESCO.

5 Restorative Practice

Modelling Key Skills of Peace and Global Citizenship

Rosalind Duke

Introduction

The difficulties facing our world are manifold—ecological degradation, climate change, ever-increasing inequity—and all these environmental, social and economic problems will increase exponentially the triggers for conflict, as indeed they already are. The need to consider peace and conflict seems then to be central to any discussion of sustainability.

Working with pre-service primary teachers in a global education project where diversity—of culture, ethnicity, attitudes, opinions, values—is a constant theme, I am struck by how often we touch on areas of potential conflict but fail to teach, and especially to model, for students how to address conflict. There is a tendency to keep conflict at bay, closing it down if it threatens to get too real, rather than exploring how we might handle it. Increasingly, I've turned to Restorative Practice (RP) in my teaching as I've become more and more aware that the skills learned through RP are foundational to notions of citizenship, global or otherwise, and also to the capacity to live and interact peacefully with others.

Restorative Practice and Restorative Justice

Restorative Practice is a set of principles and processes based on an understanding of the importance of positive relationships as central to building and maintaining inclusive community, including processes that aim to restore relationships when harm has occurred. One organisation in Dublin, Ireland, uses this definition: "Restorative Practice is both a philosophy and a set of skills that have the core aim of building strong relationships and transforming conflict in a simple and emotionally healthy manner" (TWCDI, 2016).

Restorative Practice developed out of Restorative Justice (RJ), which is a way of dealing with offending or challenging behaviour, and which prioritises repairing harm done to people or relationships over the need to assign blame and impose punishment. It aims to 'put things right' by involving all those impacted by an event or situation in a particular form of process.

RP was first used in schools as a way to deal with difficult behaviour in the school context in a way that would avoid both the exclusion of the harm-doer and leaving the persons harmed feeling angry or resentful, and therefore the school community with unaddressed conflict. Research both in the UK and in Ireland has shown that RP can be effective at this level. A Scottish report found that seven out of eight primary schools showed "significant achievement" and that the best results were in evidence in "the small number of schools where a whole school approach had been adopted" and where "the school had invested in significant staff development" (McCluskey et al., 2008, p. 415).

More recently, in Ireland, a group of schools in Tallaght, Dublin, have also shown the value of RP in improving a range of indicators relating to the well-being of the school community:

> Some school staff were initially resistant to RP, viewing it as yet another pressure in an already heavy workload. However, seeing the positive changes and what one participant identified as "the spectacular results which have taken place due to restorative practice", they now feel that RP is not only beneficial to the children, but it can make the teacher's job easier.
>
> (Fives et al., 2013, p. 44)

Restorative Practice as Skills Framework

However, a focus on behaviour management is a narrow view of the transformative effect that RP offers in schools and beyond. RP is a proactive approach which aims to build community by fostering positive relationships. It is a set of skills and practices that help to cultivate a restorative mindset which informs how we think, engage, speak, listen, and approach situations, whether in classrooms, schools or in the wider community. It requires a paradigm shift from hierarchy and control to what Lynch and Baker (2005, p. 2) call 'equality of condition' in education, in which they include equality of respect and recognition, of power, and of love, care and solidarity: dimensions which are central to RP.

In restorative classrooms, students, including disruptive ones, are treated with respect, and it has been the experience of teachers that the respect they show is usually reflected back to them. Teachers model respect by using restorative language—non-reactive, using affective statements, inviting engagement—and restorative processes. For example, they begin the day by inviting students to participate in a circle where each person receives respect and recognition for who they are; they use fair process—that is, students can rely on having the opportunity to engage, to explain, or to receive explanation, and to have clarity about expectations which they themselves help to set.

From these processes, students learn to listen actively, to listen for the feelings and needs behind others' words so that empathy can be developed. Restorative processes, by modelling the use of affective statements and allowing everyone a voice, help develop the ability to get in touch with one's own feelings so that these can be expressed in a way that gets heard and understood by others; that is, they develop emotional literacy.

Students also learn from these processes that we all see the world from our own perspective; they learn to "suspend the notion that there is only one way of looking at something" (Hopkins, 2006, p. 7), and to be able to try to 'see through someone else's lens'. These are basic skills in relationships and in peace-building: not just understandings, but concrete skills which can be experienced and practised. Learning that different perspectives are valid and should be respected and taken into account lays the foundation both for intercultural learning and for the practice of good citizenship.

In listening to others with respect, we can also learn to understand and live with diversity of perspective and opinion—not tidying it away, but learning to allow "contending voices to exist" (Davies, 2017, pp. 5–6). 'Peace' has to be able to hold space for a range of perspectives; it is about learning to live with the complexity and diversity, rather than establishing uniformity or even agreement.

When difficulties do arise and a RP conversation or process is used, participants have the opportunity to explore the causes and consequences of actions and to take responsibility for their own actions. Further, they are involved in finding ways of addressing the impacts of their behaviour; that is, becoming accountable and making decisions as agents of change.

These skills—active listening, empathy, emotional literacy, seeing others' perspectives and living with complexity, taking responsibility and making decisions—are nurtured through the RP framework. But they do not only make for more affirmative and constructive classrooms; they are key skills for global citizenship and for the building and maintaining of peaceful relationships and communities. Learning how to approach conflict and to build and maintain peace that recognises diversity of opinion is a valid way to come to an understanding of how peace has to be continually constructed from a just balancing of diverse perspectives. RP becomes a way to explore a situation and the possibilities arising from it depending on how we proceed; it is a way of learning about and coming to understand perspectives as fluid and in-the-making all the time. They are a way to explore how conflict arises and how it can bring about change if it is opened up, allowed, rather than quelled, shut down and packed away; it is a way of building peace from and through and because of conflict so that students can learn "new ways . . . for people to relate to each other, to surface and manage dissent" (Davies, 2017, p. 6)

Learning the Skills of Conflict and Peace

'Peace is usually defined as being dependent on the absence of any conflict', and in the way of such dichotomies, the assumption is made that peace is a 'good' and conflict therefore 'bad'. "Conflict is set as something that needs to be 'resolved' . . . otherwise there is no peace" (Zembylas and Bekerman, 2013, p. 4). This positioning of peace and conflict as opposites means that while education may include teaching about peace, there is no teaching about or *for* conflict. We cannot establish and maintain peace without knowledge and experience of ways to approach conflict safely and positively, and even more importantly, of how we can prevent conflict escalating into something unhelpful and instead allow it to open up debate for change. Peace understood this way cannot be static—it is always fluid. This is where RP has something valuable to offer in the educational context—as an opportunity to learn how to respect, listen to and engage with different perspectives, and thus to experience peace in the making. For as Zembylas and Bekerman put it, "peace education is a set of activities and not a set of abstract ideas—activities in the world and not ideas in the head" (p. 10).

Peace understood in this way cannot be taught; it has to be modelled, experienced in the making and practised. I'd like to draw an analogy here between this 'education for conflict and peace' and the work of psychiatrist Stuart Ablon on Collaborative Problem-Solving. Children pick up skills like problem-solving and tolerance of frustration at different rates, and those who fail to learn effective use of these skills may 'behave badly'; but rather than teach these skills in schools, we tend to punish the children who don't have them. Ablon (2014) equates this to the once-normal practice of punishing children who did not read or write correctly. Hopkins (2006, p. 195) also discusses the "tendency of teachers to be judgemental about behavioural errors", as something which should not happen and therefore should be punished, while not in fact teaching the requisite skills for more acceptable behaviour. Similarly, we cannot expect students to learn the skills of listening to diverse opinions, empathising, problem-solving in conflict and so on if we do not have a way to model and for them to practise them.

Further, Ablon points out that each time a child 'misbehaves' in class, there is an opportunity to teach the very skills that child lacks, which can only be learned in the context where they are needed. Similarly, a school classroom presents opportunities on a daily basis where RP provides a framework through which children can learn experientially and authentically about respectful listening, living with diverse perspectives, problem-solving collaboratively and decision-making: all skills in the building and maintaining of positive and peaceful relationships.

Paradigm Shift

Schools have not always modelled these skills. Many schools do aim to promote the values mentioned here and many are nurturing and respectful places. However, when rules are broken or an incident occurs, too often it is the old paradigm of blame and punishment that surfaces; and once this path is taken, effective means for exploring the feelings and perspectives which gave rise to and those which arose from the incident are closed off. Davies (2017, p. 8) speaks of the need for a new approach in schools which will provide teachers "not just with alternatives to physical punishment but shifting away from an ethos of punishment and revenge towards more restorative ways of achieving justice in schools". Research with teachers (Stowe, 2012, p. 123) shows that the letting go of the need to punish an offender presents one of the biggest obstacles to the full adoption of RP principles; many schools espouse RP for daily classroom practice but the school's Code of Behaviour still holds the right to suspend or expel students who do not behave acceptably. It seems that all our learned conceptions of 'justice' depend on punishment. This is at the heart of the very paradigm shift that opens the door for ways of thinking about community that are more inclusive, empathetic, participatory and appreciative of the value of difference. RP moves from thinking of the past to considering the future, from establishing guilt and blame to defining needs and obligations, from punishment to accountability and reparation of harm, with the ultimate focus on the well-being of the whole community and the re-establishment of peaceful relations. If our communities, and humanity as a whole, are to live sustainably and survive, the shift from denouncing difference to being willing to listen and explore that difference is essential, and children in schools can observe and learn that approach through daily experience.

Restorative Practice in Irish Education

In the Irish context, RP is being used in an increasing number of schools, both primary and post-primary. Many teachers are choosing, or being mandated by their schools, to train in RP, and Continuing Professional Development (CPD) courses in RP are being offered around the country. Where schools have introduced RP, it is often as part of a wider Community Development programme; for example, Donegal Education and Training Board received funding from an EU Peace Programme for RP to be rolled out in schools, youth training centres and further education programmes, and Donegal has become a Restorative County. Similarly, other community development organisations in Dublin and around the country are introducing RP in the community as well as in schools.

In West Dublin, the Childhood Development Initiative (CDI) supports RP across the schools in the area and in the local community. Some schools in that area have been using RP since 2007 as part of this wider RP programme in the community; in one school, the staff meet together in a community of practice to reflect on their work, and CPD is offered regularly. All new teachers in the school are required to take RP training. The principal sees multiple benefits for staff and students, in the life of the school and the community, and is clear that these benefits far outweigh the challenges of introducing and maintaining the RP approach—mostly challenges of time and maintaining commitment. In the wider community many have commented on their new approaches:

> one participant commented that she tended to argue more in the past. However, since she completed the training, she 'gives other people a chance' and asks them to recount their version of events. . . . Many participants were amazed by the power of asking restorative questions such as 'What happened?' . . . Another participant has learnt to 'take a step back', to not become as emotionally involved, and as a result is achieving more positive outcomes for the community.
>
> (Fives et al., 2013, p. 39)

Not all schools using restorative approaches have fully trained all their staff and not all use RP as a fully integrated approach throughout the school. Several have introduced some restorative practices and processes but have not (yet at least) espoused the full restorative spectrum. As mentioned above, evidence tends to show that RP really only makes a *sustainable* impact where the system of RP is carried through the whole school: where all the staff are trained, and where students find themselves in a consistent atmosphere where their voice is respected. Where a teacher, or a small group of teachers, committed to this way of working are not supported by a congruent system throughout the school, where students find themselves sooner or later up against the authoritarian application of rules and punishment, it seems inevitable that the impact will be restricted:

> A restorative approach within the school or youth work and Youthreach centre should not, then, simply focus on behaviour management and see restorative practice as some form of alternative sanction. A whole system approach focuses on changing the culture and relationships in a school to improve the overall academic and social learning processes and outcomes.
>
> (Fives et al., 2013, p. 37)

All evaluations and research into RP in Ireland have included recommendations to develop RP further, both in policy statements, and in developing the RP capacity of staff and young people.

RP is now being taught at third level, to some extent in Initial Teacher Education, but more often in Postgraduate and Masters in Education courses, and this should help in time to raise the research profile. While there have been plenty of process evaluations, there is a dearth of research into the impacts of RP in schools and communities, and funding for such research is hard to come by. Research is needed on the drop in the use of suspensions and expulsions in RP schools, as is qualitative and longitudinal research on the well-being of students and of teachers in RP schools, and on the ability to handle conflict that such students may develop. However, the studies that do exist (e.g. Campbell et al., 2013; Wilson, 2011) are clear about the value of RP not only in the school context but in the community as a whole; and anecdotal evidence from those schools which have introduced RP as a whole-school approach are almost unreservedly positive about the impact it has had on their students, teachers and wider communities.

Conclusion

RP is about building and maintaining the positive relationships which are basic to peaceful coexistence and to peace-building. 'Peace' can't be taught. We can teach about peace, but to enact peace, first we must accept the reality of conflict, and learn how to approach and deal with it; rather than trying to 'resolve' or 'manage' conflict, we must first explore what it is about, and find a way through the conflict to peace. Peace otherwise is a veneer, a failure to acknowledge underlying conflicts and problems and as such is unsustainable. John Paul Lederach describes peace "as embedded in justice. It emphasizes the importance of building right relationships and social structures through a radical respect for human rights and life" (2003, p. 4).

RP offers a way into this, a way for teachers to examine their own behaviours and to critique school structures so that we create schools which model positive and peaceful ways of being and living. Sustainable living demands peaceful conditions and evidence from schools engaging in RP shows that when undertaken as a whole-school approach, RP can indeed help us learn and teach how to "live together sustainably" (UNESCO, 2017).

References

Ablon, J. Stuart. (2014). *Rethinking Challenging Kids- Where There's a Skill There's a Way*. TED Talks. Available at: <www.youtube.com/watch?v=zuoPZkFcLVs>. Accessed 29 August 2017.

Campbell, Hugh et al. (2013). *Developing a Whole System Approach to Embedding Restorative Practices in Youthreach, Youth Work and Schools in County Donegal University of Ulster and Donegal ETB Restorative Practices Project*. Available at: <http://uir.ulster.ac.uk/27373/1/Co._Donegal_Restorative_Practice_Project%2520Research%2520Report%2520-%2520Final%2520Sept%252013.pdf>

Davies, Lynn. (2017). Justice-sensitive education: The implications of transitional justice mechanisms for teaching and learning. *Comparative Education*, 53(3), pp. 333–350. Available at: <http://dx.doi.org/10.1080/03050068.2017.1317999>

Fives, A., Keenaghan, C., Canavan, J., Moran, L. and Coen, L. (2013). *Evaluation of the Restorative Practice Programme of the Childhood Development Initiative*. Dublin: Childhood Development Initiative (CDI). Available at: <www.twcdi.ie/wp-content/uploads/2016/11/CDI-RP_Report_25.09.13.pdf>

Hopkins, B. (2006). *Implementing a Restorative Approach to Behaviour and Relationship Management in Schools—The Narrated Experiences of Educationalists*. Unpublished thesis submitted in partial fulfilment of the requirement for a Ph.D.

Lederach, John Paul. (2003). *Little Book of Conflict Transformation*. Intercourse, PA: Good Books.

Lynch, K. and Baker, J. (2005). Equality in education: An equality of condition perspective in *Theory and Research in Education*, 3(2), pp. 131–164. Available at: <http://dx.doi.org/10.1177/1477878505053298>

McCluskey, G., Lloyd, G., Kane, J., Riddell, S., Stead, J. and Weedon. E. (2008). Can restorative practices in schools make a difference? *Educational Review*, 60(4), pp. 405–417. Available at: <www.tandfonline.com/doi/full/10.1080/00131910802393456>

Stowe, Michelle. (2012). *The Implementation of Restorative Practice using a Professional Learning Community in a Post-Primary School Setting: An Action Research Study*. Unpublished Thesis in partial fulfilment of the requirements for the Degree of Master of Education, National University of Ireland, Maynooth.

TWCDI. (2016). *Restorative Practices*. Available at: <www.twcdi.ie/our-programmes/restorative-practice>. Accessed 6 September 2017.

UNESCO. (2017). *Learning to Live Together Sustainably (SDG 4.7): Trends and Progress*. Available at: <http://en.unesco.org/gced/sdg47progress>

Wilson, Derek. (2011). *Dun Laoghaire/Rathdown Comenius Regio 'Restorative Approaches' Programme 2010–2011. A Formative Evaluation*. University of Ulster. Available at: <http://uir.ulster.ac.uk/22703/1/DL_Rathdown_Restorative-Practices.pdf>

Zembylas, Michalinos and Bekerman, Zvi. (2013). Peace education in the present: Dismantling and reconstructing some fundamental theoretical premises. *Journal of Peace Education*, 10(2), pp. 197–214. Available at: <www.tandfonline.com/doi/abs/10.1080/17400201.2013.790253>

6 Into the Vortex

Exploring Curriculum Making Possibilities that Challenge Children's Responses to Extreme Climate Events

Helen Clarke and Sharon Witt

Introduction

This chapter offers insight into the power of an eco-playful pedagogy and links to the approach shared in chapter 11, where we position students of initial teacher education (ITE) as curriculum makers who possess powerful potential to make a difference to the world. In this chapter we report on research completed with primary ITE science and geography specialists and 10–11-year-old children at a Hampshire Primary School. In an imaginative storied approach to real world global and environmental issues, we explored the possibility of using small-world play to develop children's deep knowledge and understanding of our complex and dynamic earth. This positioned the children as powerful problem solvers who could readily take an active role in supporting local communities during an extreme weather event. We suggest that a range of carefully planned activities can encourage children to take a proactive response to 'disaster risk reduction' (UNESCO, 2014).

Eco-Playfulness for Hopeful Perspectives

Opportunities for curriculum making deepen and strengthen the initial training of teachers. Rich experiences for student teachers (also called 'pre-service teachers' in this volume) in turn generate significant learning for the children they teach as student teachers and as future teachers in the primary phase. We cast our aspiring teachers into the turbulent flow of alternative perspectives and deep learning to design meaningful curriculum opportunities for Education for Sustainable Development (ESD). This experience prompted us to explore the knowledge, skills and values required of young professionals in facilitating a meaningful curriculum for ESD. Tackling climate change with young learners is potentially problematic due to its complex, challenging and controversial nature. In addition, this topic often elicits a doom-laden, catastrophising approach

(Weintrobe, 2013). An eco-playful pedagogy (Witt and Clarke, 2014) takes a more hopeful perspective, inviting openness and honesty. Climate change education, handled in an age-appropriate and sensitive way (Sobel, 2008), equips and empowers children for the future. Such outcomes offer hope in uncertain times (Hicks, 2014).

Big and Little Stories

The creation of learning spaces within ITE is integral to our practice, and these spaces should take into account both the "*'little' stories individuals and the 'big' stories of the disciplines and traditions*" (Palmer, 1998, p. 76). To begin our encounter, we immersed a group of student teachers in experiential fieldwork in the village of Selborne, Hampshire. Multisensory encounters in the natural world engaged these becoming teachers in reflection on place, nature and connectedness. We then focussed on the student teachers' role as curriculum makers: a role in which they are required to balance their own experiences, their professional knowledge and skills and children's expertise as learners.

The 'Curriculum Vortex' Explored—Movement and Flight

In chapter 11, "Seeking to Unsettle Student Teachers' Notions of Curriculum", we propose the metaphor of the curriculum as a 'vortex' to represent the complex processes involved in planning learning for children. There is considerable momentum and energy in the dynamism of curriculum planning, and students are required to be agile and creative in their decisions as they respond to encounters with children and their world. This metaphor, which 'draws in' the many elements of the ESD curriculum, invites student teachers to begin curriculum making "*from anywhere, to pick up from the middle and to create a path or multiple paths*" (Coley et al., 2011). A 'rhizomatic' principle suggests space for experimentation, play and discovery of potentialities and allows an ESD curriculum to be "spontaneously shaped, constructed and reconstructed" by experiences through "multiple entryways and exits", which develop "lines of flight" (Deleuze and Guattari, 1988, p. 21). Through taking an open and broad approach that simultaneously layers experience, place, teacher and learner, these multiple trajectories avoid an ESD curriculum that is disconnected from reality and from the lives of children. Our student teachers were encouraged to find their own new trajectories and to seek innovative and creative ways to approach ESD. We hoped to unsettle the status quo in relation to their own experiences, personal knowledges and perspectives; to lead them into "the domain of potentialities" and direct them towards "becomings" (Dahlberg and Moss, 2009, p. x).

Into the Vortex—Energising Learning

In the context of ESD, the notion of the curriculum vortex provoked thinking, reflection and evaluative skills and scaffolded links between theory, experience and practice. In an act of co-construction, this discussion was also a pre-cursor to planning activities in school. We encouraged the student teachers to identify resonance (Somerville, 2008) within their thinking. One student saw the vortex as a way to represent "*connections and interconnectedness between places, ideas, themes and people*". Another viewed the curriculum in a vortex as "*flexible—something that can be moved, stretched twisted and interacted with*". For some, the metaphor captured the way "*ideas are always changing, they are dynamic—they progress—and focus your interests*". Possibilities within the vortex were recognised for "*energised learning carried out at an appropriate pace*". These ideas extended our notion of the curriculum metaphor, which was then enacted and embodied through our work in school.

Working in the Vortex—Taking Flight as Curriculum Makers

We designed a process planning model, as shown in Figure 6.1, to guide the student teachers in preparing for school-based work.

The planning model is an imaginative and storied approach to real world global and environmental issues. As educators we explored the possibility of using small-world play to develop children's knowledge and understanding of extreme weather conditions, and to position the children as powerful problem solvers who could readily take an active role in supporting local communities during such an event. As teacher educators, we recognised that the student teachers faced aspects of uncertain subject content, unfamiliar pedagogy and an unknown setting. We took a guiding and mediating role to support them to be flexible, spontaneous and responsive to the learners and their local context. Responses in the form of tutor and student teacher field jottings, photographs, online

Stages
Setting the scene and eliciting ideas
Creating a small-world environment
Posing a challenge
Planning a response
An event
Taking action in response to an event
Positive outcomes

Figure 6.1 Process planning model for environmental challenge

discussion in a 'Patchwork Text' format (Ovens, 2003), focus group conversations and the children's responses illustrate the developing practice of tutors and student teachers and also emerging themes, which offer an interpretation of the knowledge, skills and values employed by this group as they engaged in ESD.

Reflections on Context

Children were given opportunities to explore their school grounds (as in Figure 6.2) as a way to elicit discussion about microclimates and familiar weather phenomena and to establish a context for problem-solving. They observed their environment, experienced the elements and reconnected to significant places. Some children took miniature figures to seek a different view, to consider scale and perspective and to discuss scenarios. Children were then invited to engage in place-making by creating small worlds in a plastic tray; these small worlds would later be affected by simulated extreme weather events. The children drew on their familiarity with local landscapes and used a range of natural and man-made materials to reconstruct features in an act of creation, which was "*central to the thinking process*" (Robertson, 2014, p. 75).

In evaluation activities, one student teacher, Jane, identified developments in her own practice and reflected on the value of a playful approach

Figure 6.2 Exploring the school grounds

to ESD. She acknowledged that small-world play was a novel approach for her. She dealt with uncertainty and evaluated a new strategy. She supported the children to negotiate a human response to a physical phenomenon. She made explicit links between theory and practice:

> *The idea of small-world play was something new to me. Once we got into school I was really interested to see how the children would react and they seemed to really enjoy it. All of the children were thoroughly engaged with the activities they were given. We decided to plan the activities around the school as it is a familiar area for the children so that they could fully immerse themselves in the concept of storm defences. By using the school the children were able to recreate similar landscapes in their modelling trays, which created a higher level of discussion. As Dawes, Dore, Loxley, and Nicholls (2010) suggest, the context in which enquiry is carried out gives it purpose and meaning. Effective contexts are those which are already familiar to the children and make their enquiries personally significant. The children could easily relate to the idea of a storm coming to the school.*

Reflections on Real World Learning

Student teachers introduced a forthcoming weather event into the scenario in a variety of ways. They utilised video clips, weather forecasts and television and radio news reports to prompt the children to talk about existing knowledge of weather events and also to discuss the experiences of others. The students then asked the children to plan for such an event in their small worlds. To simulate extreme weather events children flooded their small worlds, created snow blizzards and modelled storm conditions. They then enacted and evaluated their risk management strategies. The children experienced agency and took control of situations. Figure 6.3 illustrates the design process.

Tim identified the value of real life scenarios. He recognised familiarity, yet challenge, on a scale where the children could respond with a practical solution:

> *I really liked how the morning's activities were about a problem which had to be faced—the storm which was forecasted to occur soon. This is a real life problem and I think it is something the children could relate to . . . the children brought their own experiences and knowledge to the conversations.*

Jane was explicit about the enquiry-based nature of her approach to ESD:

> *The puzzle of our session was to investigate how the school could be protected if there was a flood. The children were immediately*

Figure 6.3 Constructing small-world flood defences

intrigued by the situation. Throughout the activity, it was interesting to see how it enabled the children to engage with the investigation . . . they discussed their ideas and established new ways to protect the school from flooding. I would definitely use this method again as it gave the children a different perspective to work from.

Jane was tentative in her realisation of possibilities for practice:

> *It seems by immersing yourself in imaginative teaching you can promote deep and meaningful learning opportunities for the children.*

Lily shows a more confident pedagogical knowledge in the identification of higher order thinking in the investigation:

> *The children in our group started to show some aspects of meta-cognition by evaluating where they were and where they wanted to go next. This was displayed when one student asked to flood the tray again faster, in order to see if the sandbags would work as well.*

Figure 6.4 illustrates a weather event—a flood enacted in a small-world town.

Reflections on Small-world Play

Small worlds are vehicles for teachers to support children in working through life's events. Small-world play "*excites, emboldens and empowers*" (Bromley, 2004, p. 1) and enables abstract ideas of the potential effects of climate change to become accessible to learners. This approach starts from "*inside the child's world, recognising children's inherent fascinations with nature and with people, and then builds from these starting points to create sturdy community valued knowledge*" (Sobel, 2008, p. 3).

Lily reflected on the potential of play beyond the early years to explore ESD issues:

> *I liked the idea of using creative contexts, having used them regularly when working with infants, but was unsure as to how this would work with juniors. I was worried that they would be less enthused to use their imagination in the activity. However, I found the children extremely receptive to the activity, even excited at the prospect of creating and protecting 'their school'.*

However, Lily was cautious about opportunities to apply their new approach in practice:

> *There is definitely space in today's classroom for imaginative play and thinking, but not as often as we might like. Time is a valuable resource and there is just not enough of it to do all we would like.*

Figure 6.4 Flooding a small-world town

Caro responded to her peer:

> *I like the honesty in your reflections about standing back and letting the children take the role of active investigators. It is often hard to stand outside the process of learning, when experiences like this*

promote so many opportunities for further discussions and build on understanding.

Lily linked her observation to an implication for practice and identified the value of the miniature:

I found the use of small-world play focused the children's attention. I found they also tried really hard to think about the scale of what they were making in the tray.

Immy recognised theoretical significance in the use of small worlds:

In working with the children in the group it offered me insights into how to incorporate the use of role play and small-world enquiry to elicit understanding about weather and its consequences. Craciun (2010) also highlights the importance of using role-play in science as part of the constructivist idea of active learning.

Reflection on Positive Outcomes

The small-world scenarios reported here promoted sophisticated and personal responses, mediated by student teachers, using positive playful approaches. The children devised safe rehearsals of potentially serious real world events. Figure 6.5 exemplifies children's thinking about risk assessment and management.

For the student teachers too, a positive outcome is important when they have been challenged in the vortex of curriculum planning and are working outside their comfort zones. For Lucy, this work challenged her experience and offered new perspectives on practice:

The idea of a small-world enquiry unsettled my notion of curriculum experiences. The use of this imaginative teaching seemed abstract to me and I was unsure how Year 6 children would engage in an activity that was highly dependent on their imagination. However, Fettes (2005) notes that imagination is central to the process of becoming a teacher by requiring us to use our senses beyond the visible world. I found I had to become more open to a new creative teaching method which made me engage more with the task. I can see that the small world was something they all engaged with and the size helped to focus their attention due to the higher concentration level the small scale required.

ESD—Knowledge, Skills And Values—for ITE Students

Our observations and dialogue with student teachers as they engaged children with issues of environmental change extended our thinking about the knowledge, skills and values required of teachers in facilitating

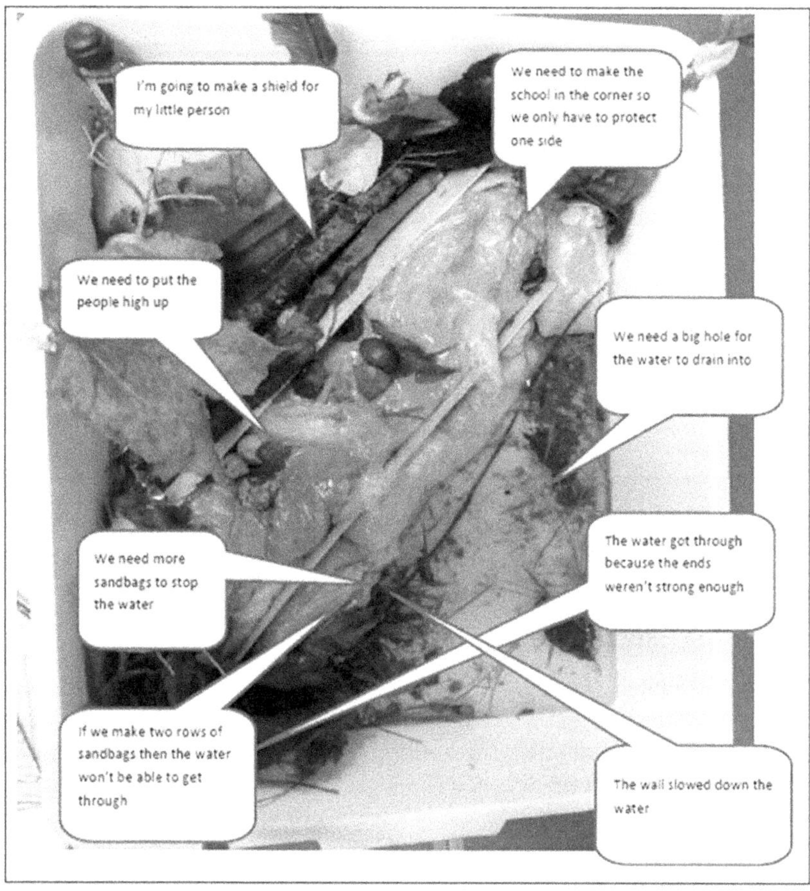

Figure 6.5 A small-world representation of the school and school grounds, protected from a flood. Children's responses show critical thinking and evaluation skills

a meaningful curriculum for ESD. The findings of our study show that students could articulate, both in discussion and practice, their emerging awareness of guiding principles of how to teach challenging, dynamic issues. Curriculum making requires student teachers "*to balance several competing priorities . . . and thus places a sophisticated form of curriculum thinking at the heart of what it means to be(come) a teacher*" (Lambert and Biddulph, 2014, p. 4). Figure 6.6 summarises the students' view of these guiding principles with regard to the knowledge, skills and values that underpin playful and positive learning experiences for children. These emerged as significant implications for our students' practice. The views offered here are not a definitive list, but are a summary of findings to date and a stimulus for others' thinking.

Knowledge	*Skills*	*Values*
Personal experiences, which bring personal knowledge	Reflection	Curiosity
Discipline subject knowledge, in this case geography and science	Humanity, human response	Respect for children's agency and teachers' agency—in a democratic approach to ESD curriculum making
Interdisciplinary knowledge—of sustainability	Flexibility and adaptability in planning	Responsiveness to children
Theoretical knowledge—of children's learning and of human response	Creative and innovative curriculum making	Creativity
Pedagogical knowledge	Willingness to try new ideas, take risks, deal uncertainty—of ideas and responses	Playful experiences
Self awareness—of reflection	Positive playfulness	Imagination
	Modelling values	Openness
		Care and love for a subject
		Confidence using the outdoors

Figure 6.6 Knowledge, skills and values of student teachers that underpin playful and positive learning experiences for children

ESD—The Human Dimension

We are prompted to reconsider some vocabulary surrounding ESD. The term 'capability' suggests a finite extent of an individual's ability. The term 'competence' denotes the ability to do something efficiently rather than deeply. The term 'capacity' suggests the maximum amount that might be contained or produced. We want our students to be more than capable, competent and capacious. Our work with these students has given us a different perspective, one that has helped us to reframe our view of ESD. It has also captured complexity, nuance and, above all, the human dimension. Our study suggests that educators would be well served by a more positive vocabulary, one that is couched in humanness. Humanness allows certain affordances in education; relations between the children and their environment afford opportunities for them to act *for* that environment. We frame curriculum making as a way of being, of "*designing teaching and learning in an interactive, learner-centred way, that enables exploratory, action-oriented and transformative learning*" (UNESCO, 2014, p. 12). An eco-playful pedagogy enhances the work of educators and prepares for hopeful futures for all.

References

Bromley, H. (2004). *The Small World Recipe Book: 50 Exciting Ideas for Small World Play*. Birmingham: Lawrence Educational Publications.

Coley, R., Lockwood, D. and O'Meara, A. (2011). *Rhizomes meet Student as Producer: Deleuze and Guattari and Media Practice*. Available at: <http://bit.ly/1MZuadR>. Accessed 3 February 2015.

Craciun, D. (2010). Role-playing as a creative method in science education. *Journal of Science and Arts*, 1(12), pp. 175–182.

Dahlberg, G. and Moss, P. (2009). Foreword. In: L. M. Olsson, *Movement and Experimentation in Young Children's Learning—Deleuze and Guattari in Early Childhood Education*. Abingdon: Routledge.

Dawes, L., Dore, B., Loxley, P. and Nicholls, L. (2010). A talk focus for promoting enjoyment and developing understanding in science. *English Teaching: Practice and Critique*, 9(2), pp. 99–110.

Deleuze, G. and Guattari, F. (1988). *A Thousand Plateaus: Capitalism and Schizophrenia*. London: Athlone.

Fettes, M. (2005). Imaginative transformation in teacher education. *Teaching Education*, 16(1), pp. 3–11.

Hicks, D. (2014). *Educating for Hope in Troubled Times: Climate Change and the Transition to a Post-Carbon Future*. Stoke on Trent: Trentham Books.

Lambert, D. and Biddulph, M. (2014). The dialogic space offered by curriculum-making in the process of learning to teach, and the creation of a progressive knowledge-led curriculum. *Asia-Pacific Journal of Teacher Education*, 43(3), pp. 210–224.

Ovens, P. (2003). Using the patchwork text to develop a critical understanding of science. *Innovations in Education and Teaching International*, 40(2), pp. 133–143.

Palmer, P. J. (1998). *The Courage to Teach. Exploring the Inner Landscape of a Teacher's Life*. San Francisco: Jossey Bank Publishers.

Robertson, J. (2014). *Dirty Teaching: A Beginner's Guide to Learning Outdoors*. Bancyfelin: Independent Thinking.

Sobel, D. (2008). *Childhood and Nature: Design Principles for Educators*. Portland, ME: Stenhouse Publishers.

Somerville, M. J. (2008). 'Waiting in the chaotic place of unknowing': Articulating postmodern emergence. *International Journal of Qualitative Studies in Education*, 21(3), 209–220.

Witt, S. and Clarke, H. (2014). Seeking to unsettle student teachers' notions of curriculum: Making sense of imaginative encounters in the natural world. *Proceedings of Teacher Education for Equity and Sustainability (TEESNet) Seventh Annual Conference*, Liverpool Hope University.

UNESCO. (2014). *UNESCO Roadmap for Implementing the Global Action Programme on Education for Sustainable Development*. Available at: <http://unesdoc.unesco.org/images/0023/002305/230514e.pdf>

Weintrobe, S. (ed.). (2013). *Engaging with Climate Change: Psychoanalytic and Interdisciplinary Perspectives*. London: Routledge.

Part 2
Curriculum

7 Moving Teachers' Experience From the Edge to the Centre

Neda Forghani-Arani

Introduction

This chapter reflects on the questions of what is involved and what is at stake in teaching for Global Citizenship (GC) within national curriculum frameworks in the transnational and transcultural space of classrooms with diverse students. In an attempt to move beyond frameworks for ESD/GC competencies, I set out to explore the experience of teaching in culturally, ethnically, nationally and linguistically heterogeneous classrooms characterised by transnational migration, in terms of practical wisdom, judgment and tact. Drawing on interview data from teachers' day-to-day experience, I try to illustrate that there is more to pedagogic competence than teachers' knowledge of and commitment to diversity and social justice. In moving teachers' experience from the edge to the centre, the language of phronesis and tact complicates the language of teacher efficacy and proves to be immensely helpful in discourses in and around teacher education.

Bringing Teachers Into Focus

Bringing teachers into focus is often associated with the growing pressure in recent years on teacher quality as one of the most, if not the most, significant factor in the quality of schooling. As Cochran-Smith (2004) writes:

> In a certain sense, of course, this is good news, which simply affirms what most educators have believed for years: teachers' work is important.... In another sense, however, this conclusion is problematic, even dangerous. When teacher quality is unequivocally identified as the primary factor that accounts for differences in student learning, some policy makers and citizens may infer that individual teachers alone are responsible for the successes and failures of the educational system despite the mitigation of social and cultural contexts, support provided for teachers' ongoing development, the historical failure of the system to serve particular groups, the disparate resources devoted

> to education across schools and school systems, and the match or mismatch of school and community expectations and values.
>
> (Cochran-Smith, 2004, p. 3)

By moving teachers from the edge to the centre, specifically by moving teachers' *experience* from the edge to the centre, I mean something quite different.

Diverse Classrooms as Spaces of Collision, Tension and Possibility

In recent years there has been an increasing interest in teaching and teacher competencies in what we call 'globalized societies', which are characterised by a "transformation in the spatial organization of social relations and transactions . . . generating transcontinental or interregional flows and networks of activity, interaction, and the exercise of power" (Held et al., 1999, p. 1). The increasing flows of people, commodities, cultures and economic and political interests across borders and the social processes that correspond to these developments prove to be highly relevant to schooling, both in terms of how they affect day-to-day life in classrooms and in how they relate to curriculum desiderata, in order for school curricula to remain relevant to our globalised social reality.

Looking at these flows and processes has been at the centre of my inquiry for a number of years, especially as they relate to curriculum and instruction. The signposts along my personal path of inquiry have been education for international understanding, peace and human rights in the 1980s, global education in the 1990s, and later intercultural education as I became increasingly involved in teacher education and teacher research. In my research in schools and with teachers, I caught sight of one specific category of transnational flows, which I observed as the most visible, present and pressing matter in day-to-day school life, namely migration and flows of people.

Migration and transnational population movements not only affect people who are themselves directly 'on the move' but also the places in which they settle, converting them to translocational spaces, thereby affecting in different ways all who live within these spaces (Anthias, 2008, p. 6). Migration has converted many a classroom to fluid social spaces that are constantly reworked through migrants' simultaneous embeddedness in more than one society (Forghani-Arani and Phelan, 2012; Levitt and Glick Schiller, 2004; Pries, 2005; Smith, 2005). These classrooms become social 'arenas' among a number of 'multi-layered and multi-sited arenas', including not just the home and host countries but other sites around the globe that connect migrants to those with whom they share the same national, ethnic, linguistic or religious memberships, identity and belonging (Levitt and Jaworsky, 2007, p. 131). A 'diverse' classroom is one such social space, constantly reworked through the cultural embeddedness of the immigrant students as they interact with their immigrant or non-immigrant teachers and classmates. And as such, it is an intersection space of collision, "collision of many layers, relations, perspectives and cosmologies" (Khagram and Levitt, 2008, p. 12).

By moving teachers from the edge to the centre, I mean taking teachers and their lived experiences in these very spaces into focus and asking: *what is it like and what does it mean* for teachers to teach in these multi-layered spaces of collision, tension and possibility?

There is much interest in these spaces of congruence-and-incongruence in the educational literature. A spectrum of conceptual, theoretical and programmatic 'solutions' have emerged in response to these alleged 'problematic' zones, often embedded in multicultural or intercultural discourses, and more recently in the context of transnational or transcultural studies (Forghani-Arani and Phelan, 2012). Whereas the term 'intercultural' is often used in a programmatic sense, the 'multicultural' is usually more descriptive (Gogolin and Krüger-Potratz, 2006, p. 110). The multicultural describes and analyses a state of affairs, for example, the multicultural society or the multicultural set-up of a classroom. The intercultural is a normative stance in response to multiculturality. It has to do with the requisites of adequate pedagogical handling of multicultural setups. In educational policy and public debates both terms are often used interchangeably. Transcultural approaches in education are often based on a conceptualisation of culture as empirically and normatively 'transcultural'; mutually delimiting, ethnically founded and socially homogenous cultures are in reality internally plural and externally transboundary (Adick, 2010, p. 107).

Literature on diversity competence of teachers is often based on the premise that teaching efficacy in diverse classrooms depends on the teachers' consciousness of their own enculturation, cultural identities, assumptions, perspectives and biases, as well as of the cultural identities of others (Gay, 2000; Guyton and Wesche, 2005; Ladson-Billings, 1995). The literature suggests that teachers tend to introduce their own cultural beliefs into the curriculum and ignore the cultural heterogeneity of their students (Gay, 2000). When teachers become conscious of their own cultural identities, it is argued, they become culturally efficacious individuals who can move between two or more cultures and also become advocates for those from cultures other than the dominant one (Guyton and Wesche, 2005). Researchers and practitioners have developed tools such as the Multicultural Teacher Efficacy Scale (Guyton and Wesche, 2005) and the Multicultural Dispositions Index (Thompson, 2009) to assess culturally responsive teaching (Forghani-Arani and Phelan, 2012).

More recent discourse takes a critical stance on the predominant praxis of intercultural communication and intercultural education (Forghani-Arani and Phelan, 2012; Phelan and Forghani-Arani, 2014). Training programmes for intercultural competence are criticised for being limited to imparting culture-specific knowledge in an attempt to decipher the 'foreign' and, therefore, for their 'culturizing' and 'ethnicizing' tendency (Auernheimer, 2002; Mecheril, 2002). It is argued that there is little acknowledgement of the complications of intersectionality—the weave and intersection of race/ ethnicity, gender, class, religion, sexual orientation, age and ability within individual lives (Bhopal and Preston, 2012)—and translocationality—the defining and redefining of identity across different spatial and cultural locations at different historical moments (Anthias, 2008).

What Is It Like and What Does It Mean?

The central question of the paper, *what is it like and what does it mean* for teachers to teach in diverse classrooms, is set against this backdrop. The '*what is it like*' purposefully departs from catalogues of required competencies (objectified as measurable outcomes) that teachers need to acquire so that they can be made fit for life in heterogeneous classrooms. Moving beyond the frame of catalogues, criteria and yardsticks of teachers' competencies means a search for another vocabulary. Recalling Wittgenstein's caution (2001, p. 119) that "*the limits of my language mean the limits of my world*", I set out to examine the possibilities to be found in the language of pedagogical tact (Forghani-Arani and Phelan. 2012).

I have been asking teachers the '*what is it like and what does it mean*' question in my empirical research. Here I draw on a vignette from an interview with a high school teacher in Vienna. Klaudia is a mainstream, white, middle-class Austrian teacher in an urban high school. The student body at her school is diverse in terms of culture, religion, nationality, ethnicity and language. In the interview, Klaudia describes her school and her class:

> *My students are the most colourful bunch. I have students from—let's say—twelve different nationalities. Many of them are from India, one from Iran—her father is from Iran, her mother is from Iraq, very interesting—there is one from Sri Lanka, two from Croatia, from Poland, three from Nigeria, actually there are only two Austrians.* (I-1)

Klaudia clearly uses the diversity of her students as a curriculum resource. While describing her efforts to recognise and include diversity of cultural, religious, ethnic backgrounds in her curriculum, she relates the following story:

> *A student of mine from Sri Lanka, he went to the, he went to Hajj, you know the Muslim pilgrimage, and I could tell he was different, when he came back. He was just so filled with faith when he came*

> *back from Mecca. Imagine, there are millions of people circumambulating the Kaaba, and you are part of it, I mean for a thirteen-year-old. Shortly after that we were doing major religions in history, and I said: "Well, tell us about it, you were there" . . . and then he took his Koran, stood in the corner of the class and chanted a prayer for us with all the movements that go with the phrases. Everything turned so quiet. Then he told us about his religious beliefs. He made it very clear that he would never ever marry a girl who doesn't wear a headscarf, and that he persuaded his mother and his sister to wear the hijab after he came back. He said: "otherwise a woman's hair would catch fire". That's when I said: "Let's change the topic".*
>
> (I-1)

Attempting to read, understand and make sense of Klaudia's account of lived experience, a number of questions arise:

- What is it like for teachers to teach in these multilayered spaces of collision, tension and possibility?
- How do teachers experience these moments (pedagogical moments) of collision, tension and possibility?
- How do they act? How do they know what is the right thing to do?
- How do they spontaneously assess, judge, decide and act?
- What is involved and what is at stake in handling the ambiguity and uncertainty of these pedagogically significant situations?
- What vocabulary can articulate the process of spontaneous assessing-judging-deciding-and-acting involved?

In an attempt to move beyond the frame of propositional criteria of teachers' competencies, I change epistemological tracks from episteme to phronesis, from propositional expert knowledge (i.e. predefined criteria of teacher efficacy), theoretically grounded universal assertions and inherently coherent principles (e.g. social justice, human rights, diversity, values and perceptions, sustainable development and global citizenship), into the practical realm of specific, concrete situations (i.e. day-to-day classroom situations), into spaces of legitimate uncertainty, ambiguity and disagreement. In oversimplified terms, I change tracks from a conception of knowledge and knowing in terms of Plato's episteme, the objectivity and universality of ever-abiding truths, to the Aristotelian concept of phronesis as practical wisdom in specific situations, as a contextual kind of knowing, as situational appreciation and discernment.

Here I draw on a construct from the rich tradition of German pedagogy which has found its way into international discourse, namely the concept of pedagogical tact (Herbart, 1802). Johann Friedrich Herbart, who is considered the founder of pedagogy as a scientific discipline, introduced tact in his first lectures in teacher education in 1802, as a mediator of educational theory and practice, as instantaneous assessment and decision-making of the educator to meet the necessities of the situation, and as thoughtfulness, genuine interest and moral commitment to the individual at hand (Asmus, 1982; Herbart, 1802; Müßener, 1983; Muth, 1962). Herbart posited that tact occupies a special place in practical educational action. Tact is the immediate ruler of practice. It manifests itself in everyday teaching in the process of making instant judgments and quick decisions, and forms a way of acting which is first of all dependent on *Gefühl* (feeling or sensitivity) and only more remotely on convictions derived from theory (Forghani-Arani, 2012). Pedagogical tact is sensitive to the requisites of the particular situation and slips in to position the prevailing condition of the student within his or her entire growth process. Tact is a ruler of practice, which rules in response to the call of the moment, moved by a concern for the long-term development and wholeness of the child (Forghani-Arani and Phelan, 2012).

Was it pedagogical tact slipping in when the teacher responded to the situation by changing the topic? Or was it a plain lack of tact? The purpose of raising the question of tact in the context of this inquiry is not to come to a judgmental conclusion on the prudent tactfulness or the oblivious tactlessness of the teacher in the given situation. The rationale of drawing on the construct of tact is that tact brings distinctive moments into focus where teachers assess, judge, decide and act—on the spot—in the process of action. Tact brings the practical realm of specific, concrete situations into focus and as such resonates with the phronetic turn in this inquiry.

Reading the vignette through the lens of pedagogical tact, the classroom moment calls for a response and tact slips in, as mediator of theory and practice in the midst of practice, and as teachers' instantaneous and intuitive assessment and decision-making to meet the necessities of the situation, with a thoughtful commitment to the individual case at hand. Klaudia essentially makes two key decisions: (1) to invite the student to speak, and the reverse, (2) to put an end to the student's speech. Her first decision is to include diversity. She notices that Kulasiri, a student from Sri Lanka now living in Vienna, has just returned from pilgrimage. Seeing an opportunity to include values and perspectives of her diverse student body in the context of a history class on world religions, Klaudia calls on Kulasiri to tell his classmates about the pilgrimage. She possibly expects a description, a narrative account and some information about the pilgrimage. The student however, "*took his Koran, stood in the corner of the class and chanted a prayer with all the movements that go with the phrases*" (I-1). "*Everything turned so quiet*" (I-1). Instead of a factual account or description, religion is presented as embodied belief. It appears as if the teacher can provide space for this introduced difference. As Kulasiri begins to relate 'his religious beliefs' regarding women, however, Klaudia becomes uneasy. The difference he introduces in his argumentation about womens' hair coverage cannot be contained within the assumed rationalism of the study of world religions in a history lesson. The plurality initially sought by the teacher can no longer be managed as a curriculum resource intended to enrich the topic of major religions. The potential response from the other students to Kulasiri's statement about women's hair catching fire renders the event sufficiently 'scary', in the teacher's view, to shut down the discussion before it becomes ignited: "*Let's change the topic*" (I-1).

What Is at Stake?

Klaudia shares the reasoning behind her decision to 'change the topic' and explains:

> *This is always extremely sensitive. As a teacher, if I contradict him, I'd create resistance and opposition on his part. I would end up shoving him into a corner and that is exactly what I want to avoid as a teacher. That's not my job, that's not what I'm here for, that's not my role. If I let it pass and let the other kids take over the discussion . . . well actually I didn't even think of that option. You have absolutely no idea what would turn out. You never know, someone could get up and say: "rubbish" or "that's nonsense" or something like that. So . . . I simply turned it off. I said: "That's enough for now" because it was getting out of hand, it was actually kind of scary. I was somehow perplexed. You have to be so careful. It's like walking in a minefield.*
>
> (I-2)

What is at stake in these multilayered spaces of collision, tension and possibility? Klaudia's second decision to put an end to the child's speech stems from her stated concern that some harm could befall the child or his classmates. If the topic prevails, she would be compelled to contradict the student's statement. She fears, however, that harm could result from telling him that he is wrong. To do so, in Klaudia's view, would be to isolate the student; "*shoving him into a corner*" (I-2) would mean to literally move the child and his difference to the periphery and margins of acceptability, to marginalising the othered child, exactly the opposite to the inclusion of difference she is committed to.

What is at stake when walking in a minefield with a "*colourful bunch*" (I-1) of children? Harm could result. The othered child could get hurt by his classmates: "*someone could get up and say: 'rubbish' or 'that's nonsense' or something like that*" (I-2). "*You have absolutely no idea what would turn out. You never know*" (I-2). Something could blow up and someone could get hurt. "*You have to be careful*" (I-2). The teacher also wants to protect her students from Kulasiri. In this instance, she is moved by a commitment, in the sense of responsibility for the wholeness of the child or the children, that competes or actually overpowers her commitment to opening up the classroom space to plurality of values and perspectives. While the teacher's decision to invite the student to speak was shaped by general principles (e.g. diversity and intercultural, interreligious education as a matter of principle), her decision to 'change the topic', thereby silencing the student and the alienating difference he introduces, appears less principle-driven and more situational.

We encounter conflicting sources of disparate commitments, where ironically the commitment to include and to not-marginalise the immigrant child gets in the way of the commitment to diversity, plurality, difference and openness. A commitment takes over that subdues an open dialogue of perspectives: a commitment that may or may not have to do with tact, but it has its own reasoning. Bill Green (2009) writes that phronesis—and I would add tact—is essentially an aporetic state wherein the ethics of undecidability confronts the politics of decision-making. The moment calls for a response, and in the urgency and drama of the moment, tact slips in to provide knowing that "*you never know*" (I-2); "*It's like walking in a minefield*" (I-2).

While it is difficult to argue with Klaudia's sense of obligation to do no harm, some complex questions emerge about commitment to our agendas in the midst of practice: what is lost and gained in the call of such moments? What sources of commitment are at play in the midst of pedagogical practice? Klaudia's case study takes us to those layered, loaded, significant spaces of tensionality and potentiality where, ironically, the very agenda of inclusion runs the risk of marginalisation.

In moving teachers' experience from the edge to the centre, we start to discern *what it is like, what is involved and what is at stake* in teaching for diversity and plurality of values and perceptions within curriculum frameworks in the transnational, transcultural and translocational spaces of classrooms with diverse students. In moving teachers' experience from the edge to the centre, we also move the contextual, the situational, the specific and never-the-same pedagogic situations into the forefront, in a space usually occupied by the propositionals, the principles, the universals, the oughts and 'shall-be's. And in moving teachers' experience from the edge to the centre we come across moments of conflicting pedagogical commitments, where for example commitment to diversity ironically collides with the commitment to include, or to not-marginalise. We come to see that there is more to teaching for diversity than teachers' knowledge of and commitment to diversity and plurality.

Conclusion

These ideas only begin to outline the contours of needed pedagogical concepts and vocabularies to talk about teaching under our current conditions of uncertainty. Drawing on the resonance between Aristotle's *phronesis* and Herbart's pedagogical tact, one can start to think along the lines of a 'transcultural pedagogical tact', or of a 'pedagogical diversity tact' as possible vocabularies to articulate what is called for in handling the uncertainty of current migration-driven diversity pedagogically. The inquiry at hand embarked on this venture.

The ideas proposed here also point to contents, methods and spaces in teacher education that can foster or hinder the development of pedagogical competence in terms of fostering diversity, sustainability and global citizenship. This means to enter the complex terrain of teacher education and teacher professional development. The complexity of the field is twofold; questions about teacher education and teacher development have an exceptionally high level of theoretical complexity, and at the same time the discussion in the field is invested with increased *political* complexity (Biesta, 2012). In times of (radical) uncertainty, politics and policies begin to take even more control over education, over the schools, and over teachers and their formation. It is precisely under these conditions that we need to take a close look at current underlying assumptions about school education, about teaching and being a teacher, and as such to resist conceptions of "teaching that ultimately undermine the very education teaching should seek to make possible" (Biesta, 2012, p. 45). Moving teachers' experience from the edge to the centre, and complicating the otherwise rather technical language of teacher efficacy through a language of tact and phronesis, could open up discourses in and around teacher education in globalised societies.

References

Adick, C. (2010). Inter-, multi-, transkulturell: uber die Muhen der Begriffsarbeit in kulturübergreifenden Forschungsprozessen. In: Alfred Hirsch and Ronald Kurt (eds.), *Interkultur—Jugendkultur*: *Bildung neu verstehen*, 105–133. Wiesbaden: Springer.

Anthias, F. (2008). Thinking through the lens of translocational positionality: An intersectionality frame for understanding identity and belonging. *Translocations: Migration and Social Change*, 4(1), pp. 5–20.

Asmus, Walter, ed. (1982). *Pädagogische Schriften*. Bd. 1. Stuttgart: Klett-Cotta.

Auernheimer, G. (2002). Interkulturelle Kompetenz/ein neues Element pädagogischer Professionalität? In: Georg Auernheimer (ed.), *Interkulturelle Kompetenz und pädagogische Professionlität*, 183–205. Opladen: Leske-Budrich Verlag.

Bhopal, K. and Preston, J. (eds.). (2012). *Intersectionality and Race in Education*. New York: Routledge.

Biesta, G. (2012). Giving teaching back to education: Responding to the disappearance of the teacher. *Phenomenology & Practice*, 6(2), pp. 35–49.

Cochran-Smith, M. (2004). Taking stock in 2004: Teacher education in dangerous times. *Journal of Teacher Education*, 55, pp. 3–7.

Forghani-Arani, N. (2012). In the Finite Province of Pedagogic Working: Teachers' acting and (t)acting in-between familiarity and strangeness. In: Projektteam

NOESIS (Hg), *Eine Schule für alle? Zur Evaluation der Nieder-österreichischen Mittelschule*, 153–180. Graz: Leykam.

Forghani-Arani, N. and Phelan, A. M. (2012). Teaching in heterogeneous classrooms: The play of reason and unreason. In: B. T. Schröttner and A. Pilch-Ortega (Hg), *Transcultural Spaces and Regional Localization; Social Networks, Border Regions and Local-Global Relations*, 191–204. Münster: Waxmann.

Gay, G. (2000). *Culturally Responsive Teaching: Theory, Practice, & Research*. New York: Teachers College Press.

Gogolin, I. and Krüger-Potratz, M. (2006). *Einführung in die Interkulturelle Pädagogik*. Opladen. UTB: Einführungstexte Erziehungswissenschaft, 9.

Green, B. (2009). The (im)possibility of the project. *Australian Educational Researcher*, 37(3), pp. 1–17.

Guyton, E. and Wesch, M. (2005). The multicultural efficacy scale: Development, item selection, and reliability. *Multicultural Perspectives*, 7(4), pp. 21–29.

Held, D., McGrew, A., Goldblatt, D. and Perraton, J. (1999). *Global Transformations: Politics, Economics, Culture*. Cambridge: Polity.

Herbart, Johann Friedrich. (cit. 1802). Erste Vorlesungen über Pädagogik. In: Walter Asmud (ed.), *Pädagogische Schriften*, Bd.1. Stuttgart: Klett-Cotta, 1982.

Khagram, S. and Levitt, P. (eds.). (2008). *The Transnational Studies Reader: Intersections and Innovations*. New York: Routledge.

Ladson-Billings, G. (1995). Toward a theory of culturally relevant pedagogy. *American Education Research Journal*, 32(3), pp. 465–491.

Levitt, P. and Glick Schiller, N. (2004). Conceptualizing simultaneity: A transnational social field perspective on society. *International Migration Review*, 38(3), pp. 1002–1039.

Levitt, P. and Jaworsky, B. N. (2007). Transnational migration studies: Past developments and future trends. *Annual Review of Sociology*, 33(1), pp. 129–156.

Mecheril, P. (2002). "Kompetenzlosigkeitskompetenz". Pädagogisches Handeln unter Einwanderungsbedingungen. In: Georg Auernheimer (ed.), *Interkulturelle Kompetenz und pädagogische Professionalität*, 15–34. Opladen: Leske-Budrich Verlag.

Müßener, Gerhard. (1983). Pädagogischer Takt qua ars iudicandi. Ein historisch systematischer Beitrag zu einem hochschuldidaktischen Obligatum in der Lehrerausbildung. *Vierteljahresschrift für wissenschaftliche Pädagogik*, 2/83, pp. 159–170.

Muth, Jakob. (1962). *Pädagogischer Takt: Monographie einer aktuellen Form erzieherischen und didaktischen Handelns*. Heidelberg: Quelle and Mayer.

Phelan, A. and Forghani-Arani, N. (2014). Teacher as stranger at home. In: A. Phelan (ed.), *Teacher Education and Curriculum Theorizing: Complicating Conjunctions*. London, UK: Routledge Press.

Pries, L. (2005). Configurations of geographic and societal spaces: A sociological proposal between 'methodological nationalism' and the 'spaces of flows'. *Global Networks*, 5(2), pp. 167–190.

Smith, M. P. (2005). Transnational urbanism revisited. *Journal of Ethnic and Migration Studies*, 31(2), pp. 235–244.

Thompson, F. (2009). The development and validation of the multicultural dispositions index. *Multicultural Perspectives*, 11(2), pp. 94–100.

Wittgenstein, L. (2001). *Tractatus Logico Philosophicus*. New York and London: Routledge.

8 Bridging 4.7 with Secondary Teachers

Engaging Critical Scholarship in Education for Sustainable Development and Global Citizenship

Karen Pashby and Louise Sund

Introduction

The United Nations Sustainable Development Goals (SDGs) set an agenda for action to contribute to effectively improving life on our shared planet. In effect, they set a policy direction aiming for significant improvements by 2030. Goal 4 attends to the need for quality education for all, and target 4.7 requires that all learners acquire the knowledge and skills needed to promote sustainable development, including explicit Education for Sustainable Development and Global Citizenship. Whereas the former UN Millennium Development Goals focussed on supporting action in so-called 'developing countries', the current SDGs call for action in all signatory countries, recognising the interdependent nature of sustainability issues. Given the continued inequality and ethical concerns around responsibilities in regards to who contributes to and who is most negatively impacted by global issues such as, for example, climate change, SDG 4.7 raises important questions about how teachers in the 'Global North' are resourced to teach for sustainable development and global citizenship.

In this chapter we consider key points of criticism of Global Citizenship Education (GCE) and Education for Sustainable Development (ESD) in scholarly literature. We propose an analytical tool, the HEADSUP checklist (Andreotti, 2011), that could support ethical global issues pedagogy while responding to these critiques. Then, we share some findings from a project working with secondary teachers in England, Sweden and Finland where we shared and gained feedback on the tool. We offer three classroom snapshots from visits to classes where teachers volunteered to apply HEADSUP. We then discuss some challenges and possibilities emerging from our project and suggest directions for further work in this area.

Engaging Critiques of ESD and GCE

As educators and researchers in the areas of critical GCE and environmental and sustainability education (ESE), we recognise the extent to which SDG 4.7 represents an important imperative for educational work. We are also concerned about the extent to which education initiatives in support of 4.7 will inherit problematic constructs inherent to extant approaches. Research has demonstrated that despite very good intentions, ESD/GC can reinforce colonial systems of power. In both non-formal school-wide initiatives and in formal curriculum and resources, research has pointed to a problematic trend whereby 'we' in the 'Global North' learn about and help solve the problems of 'those' in the 'Global South' (Andreotti, 2006; Martin, 2011). Scholars in the field of critical GCE highlight the ways superficial approaches can serve to step over complex ethical issues and contribute to the unconscious reproduction of colonial systems of power (e.g. Andreotti, 2011; Bryan et al., 2009; Martin, 2011; Andreotti and Souza, 2012; Pashby, 2012, 2018). As Shultz and Pillay (2018) assert

> More often than otherwise, global citizenship literature and theorizing represents the continuing dominance of western discourses and related epistemic constructions that do little challenge the citizenship or educational needs of those who need them the most. . . . Indeed as global citizenship education scholarship [has] increased, the equity gap between global as well as national citizens has widened tremendously.
>
> (p. 1)

Similarly, research conducted in the field of ESE has raised concerns about approaches to ESD, specifically for mobilising universalising approaches in educational sustainability policies (e.g. Wals, 2009; McKenzie, 2012; Sund and Öhman, 2014) and supporting a neo-liberal agenda focussed on individualism and competition (e.g., Jickling and Wals, 2008; Van Poeck and Vandenabeele, 2012). Recent work in the field has pointed to the need to centre historical and current contexts of colonisation in education and in relation to land education (e.g. Tuck et al., 2014), with Blenkinsop et al. (2017). calling for "an anti-colonial praxis for ecopedagogy" as a reminder to listen to "the voices of the silenced" (p. 349).

HEADSUP as a Framework for Ethical Global Issues Pedagogy

While SDG 4.7 represents an important focus for teachers in the Global North to directly contribute to the SDGs more broadly, it is essential that attention to colonial systems of power remain at the centre of curricular and pedagogical initiatives. It is also important to connect the scholarly critiques to day-to-day life in classrooms, a particular focus for this edited collection. As scholars working in GCE and ESE respectively, we both draw on the work of Vanessa Andreotti on explicitly taking up colonial systems of power. Andreotti's (2012) work applies postcolonial analyses to the concepts of 'critical literacy' and 'reflexivity' as an educational practice and could be considered a tool towards, as Simpson calls for in her contribution to this book, unlearning. Specifically, we draw on her HEADSUP framework (Table 8.1), originally created in response to the Kony 2012 phenomenon when youth from around the world shared via social media a video created by NGO Imaginary Children. The video used compelling video production and testimonies to urge the raising of monetary support to assist the Ugandan government to imprison warlord Joseph Kony. The video was viewed over 100 million times in ten days and became "the most publicized online humanitarian campaign ever produced" (Engelhardt and Jansz, 2014). The video was later criticised for presenting a simplistic view of the issue and the NGO in question was the source of much criticism (Gregory, 2012).

Reflecting on how to support young people to critically engage with these types of campaigns more broadly and to support a complex treatment of global issues in educational arenas, Andreotti (2012) created the HEADSUP tool. The acronym includes seven interrelated historical patterns often reproduced through global issues treatment: Hegemony—Justifying superiority and supporting domination; Ethnocentrism—projecting one view as universal; Ahistoricism—forgetting historical legacies and complicities; Depoliticisation—disregarding power inequalities and ideological roots of analyses and proposals; Salvationism—framing help as the burden of the fittest; Un-complicated solutions—offering easy and simple solutions that do not require systemic change; Paternalism—seeking affirmation of authority/superiority through the provision of help and the infantilisation of recipients (Andreotti, 2012, p. 2).

This framework, we argue, together with other critical literacy tools (such as Andreotti et al., 2006), can support educators to reflect upon and direct work in secondary classrooms towards SDG 4.7 in such a way as to respond to critiques rather than reinforcing extant approaches by making explicit and critically engaging with historical patterns reproduced through ESD and GCE (see also Andreotti et al., 2018).

In a project conducted over one year in 2018 and funded by the British Academy's Tackling the UK's International Challenges Programme, we hosted workshops for secondary school teachers (teaching within the fourteen- to eighteen-year-old range) in England, Finland and Sweden. At the workshops, we presented the HEADSUP tool and sought input into its applicability in the classroom. The locations were selected based on the researchers' locations and access to networks who could help recruit participants within the short project timeline. There are also direct curricular links in all three national contexts to support global issues and sustainability. Twenty-six teachers were involved in the workshops.

Table 8.1 Andreotti's HEADSUP tool

Hegemony (justifying superiority and supporting domination)	a) does this initiative promote the idea that one group of people could design and implement the ultimate solution that will solve all problems?	b) does this initiative invite people to analyse things from different perspectives, including complicities in the making of the problems being addressed?
Ethnocentrism (projecting one view as universal)	a) does this initiative imply that anyone who disagrees with what is proposed is completely wrong or immoral?	b) does this initiative acknowledge that there are other logical ways of looking at the same issue framed by different understandings of reality?
Ahistoricism (forgetting historical legacies and complicities)	a) does this initiative introduce a problem in the present without reference to why this problem exists and how 'we' are connected to the making of that?	b) does this initiative offer a complex historical analysis of the issue?
Depoliticisation (disregarding power inequalities and ideological roots of analyses and proposals)	a) does this initiative present the problem/solution as disconnected from power and ideology?	b) does this initiative acknowledge its own ideological location and offer an analysis of power relations?
Salvationism (framing help as the burden of the fittest)	a) does this initiative present helpers or adopters as the chosen 'global' people on a mission to save the world and lead humanity towards its destiny of order, progress and harmony?	b) does this initiative acknowledge that the self-centred desire to be better than/superior to others and the imposition of aspirations for singular ideas of progress and development have historically been part of what creates injustice?
Un-complicated solutions (offering easy and simple solutions that do not require systemic change)	a) does this initiative offer simplistic analyses and answers that do not invite people to engage with complexity or think more deeply?	b) does this initiative offer a complex analysis of the problem acknowledging the possible adverse effects of proposed solutions?
Paternalism (seeking affirmation of authority/superiority through the provision of help and the infantilisation of recipients)	a) does this initiative portray people in need as people who lack education, resources, maturity or civilisation and who would and should be very grateful for your help?	b) does this initiative portray people in need as people who are entitled to disagree with their saviours and to legitimately want to implement different solutions to what their helpers have in mind?

Source: Andreotti 2012, p. 2.

Across the contexts, participants expressed in surveys after the workshop that there was a great deal of interest and support for such an approach. Teachers felt the workshop inputs reinforced what they "intuited and practiced" (Finnish participant) and found the HEADSUP tool to be "*an interesting way to question our subjects*" (Swedish participant). Many said they would use HEADSUP to prepare new units and would modify it to use with their students. A participant from Sweden summed up how the HEADSUP tool was useful for both self-reflection and pedagogical application:

> *What comes to mind first of all is really being mindful of many perspectives and help the students see the complexity. I'm also thinking a lot about being mindful of my own practices and thinking critically about the way I teach. I will definitely give the heads up model a chance and think about how I can use it in my teaching.*

Participants also raised important dynamic concerns, particularly in regards the challenge of explicitly treating complexity and power inequalities while also keeping a sense of hope and inspiration that youth can work towards a better world. When asked what challenges they anticipate, a participant from Sweden answered:

> *First of all that trap of strengthening the idea that I represent a politically-correct establishment and also the time constraints that make it difficult to deal with the complexities fully. However, I think that trying out a new practice [such as HEADSUP] is always challenging in the beginning and with some time it becomes easier.*

This response demonstrates both the institutional constraints experienced by teachers as well as the challenge of taking up political ideas. This participant also expressed a commitment to continuing critically reflexive practice.

One participant took HEADSUP with the guiding questions created by Andreotti (2012; see Table 8.1) into her Geography classes (Years 7, 8, 10 and 12, spanning ages fourteen to eighteen) making no adaptations of language and used it to review the KONY 2012 video. She found that all classes got a lot out of it, even if some of the younger students were not as comfortable with the language. She shared her reflections:

> *I think with our [younger students] we structure things so much that they don't feel like they're actually doing the work, so something like this [HEADSUP list], it was tough and we did get through it and they were so invested in it in the lesson. They were able to walk away understanding like maybe there's more situations than I think, there's certain factors that I can look for that would suggest to me*

> *that maybe I'm not getting the whole story. So with my Year 8s it was less about them comprehending each one of these [HEADSUP concepts] and more about them understanding the dynamic that like news, media, stuff like that, stories sometimes are very simple and we need to listen to them critically and figure out what we're not being told and maybe there's room to explore further.*

In the next section, we will share snapshots of three classroom lessons in which workshop participants who volunteered to apply the HEADSUP to a lesson invite a researcher to observe, and participate in a reflection interview afterwards. We share three such lessons and reflections from the teachers in order to then discuss the implications for an ethical global issues pedagogy that supports SDG 4.7 in Global North contexts.

Classroom Snapshot 1

In a Year 9 class in the Midlands in England, Geography teacher Sam led a class about the Kibera area of Nairobi (n.b., pseudonyms are being used to protect the anonymity of all participants in the study). He adapted HEADSUP, "*breaking [it] down, making it a little bit more straightforward for the students and put it into categories and thinking of ways to do it*". He plans to use more complex language for his A level students (sixteen- to eighteen-year-olds), but for the Year 9 (thirteen- to fourteen-year-olds) groups that day, he used these terms and questions: leadership (who is in charge in this situation?), opinions (what are the different viewpoints of this situation?), background (what have been the main causes of this situation?), fairness (what are the main issues or problems here?), responses (what is the best way to respond to this situation?) and future (what do you think Kibera will be like in the future?). Reflecting on the lesson and the idea of trying to add complexity by adapting HEADSUP, Sam said, "*This is just as a starting point. I thought this worked quite well and it comes up with some good questions which I will then use again*".

The lesson was part of a larger unit looking at Kenya. In previous lessons, students had been looking at rural issues, population distribution and density, and push/pull factors contributing to urbanisation. In this lesson, the students learned some key characteristics of the Kibera slum in Nairobi, looked at some images to explore different characteristics, ranked different priorities and then answered questions based on the adapted HEADSUP list. Having answered a question connected to each of the terms, Sam then asked students to come up with alternative questions. He intended to challenge his own power and raise the question of who gets to set the questions, hoping this would encourage them to think of multiple perspectives on how a problem is framed. Sam was impressed by the alternative questions developed by the students. When reading through the student work he highlighted one in particular: "*That's a great alternative question, to go from who's in charge of the situation to who can change or influence people, it's like spot on!*". He also remarked as to how some lower-performing students were highly engaged and produced some of the most thoughtful and complex alternative questions:

> *some of them really got into it, some of them didn't so much and what was really interesting actually, a lot of the less able kids really enjoyed it and really got on and actually came up with some incredibly good questions and just their lateral thinking of it. I think it's something that if I had a bit more time I'd probably develop it for maybe twenty minutes and keep going.*

In particular, the prompt for students to compose an alternative question was something he would do again.

Sam did feel that the students tended to have a neutral understanding that the government should 'do more' and 'fix things', and he suggested he would particularly adjust the first question related to 'leadership' to consider more complexity around how power is determined and distributed politically. Also, he will continue to work on how to make links between the urbanisation issues in Kibera and issues in the UK context:

> *I think it's also important to get them . . . to read, especially if you've got an image and an issue, say 'how does that compare to the UK? Would that happen in the UK? Do we get that?' You might if you, let's say you're doing it at A-level they might be more aware of things like places like Grenfell and what's happened recently and other things, because there are similarities and obviously.*

Classroom Snapshot 2

Another classroom application occurred in a small town about a forty-minute drive outside of Manchester, England. The Geography lesson, planned and facilitated by Laura, also involved Year 9 students (fourteen-year-olds) and engaged them in a critical examination of the favelas in Sao Paulo, Brazil. They considered how a resident from the favela can have contradictory and complex perspectives and examined the extent to which a mainstream perspective on helping communities 'develop' fails to account for the lived realities and desires of different stakeholders.

When asked how she felt about applying HEADSUP, Laura responded: "*I think it actually was really positive. I think that they thought more deeply than I expected, like the answers they gave were more well-reasoned and much higher-level than I expected. They really did see things from multiple perspectives*". She reflected specifically on one of the warm-up activities in which she presented different viewpoints on

PowerPoint slides and asked the students to guess what person would have that perspective:

> *I wanted to see if they could think a bit differently, so rather than telling them whose opinion it was, give them the opinion, see if they could actually work it out. . . . So, they thought that [one of the more negative opinions] was from someone living in a slum, shanty town, but it's actually someone living in what would be seen as solution. So, they found that quite surprising.*

Laura elaborated on one example from that activity where one perspective shared expressed a deep connection to the favela, connecting its history to a personal history. This person appreciated the family networks and community support in the favela. The next slide present an opinion expressing deep concern about the violence. The students did not guess that this view was from the same person as the perspective on the previous slide. Laura felt the plurivocality of the issue came across and added complexity to the way she taught the issue: "*So, trying to get them to see that people can hold multiple perspectives of the same area*".

For the bulk of the lesson, students went to different stations, where they explored various perspectives about approaches to improving life in the Sao Paulo favelas through reading short articles and watching videos about art projects, tourism initiatives and resettlement projects. Using prompts inspired by HEADSUP, they wrote their various responses on sheets of paper, generating multiple responses to each station. Laura asked to consolidate their learning at the end by writing a response suggesting what would be the best way to improve the favelas if they accepted they needed improving. As she is trying to prepare them for their General Certificate of Secondary Education (GCSE) exam in this subject, she wanted students to be able to practice defending a solution as they will need to in the exam; however, she also wanted to ensure they took a complex approach. Many students were able to recognise that the situation was very complex and that there are multiple perspectives.

In reading one of the students' responses, Laura felt the student reached a level of complexity she had not seen in previous lessons:

> *This student wrote 'I think it's good that they are building new houses for people of the favela, but it doesn't involve their opinion as to how they want to live. I think relocating them is a bad thing because it doesn't get over the fact that there are still areas who are unsustainable and doesn't really improve anything for the area'.*

She noted that the students were picking up on the synopticity which is also a key concept in the course, and was particularly impressed by the work of a 'weaker' student who responded in a way that took up a complex perspective: "*One of them has written 'I think that the favelas do need improving, they would be better if they had running water and toilets, however everyone in the favela feels like a community, that sense shouldn't be ruined'. That is a weaker student, yay!*". Laura was able to apply HEADSUP in a way that felt consistent with her overall goal of preparing students for their GCSE exam.

Classroom Snapshot 3

In a classroom in one of the bigger cities of Sweden, students critically examined ethnocentrism in considering their international fieldwork experiences on farming issues. During the classroom observation, the students were preparing the oral presentations of their diploma projects (grade 12 essay) based on fieldwork they conducted in India (3-week-trip). Using some of the concepts that had been introduced through HEADSUP at the workshop facilitated by the researchers the month previous, Anna reminded the students about being critical and mindful of binary and hierarchical concepts. Specifically she talked about the need for them to consider one-dimensional/multidimensional views of development, homogenous/heterogeneous groups and central/peripheral values when preparing their presentations.

In a student discussion with five female students who focussed on agriculture and development as part of the field study, certain issues related to the teacher's instructions came up. A group of students mentioned what they referred to as a 'Western view of development' in relation to the question of the well-being of a population who relied on agriculture/farming and economic growth. The students found that farming and being able to support their family on what they produced made the farmers feel happy with their lives, and that seemed to be a more important factor that economic growth and 'earning or producing more'. The students also reflected on the concept of poverty and concluded that 'being poor' is highly contextual and that their view on poverty was quite one-dimensional. This surprised them somewhat as they had worked with a multidimensional and complex method when analysing the lives of people experiencing poverty and disadvantage when preparing the fieldwork, and they referred to this as a real eye-opener.

In a follow-up discussion with the researcher reflecting on the student discussions, Anna described that the purpose of the lesson was "*to make different perspectives on development visible, the dominant ones and also the non-dominant ones and to discuss which theories and approaches that are useful to get a more balanced picture*". She commented on the model described by the students which aligns with what was described by the students and their reflective approach to development:

> *Its fundamental ideas are that development is multidimensional; that the reality of people is complex and shifting, and that you focus on assets and opportunities rather than needs and shortages. . . . It gives*

> *a comprehensive view on the living conditions of people, and not just income. And it makes visible the interplay and connection between macro and micro, and that they affect and shape each other . . . and assumes that individuals and groups have a number of resources, or capital.*

Anna also stressed the need for reflective tools to support the development of critically reflective teaching practice beyond learning the theoretical constructs to applying them deeply:

> *I mean a little of what I tried to present in the class today, like how . . . they are not supposed to discuss eurocentrism, but how can they involve that when reflecting and discussing the conclusions? Can they apply that approach? And to me, that's like . . . well, I do have some of these tools anyway, but I think I could need a more up-to-date package, like a tutorial". Similarly to Sam, she expressed a need for resources to support linking to issues in Sweden: "when I need to think of which examples I should bring up when I want to talk about Swedish welfare for example . . . some of those concepts that help you being norm critical, and . . . I like that word norm-creative.*

Anna's students have the privilege of participating in experiential learning in India and studying at a school where global issues are embedded throughout the curriculum. However, her example demonstrates that it is both important and possible to raise deep issues around Westerncentrism and power imbalances regarding who gets to frame, who experiences and who is impacted by global issues and their proposed solutions. As an experienced and lead teacher, Anna also drew parallels to a recent lecture she gave for student teachers who wanted to improve their knowledge of global development issues by participating in fieldwork in a developing country for eight weeks. Anna discussed the importance of critical literacy in teacher education, and to prepare the student teachers for their field study abroad she used the concept of reflexivity that was discussed at the workshop.

> *Now I was thinking as an active way to challenge their beliefs and picture of the world, and also like considering whether it matters if you believe in some other way. . . . So I showed them the trend for Sweden with regards to economic development, and afterwards they got to draw the trend for the country they thought they would [need economic development. . . . And they could basically not draw anything, but plenty of questions came up, because they realized that it was not just that simple to. . . . Well, partly maybe they didn't know that much. So we looked at what it was really like. And then I think it works well if you first try to look at the preconceived notions/*

> *assumptions that are there. . . . You really have to start doing something with that.*

This comment relates strongly to what Martin and Pirbhai-Illich suggest in their contribution to this book regarding the importance of directly engaging with the idea of relationality in teacher education.

While these three snapshots of classes where teachers applied the HEADSUP tool represent somewhat exceptional cases with teachers who volunteered to come to the workshop and then to invite researchers to their classrooms, this small project seeks to exemplify that both teachers and students are able to engage in deep and complex discussions about global issues. Each teacher has taken up a specific aspect or sets of aspects related to HEADSUP for use in her or his context and students have responded in turn. And, across the three national contexts, there was both a sense that teachers are already engaged in taking up complexity and that they could use further resources, particularly to develop deep links between local and global issues. Anna's example with the student teachers also speaks to the importance of criticality and of understanding origins of assumptions and about challenging and providing space for student teachers to reflect on their own and others' 'root narratives', as stressed by Andreotti (2006).

Conclusion

According to UNESCO (2014), a main aim of GCE is: "Support learners to revisit assumptions, world views and power relations in mainstream discourses and consider people/groups that are systematically underrepresented/marginalized" (p. 12).

The examples presented in this chapter suggest that teachers are teaching in a way that takes up key ethical issues. We suggest this particular aim of Global Citizenship Education be a central bridging aim for 4.7, inclusive of Education for Sustainable Development (see also Pashby, 2018). There is an opportunity to mobilise around SDG 4.7 in a way that to a significant extent takes up rather than extending the scholarly critiques of ESD and GCE which raise concerns about superficial approaches reinforcing colonial systems of power. The teachers featured here are explicitly taking up issues like ethnocentrism, power, and multiple and contradictory perspectives, thereby bringing the ethical implications of the consequences of global issues into teaching and learning. Widdows argues (2014):

> A pedagogy of global ethics would not involve proposing 'a' global ethic, but would explicitly consider how teachers and learners can engage with the plurality of contexts and ethical considerations that define today's pressing global issues. . . . What matters is not just the

> consideration of global issues, but how these issues are approached and the methodology, ethical framework and assumptions adopted.
> (Widdows, 2014, p. 5)

These three teachers demonstrate a pedagogy of global ethics rooted in directly taking up mainstream perspectives and marginalised voices. As well, all three express the challenge of connecting deep issues of power inequalities to local contexts and connecting issues in the Global South to ongoing issues in their own national and regional contexts. Indeed, our study has indicated some key challenges of applying HEADSUP include working against a neutral understanding of power as government in Sam's case, a point that is reinforced in the post-workshop comment from a Swedish participant in regards to concerns about how to handle political correctness in the classroom. In Laura's case a challenge is pushing from within an exam culture that wants students to defend one approach, a challenge she felt she was able to meet. And, Anna raised the challenge of needing to keep up-to-date and continually work on how to apply key theoretical constructs like ethnocentrism. Whereas the students in England were learning in an exam-driven context, the students in Sweden were engaged in experiential learning abroad; yet, all three teachers found ways to adapt the HEADSUP tool, suggesting it can be useful across contexts. Significantly, however, while our workshops encouraged teachers to apply HEADSUP to the study of global environmental issues, the classroom applications tended to focus more on social and political dimensions. Further research and praxis also need to engage more explicitly with the links between a natural science approach to studying environmental issues and tackling the deep historical and present-day inequalities in which such issues are deeply entrenched.

We suggest continued research with teachers to engage with theoretical tools and classroom application, as our participants indicated this is missing for even those teachers most likely to be open to such praxis. The HEADSUP tool seems to have helped the teachers in this study deepen their existing pedagogical approaches, but we did not gather data in regards to the extent to which it relates to how they engage in their own approach to relating to others in the world, including within their own classrooms. Thus, in line with what Martin and Pirbhai-Illich propose in their chapter in this book, we also suggest further work to consider the importance of critical cultural literacies as integral to ethical global issues pedagogy. Ethical global issues pedagogy will require resourcing at pre-service and in-service levels as well as ongoing reflection and work. We will not arrive at one approach, and we hope this chapter has shed some light on both the real possibilities and important work being done currently in classrooms and the challenges framing this ongoing and important work.

References

Andreotti, V. (2006). Soft vs. critical global citizenship education. *Policy and Practice: A Development Education Review*, 3, pp. 40–51.

Andreotti, V. (2011). *Actionable Postcolonial Theory in Education*. New York: Palgrave Macmillan.

Andreotti, V. (2012). Editor's preface: HEADS UP. *Critical Literacy: Theories and Practices*, 6(1), pp. 1–3.

Andreotti, V., Barker, L. and Newell-Jones, K. (2006). *Critical Literacy in Global Citizenship Education: Professional Development Resource Pack*. Open Spaces Dialogue and Enquire Methodology Initiative. Derby, England: Centre for the Study of Social and Global Justice. Available at: <www.osdemethodology.org.uk/keydocs/pdresourcepack.pdf>

Andreotti, V. and Souza, L. M. T. M. (eds.). (2012). *Postcolonial Perspectives on Global Citizenship Education*. New York: Routledge.

Andreotti, V., Stein, S., Sutherland, A., Pashby, K., Susa, R. and Amsler, S. (2018). Mobilising different conversations about global justice in education: Toward alternative futures in uncertain times. *Policy and Practice: A Development Education Review*, 26, pp. 9–41.

Blenkinsop, S., Affifi, R., Piersol, L. and Sitka-Sage, M. (2017). Shut-up and listen: Implications and possibilities of Albert Memmi's characteristics of colonization upon the 'natural world'. *Studies in Philosophy and Education*, 36(3), pp. 349–365.

Bryan, A., Clarke, M. and Drudy, S. (2009). Social justice education in initial teacher education: A cross border perspective. A report for the standing conference on teacher education north and south (SCoTENS). Available at: <http://scotens.org/docs/2009-Social%20Justice%20Education%20in%20Initial%20Teacher%20Education.pdf>

Gregory, S. (2012). Kony 2012 through a prism of video advocacy practices and trends. *Journal of Human Rights Practice*, 4(3), pp. 463–468.

Jickling, B. and Wals, A. E. J. (2008). Globalization and environmental education: Looking beyond sustainable development. *Journal of Curriculum Studies*, 40(1), pp. 1–21.

Martin, F. (2011). Global ethics, sustainability and partnership. In: G. Butt (ed.), *Geography, Education and the Future*, 206–224. London: Continuum.

McKenzie, M. (2012). Education for y'all: Global neoliberalism and the case for a politics of scale in sustainability education policy. *Policy Futures in Education*, 10(2), pp. 165–177.

Pashby, K. (2012). Questions for global citizenship education in the context of the 'new imperialism'. In: V. de Oliveira Andreotti and L. M. T. M. de Souza (eds.), *Postcolonial Perspectives on Global Citizenship Education*, 9–26. NY: Routledge.

Pashby, K. (2018). Global citizenship education as a UNESCO key theme: More of the same or opportunities for thinking 'Otherwise'? In: L. Shultz and T. Pillay (eds.), *Global Citizenship, Common Wealth and Uncommon Citizenships*, 160–174. Leiden: Koninklijke Brill NV.

Shultz, L. and Pillay, T. (2018). Global citizenship, common wealth, and uncommon citizenships: An introduction. In: L. Shultz and T. Pillay (eds.), *Global*

Citizenship, Common Wealth and Uncommon Citizenships, 1–8. Leiden: Koninklijke Brill NV.

Sund, L. and Öhman, J. (2014). On the need to repoliticise environmental and sustainability education: Rethinking the postpolitical consensus. *Environmental Education Research*, 20(5), pp. 639–659.

Tuck, Eve, McKenzie, Marcia and McCoy, Kate. (2014). Land education: Indigenous, post-colonial, and decolonizing perspectives on place and environmental education research. *Environmental Education Research*, 20(1), pp. 1–23.

UNESCO. (2014). *Global Citizenship Education: Preparing Learners for the Challenges of the Twenty-First Century*. Available at: <http://unesdoc.unesco.org/images/0022/002277/227729E.pdf>

Van Poeck, K. and Vandenabeele, J. (2012). Learning from sustainable development: Education in the light of public issues. *Environmental Education Research*, 18(4), pp. 541–552.

Von Engelhardt, J. and Jansz, J. (2014). Challenging humanitarian communication: An empirical exploration of Kony 2012. *International Communication Gazette*, 76(6), pp. 464–484.

Wals, A. E. (2009). A mid-DESD review: Key findings and ways forward. *Journal of Education for Sustainable Development*, 3(2), pp. 195–204.

Widdows, H. (2014). *Global Ethics: An Introduction*. Durham: Acumen.

9 Bat Conservation in the Foundation Stage

An Early Start to Education for Sustainability

Zoi Nikiforidou, Zoe Lavin-Miles and Paulette Luff

Introduction

This chapter highlights the essential role of early years teachers and teacher educators in delivering an educational response to promoting a just and sustainable world. Education for Sustainable Development and Global Citizenship (ESD/GC) has expanded in schools and in further and higher education but has received less attention in early years, particularly in England. In the light of this, we offer an account of a practical project that provides an exemplar of ESD/GC in the early years—the Bat Conservation Project. The Bat Conservation Project has been implemented with young children in England and in a parallel project in Kenya and then used as the basis for a professional development resource for early years teachers. The Bat Project training resource comprises three phases/sections; teachers' own perceptions, attitudes and broader understanding of ESD are brought together with the implementation of a project with young children under the Early Years Foundation Stage (EYFS) principles and active learning approach, culminating in a review and future considerations of ways to enhance ESD. Precisely, in phase 1 the project proposes activities that focus on teachers' personal and shared understanding of ESD; phase 2 is about exploring with pre-schoolers the worldwide issue of conservation of protected species (in this case bats); and phase 3 consists of assessing provision and planning further steps in promoting ESD in the early years classrooms. All the proposed activities are flexible and can be used by individuals and groups, face-to-face or online. Using this project as a basis, we then explore some of the possibilities and challenges of introducing meaningful curriculum for ESD/GC in the earliest years of education. We draw parallels between the opportunities for experiential learning on offer to the children and strategies for the training and professional development in order to build the knowledge, skills, values and capabilities of early years teachers and other early years practitioners. World Organisation for Early Childhood Education and Care (OMEP) and OMEP UK have been working in this direction by addressing the necessity and urge to consider ESD from early childhood onwards, in accordance with the United Nations' 2015–2030 sustainable development goals.

Education for Sustainable Development in Early Childhood

Education for Sustainable Development (ESD) both as a content area and a way of working with children has recently gained attention within Early Childhood (EC) (Pramling Samuelsson, 2011; Davis and Elliott, 2014; Davis, 2015). Frequently, ESD is connected with environmental education and engagement with issues that relate to the environment and nature. Educating all children, including the youngest, about the intrinsic value of their physical environment is key for a sustainable future. Sustainable development means working for a world that is diverse, fair, just and peaceful, with careful use of limited resources and concern for the well-being of people and the planet. As such, children from a young age can be introduced to and become aware of aspects related to the three key pillars of sustainable development: environmental and ecological concerns, social and cultural implications, and economic aspects (Brundtland, 1987). Pramling Samuelsson and Kaga (2010) propose seven notions that are embedded in a sustainable environment for social life and economy: respect, reduce, reflect, reuse, repair, recycle and responsibility. These '7Rs' underline the basic principles children need in order to foster love and respect towards nature. The purpose of ESD in EC is "fundamentally about values, with respect at the centre: respect for others, including those of present and future generations, for difference and diversity, for the environment, for the resources of the planet we inhabit" (UN, 2005, p. 23).

While discussing ESD in EC, and in particular environmental issues, Davis (2009) proposes the distinction between *education in the environment*, *education about the environment* and *education for the environment* (p. 235). Today, environmental behavioural modifications indicate and align with more participatory approaches, where children are seen as competent, active agents, with the right to be involved and be heard (James and James, 2004). They become global citizens in the sense that they learn to become independent knowledge constructors, problem solvers and critical thinkers (Johansson, 2009) about issues that matter. These issues link to the wider natural and social environment and are connected with values, practices and behaviours that promote a sense of justice, responsibility, exploration and dialogue.

A significant factor related to the pedagogical implications of ESD in Early Childhood is the role and attitude of the practitioner. Firstly, practitioners can draw and direct children's attention to particular aspects related to ESD (Pramling Samuelsson, 2011; Davis, 2015). With teachers' support, children can engage with and understand themes and topics linked to ecological cycles, people's lifestyles, nature, society and culture. Furthermore, Thulin and Pramling (2009) found that the way the teacher introduces tasks influences the outcome and how children will participate in the project. Dialogue, questions, questioning are also techniques that will generate active engagement. The practitioner should provide safe and enabling environments for children's meaning-making. Even though the practitioner should have knowledge and understanding of the topic under investigation, children should be encouraged to explore, create meanings and develop skills, attitudes and understandings that are driven by their own interests and experiences (Pramling Samuelsson and Asplund Carlsson, 2008; Davis, 2015).

In addition, ESD in EC should be based on a play-based pedagogy and the principles of playful learning (Wright et al., 2014). Edwards and Cutter-MacKenzie (2011) found, specifically, that a play-based pedagogy in combination with intentional teaching can support children's knowledge and understanding of sustainability. Another pedagogical aspect of ESD relates to the fact that activities should enhance opportunities for communication, participation and interaction (Pramling Samuelsson, 2011). These opportunities have many facets: children and nature, children and others, children and tradition, children and themselves, children and the wider community, children and economy. Accordingly, early learning for sustainability can take place in different settings: in families, communities, schools, early childhood settings. According to Kaga (2008), formal, non-formal and informal spaces should all be used in promoting awareness that everyone is responsible for making societies sustainable. She proposes that cultural resources (e.g. local folk tales and songs, traditional ceremonies), economic resources (e.g. businesses), social and political resources (e.g. NGOs, governments) must be organised for making learning experiences relevant to sustainability and meaningful for young children. In the case study project, reported here as an exemplar of ESD/GC in early years education, these pedagogical principles are implemented within a project on conservation of bats (see also Luff et al., 2015).

Exploring the Worldwide Conservation of Protected Species and Pre-School Children: The Bat Conservation Project

Animal or environmental protection are often left to the 'experts' deemed responsible for the protection of ever decreasing wildlife and habitats. The attitude would be, 'why bother? what is the relevance to me now?'. The answer lies in our children; the legacy of our indifference will exact a significant price from them in the future if we do not start to raise awareness of the fragility of our world from the early years. ESD will allow every child to develop skills, attitudes and the determination to shape their future to meet their needs.

Why bats? This particular species is a threatened and protected species around the world and, in Kenya (the partnership country for this project), the bat is synonymous with myths, and so feared as carriers of evil spirits and ghosts. They are also reservoir hosts of many parasites including malaria and, more recently, Ebola, which does not add to their popularity. In the UK, the bat has a long history associated with Halloween and other media generated stereotypes. A lack of knowledge leads to myths such as 'bats get into your hair', which fuel the paranoia. The greatest devastation to bats in the UK and Kenya is from home-building, persecution, deforestation and general habitat loss.

The importance of these animals to our eco-systems is much less understood. This is an area in which the early years can gain their first 'experience' of this animal and of other species that are essential for our food security. Two of the UK's most common species of bat are the *Common* and *Soprano pipistrelle*, living within housing estates, woodlands and arable land. This latter species, in Asia and elsewhere, has recently been found to be "a very convenient sustainable hazard free alternative to pesticides", with evidence of "the ability of the Soprano Pipistrelle to control the rice borer moth (*Chilo supressalis*), a major pest of rice around the world" (Puig-Montserrat et al., 2015). In addition to controlling borer infestations, in the UK they can consume up to 3000 *Lepidoptera sp.* per night. In Kenya, two of the rarest bats are *Cardioderma cor* (Insect bat) and *Epomophorus whalbergi* (Fruit bat); and Kenbats (the Kenyan bat conservation trust) are urging for more education to help reduce the myths surrounding them. Bats in Africa are pollinators for over 500 species of fruits and plants, including mango, banana and cocoa, arguably the main economically important fruits in Africa.

In Sunbeams Nursery at Alderholt, Dorset, UK, a project was launched in 2015 for three weeks, run by the staff members of the setting (Table 9.1). The three weeks were interspersed with four sessions from an Environmental Educator under the headings: Introduction to Bats; Echolocation or 'See with Sound'; Evening of Bat Detecting; and Bat Habitat Sharing. The aim was to familiarise the children with this species as an important, protected and exciting animal. Children engaged through a diversity of activities and play-based tasks in connection with the Early Years Foundation Stage learning and development areas (DfE, 2014) (see Table 9.1); also, the community was brought in with an evening bat walk. The Sunbeams Nursery sessions video is available to view at www.youtube.com/watch?v=w19GMXRAd70&feature=youtu.be.

Table 9.1 Outline of the pedagogical sessions of the Bat Conservation Project

Activity	*EYFS—areas of learning and development*	*Resources*
Introduced bats to children—story for three weeks, twice a week.	**C&L**—Listening to stories with increased attention. **Lit**—Repetition of words with the children each week. **UW**—Becoming familiar with the natural world around.	Story book—*Bat Loves the Night* with Bat Toy to go to Kenya
Bats love bugs—followed from a bug hunt in the grounds from educator.	**Maths**—Bug to be placed in numbered baskets 1–5, count out and place with support.	Rubber bugs Laminated habitat
The children learnt about the positions of the bats in their homes (habitats) and how bats 'hang upside down'. They made their bats and hung them around the nursery.	**EA&D**—Make a bat that hangs. Egg box for younger children and loo roll for older ones. Exploring using various construction materials.	Egg boxes, loo rolls, pipe cleaners, paint, tape, glue, googly eyes, "Can you find somewhere to hang?"
The children re-enacted being a bat and flew around 'like a bat' avoiding obstacles to follow the 'echolocation' song and video and 'sound to see session' from educator.	**PD**—Moving and handling. Runs skilfully and negotiates space, successfully adjusting speed or direction to avoid obstacles.	Bat capes Cones Stands
Bat songs sung twice a week over three weeks.	**Maths**—Number and counting songs from bat song sheets. **EA&D**—Song and music expression.	Song sheets
After the bat was made and hung, the children over two weeks started to think about where a bat might live, following habitat session from educator.	**UW, EA&D, C&L**—Draw, design and make a home for a bat, using prompt sheets for ideas.	Paper Pencils Prompt for questions to ask children
Children took the toy bat to show him/her their favourite thing to do and record, photo to show children in Kenya.	**PSED**—The toy was filmed and given to Kenya/UK OMEP partnership to take to Kenya.	Bat teddy—Emily

(*Continued*)

Table 9.1 (Continued)

Activity	*EYFS—areas of learning and development*	*Resources*
Played in a 'bat cave' extending and elaborating play ideas, building role-play activities with other children.	**PSED**—Bat tent cave—provide props for the children to engage in role-play scenario.	Tent Bat toys Capes Cushions
Bat threading—handled tools, objects, construction and malleable materials safely with control.	**PD**—Thread wool through the holes around a bat silhouette.	Bat shape Wool Tape to fasten

Key:
Communication and language development (C&L)
Physical development (PD)
Personal, social and emotional development (PSED)
Literacy development (Lit)
Mathematics (Maths)
Understanding the world (UW)
Expressive arts and design (EA&D)

Implications

The Bat Conservation project in the EYFS, including the link with pre-schools in Kenya, offers an example of how cross-curricular, experiential learning can be used to engage young children with complex environmental topics in ESD/GC through learning about a local species. We argue that this strategy could and should be used more widely to foster appreciation of present eco-systems and encourage young children, and their families, to consider and protect the natural world. The earliest years of education are a vital period in which the values, knowledge and skills of ESD/GC can be introduced (Pramling Samuelsson, 2011; Davis, 2015). The principles that underpin the EYFS curriculum support an ecological approach, sustaining the optimal growth, learning and development of each unique child through positive relationships and within an enabling environment (DfE, 2014). The challenge is to make these implicit values more explicit and to link them firmly to ESD/GC.

Whilst ESD/GC is well established in schools, colleges and universities, in England, early years education lags behind other sectors, and work during the United Nations Decade of Education for Sustainable Development appears to have made little impact. Recently, and at the present moment, 'sustainability' in early years education is about maintaining provision in an era of low funding (e.g. Morton, 2015), and there is little capacity to embrace a wider commitment to global concerns. Early years practitioners of all types, and with a wide range of qualifications (including both those with the new Early Years Teacher status and those with Qualified Teacher status who work in the EYFS), are deeply committed to the present and future well-being of the children in their care but, arguably, often have limited knowledge of complex economic, political, social and environmental issues. They may also lack confidence in their own abilities to understand the intricacies of ESD/GC and to incorporate it within their work with children and families. It is in this context that we anticipate the United Nation's 2015–2030 sustainable development goals and the challenge of inspiring early years teachers and other early years practitioners to embrace ESD/GC. This will require imaginative training and professional development in order to consider values, build knowledge, develop skills and extend capabilities.

Conclusion

ESD/GC is only recently starting to become part of early years provision in an explicit and intentional manner. There are many examples of daily practice where children experience and experiment with ideas related to the three pillars of sustainable development: environment, economy and society. However, there is still a long way to go before practitioners feel fully equipped to promote ESD/GC in Early Years and before ESD/GC becomes an educational goal, process and attitude. A way forward is to focus on highlighting existing practices within early years settings (such as listening to children, encouraging co-operation, promoting outdoor play in nature, furthering inclusive practice and the embracing of diversity) and to link these overtly to ESD/GC. Another way is to increase awareness of responsibilities for local and global citizenship and find ways to challenge and change complacency and consumerism. This latter task is daunting but essential. The practitioners who were involved in the case example of the Bat Conservation Project presented learned alongside the children through playful child-led and adult-directed activities. This co-construction of knowledge provides a model for a practical and investigative approach that could prove fruitful for early years teacher professional development for ESD/GC.

OMEP, World Organisation for Early Childhood, is an international non-governmental and non-profit organisation with Consultative Status at the United Nations and UNESCO. Since 2010, OMEP have led projects on ESD in order to raise awareness among members in more than seventy countries, and so influence young children and their families and make a difference in early childhood education at large (for details, see link below). The Bat Conservation project, described above, is part of the OMEP UK contribution focussed upon resources for teacher education that embeds ESD/GC within the EYFS for an earlier start to Education for Sustainability.

References

Brundtland, G. (ed.). (1987). *Our Common Future: The World Commission on Environment and Development*. Oxford: Oxford University Press.

Davis, J. M. (2009). Revealing the research 'hole' of early childhood education for sustainability: A preliminary survey of the literature. *Environmental Education Research*, 15(2), pp. 227–241.

Davis, J. M. (ed.). (2015). *Young Children and the Environment: Early Education for Sustainability*. 2nd edition. Melbourne: Cambridge University Press.

Davis, J. M. and Elliott, S. (2014). *Research in Early Childhood Sustainability: International Perspectives and Provocations*. London: Routledge.

Department for Education (DfE) (2014). *Statutory Framework for the Early Years Foundation* Stage. Available at: <www.gov.uk/government/uploads/system/uploads/attachment_data/file/335533/EYFS_framework_from_1_September_2014__with_clarification_note.pdf>

Edwards, S. and Cutter-Mackenzie, A. (2011). Environmentalizing early childhood curriculum through play-based pedagogies. *Australasian Journal of Early Childhood*, 36(1), pp. 51–59.

Edwards, S. and Cutter-Mackenzie, A. (2013). Towards a model for early childhood environmental education: Foregrounding, developing and connecting knowledge through play-based learning. *The Journal of Environmental Education*, 44(3), pp. 195–213.

James, A. and James, A. L. (2004). *Constructing Childhood*. Basingstoke: Palgrave Macmillan.

Johansson, E. (2009). The preschool child of today—the world-citizen of tomorrow? *International Journal of Early Childhood*, 41(2), pp. 79–97.

Kaga, Y. (2008). Early childhood education for a sustainable world. In: I. Pramling-Samuelsson and Y. Kaga (eds.), *The Contribution of Early Childhood Education to a Sustainable Society*, 53–56. Paris: UNESCO.

Luff, P., Miles, Z. and Wangui, C. (2015). A bat conservation project in the UK and Kenya. *Early Education Journal*, 76, pp. 14–15.

Morton, K. (2015). *Sector Fears Over Delivery of 30 Hours Free Childcare Pledge*. Nursery World, 1 June. Available at: <www.nurseryworld.co.uk/nursery-world/news/1151793/sector-fears-over-delivery-of-30-hours-free-childcare-pledge>

Pramling Samuelsson, I. (2011). Why we should begin early with ESD: The role of early childhood education. *International Journal of Early Childhood*, 43(2), pp. 103–118.

Pramling Samuelsson, I. and Asplund Carlsson, M. (2008). The playing learning child: Towards a pedagogy of early childhood. *Scandinavian Journal of Educational Research*, 52(6), pp. 623–641.

Pramling Samuelsson, I. and Kaga, Y. (2010). Early childhood education in transforming cultures for sustainability. In: E. Assadourian (ed.), *State of the World 2010. Transforming Cultures: From Consumerism to Sustainability*, 57–61. Washington, DC: Worldwatch Institute.

Puig-Montserrat, X., Torre, I., Lopez-Baucells, A., Guerrieri, E., Monti, M., Rofols-Garcia, R., Ferrer, X., Gisbert, D.,and Flaquer, C. (2015). Pest control service provided by bats in Mediterranean rice paddies: Linking Agro-ecosystems structure to ecological functions. *Mammalian Biology*, 80(3), pp. 237–45. Available at: <www.sciencedirect.com/science/article/pii/S1616504715000348>

Thulin, S. and Pramling, N. (2009). Anthropomorphically speaking: On communication between teachers and children in early childhood biology learning. *International Journal of Early Years Education*, 17(2), pp. 137–150.

United Nations. (2005). *UN Decade of Education for Sustainable Development 2005–2014. International Implementation Scheme*. Paris: UNESCO.

Wright, H., Emre, C. and Luff, P. (2014). Early childhood play with reclaimed resources: Potential benefits for young children. Paper presented at the Erasmus Intensive Program Project; Play, Toys and Culture Seminar at Marmara University, Istanbul, 26–27 September.

10 Advocating for Democratic, Participatory Approaches to Learning and Research for Sustainability in Early Childhood

Mallika Kanyal, Paulette Luff and Opeyemi Osadiya

Introduction

One hundred years on from the publication of John Dewey's *Democracy and Education*, in this chapter we explore aspects of sustainable education with an emphasis upon concepts of experience, enquiry, critical reflection and dialogue as a basis for participatory learning and teaching. The aim is to bring forward, and attempt to reconcile, some of the implicit questions that divide education into dichotomous discourses: on the one hand consumerism and marketisation and, on the other, inclusion, reciprocity and potential for social transformation. Drawing upon DEEEP's recommendations for transformative approaches to education and work towards sustainable development and active global citizenship (Fricke and Gathercole, 2015), we explore relational pedagogies in early childhood education and in higher education, and argue for learner-centred, participatory methods. Specifically, we present and analyse two parallel examples from our research and practice, one from the early childhood sector and another from higher education. The first example is from an action research study in a nursery setting involving young children and members of staff in the creation of a wildlife garden, as a basis for co-construction of understandings of sustainability. The second reports a project in which early childhood studies (ECS) students participated in the development of a learning space in their university. Both are used to illustrate a collegial model of working with early childhood stakeholders and the participatory, relational pedagogical approaches that we advocate.

Sterling (2001, 2011), in response to challenges to education posed by Schumacher (1973), argues for transformative learning, teaching and educational research. This calls for creative, participatory and collaborative approaches at every level of education (from early childhood through to university and lifelong/lifewide learning). Further, prominence is given to social and environmental concerns, which may challenge institutional values and priorities. This is echoed in the conceptual basis for Education for Global Citizenship proposed by DEEEP, which highlights "the purpose of education as going beyond the acquisition of knowledge and cognitive skills, to transforming the way people think and act individually and collectively" (Fricke and Gathercole, 2015, p. 10). It is in this context that we raise questions for our own practice and research. This chapter begins with an exploration of education for sustainability within early childhood education and in early childhood studies at university. Working within current systems and processes, with awareness of some of the associated tensions and pressures, the focus here is upon democracy and participation with regard to what is taught, learned and assessed.

Education can be seen as a lifelong learning process that supports people in becoming active and competent global citizens. In our context, this concerns the development of sustainable participatory spaces that help to engender a sense of belonging amongst the participants, as well as promoting their ability to relate to the environment and wider community needs. It is the participatory nature of learning which is at the heart of our practice. The co-construction of knowledge amongst various participants not only helps to bring forward the notions of equality through participation and democracy but also places value upon participants' previous learning and experiences. Within participatory learning, 'democracy' becomes a central ethical imperative in education (Dewey, 1903, 1916). Democracy, from an ethical perspective (rather than a technical one), facilitates the building of relationships of responsibility as well as freedom of mind and discovery between students and tutors. If the tutor, as Dewey asserted, shows the power of initiation and knowledge co-construction, the students can flourish within conditions where they develop their individual mental powers and adequate responsibility for their use (ibid.). It is on these principles of democracy that we present the following two case studies, which are built on a participatory framework of enquiry, promoting dialogue, critical thinking, reflection and experiential learning, and therefore offering transformative potential to all participants.

Case Studies

Human learning begins from birth, and so, arguably, the early years are especially important for Education for Sustainable Development (ESD) as they represent the first and most influential stage of each child's learning life course, and also the period during which the foundations of many fundamental attitudes and values are formed (Engdahl, 2015). There is, therefore, great potential to instigate changes for a more sustainable world and a better future from the early years (Pramling Samuelsson and Kaga, 2008; Engdahl, 2015).

In a similar vein, universities are also ideally positioned to make critical contributions to sustainable development through research and teaching (Sterling, 2012). Current tensions in higher education, especially with regards to its structural rigidity, consumerist culture and disassociated research from local realities, point towards consideration of a paradigm shift in learning, teaching and research approaches (Taylor and Fransman, 2004, Carey, 2013). A university's role is not restricted to the engineering of employees but encompasses a wider aim of education for change that can assist in the production of complete citizens who are able to think for themselves (Nussbaum, 2010). This can be achieved through the promotion of student participation and participatory teaching and learning (see Seale et al., 2015; Kanyal, 2014, 2017). In an Early Childhood Studies (ECS) context, a majority of undergraduate students either aspire to professions where they can work with young children and families, or, are already practitioners in the sector at the time of studying. The notion of ECS academics working with prospective and current early childhood practitioners, therefore, puts us in a strong position to advocate and build capacity for a participatory learning and working environment that has the potential for transformation at a community level.

It is within this conceptual framework of participatory learning that both case studies are situated. They are used to illustrate a collegial model of working with early childhood stakeholders and utilise participatory, relational pedagogical approaches. Case study 1 is an ongoing project and the chapter refers to its initial findings; case study 2 is completed and the chapter draws more from its reflection and recommendations.

Case Study 1—'A Garden for the Bees'

Case study 1 explores opportunities and challenges for monitoring and evaluating education that supports sustainability attitudes and values. It is drawn from action research with practitioners and children in one early years setting. Action research is a social and educational process which offers an opportunity to create forums where people can join together as co-participants in the struggle to remake the practices in which they interact. It is a respectful process of collaborative learning realised by groups of people who desire to change the practices through which they interact in a shared social world in which, for better or worse, we live with the consequences of one another's actions (Kemmis and McTaggart, 2007). In examining what is valuable in the context of ESD, listening to children's and nursery practitioners' voices is of central importance. This is evident in this study, where members of staff proposed the creation of a wildlife garden with the aim of attracting bees, an important issue in sustainable development, and this then became a basis for co-construction of understandings of sustainability.

The Context

The study was designed in response to calls for ESD to begin from the earliest years of education. Ecological and social crises, overconsumption of limited planetary resources and growing awareness of significant threats to the present and future well-being of humanity require shifts in values, awareness and practices. It is important to start from early childhood in order to lay sound intellectual, emotional, social and physical foundations for development and lifelong learning. Young children are not passive in this process but active agents in creation of better conditions (e.g. see: Davis, 2007, 2008; Pramling Samuelsson and Kaga, 2008; Liu and Liu, 2008; Siraj-Blatchford et al., 2010; Mackey, 2012; Engdahl, 2015).

Aim

The case study is part of a research study that aims to develop and describe processes through which sustainability thinking, attitudes and practices can be understood and promoted within a day nursery setting. ESD, within the study, is organised in an interdisciplinary and authentic way with children and practitioners. The initial phase involved a wildlife gardening project.

Setting and Participants

The case study took the form of action research, in conjunction with nursery practitioners and children from a day nursery, in a town in the East of England. The nursery is run by the Pre-school Learning Alliance, serves the local area and is accessible to all children. It operates from two playrooms, and there is an enclosed area available for outdoor play. There were sixteen practitioners in total, all female, and thirty-eight children (aged 2–4 years): thirteen boys and fifteen girls.

Methods

The first cycle of the action research engaged with ESD through a wildlife gardening project. Gardening enables children to connect with nature and to channel their interests in all things living into a genuine appreciation of, and even a scientific curiosity about, their environment (Dewey, 1908; Brook, 2010). As participation and involvement are basic components of ESD, gardening encompasses community learning, which lends credence to its power to bring families together in projects that benefit not only children but everyone who participates (Starbuck and Olthof, 2008; Engdahl, 2015).

The gardening project enabled children in the nursery to experience and understand topics linked to sustainable development with support from practitioners. They were encouraged to explore, create meanings and develop skills, attitudes and understandings driven by their own interests and through activities arising from the bee project to support learning with the Early Years Foundation Stage curriculum (DfE, 2017).

The work of sowing seeds, caring for the wildlife garden and observing insects can then be translated into children's understandings of the importance of bees to the planet (Friends of the Earth, 2017).

Data Collection and Analysis

The data collection process was based on Rinaldi's (2006) 'pedagogy of listening', which was adopted to capture participants' voices through dialogic conversations and questioning to generate active engagement. In addition, data was collected through observations, group interactions/interviews and practitioners' reflections. Analysis is in progress and is being developed to explore practitioners' perceptions of Education for Sustainable Development and gain understanding of the meanings that participants give to this new, complex and challenging area of work. The action research in many ways mirrors the open-ended project-based approach to learning about aspects of ESD. The project is in its early stages, but it can already be seen that collaborative enquiry-based methods, in which there is openness to contributions from all participants, offer great promise as teaching and learning processes for ESD.

Case Study 2—An Early Childhood Learning Space

The second case study reports another participatory project in which ECS university students participated with staff in the development of a learning space within their institution.

The Context

The case study is based in a Higher Education Institution (HEI) in England, where, at a sector level, huge changes are underway with regards to standardised and marketised approaches to learning, teaching and assessment (Shore, 2008). Student participation is generally offered through mechanisms such as module evaluations, student surveys and student representation in various institutional meetings and governance processes. There is, however, a general reluctance from the students towards representational notions of democracy (NSF Annual Report, 2010). Case study 2, therefore, offers an alternative form of democracy, drawn from Dewey's ethical imperative (Dewey, 1903), where students worked with staff and with each other to create a shared vision for pedagogy and pedagogical space.

Aim

The aim of the research from which this case study is drawn was to analyse the application of participatory approaches in creating a pedagogic space (Early Childhood Resource and Research Room—ECRRR) and analyse the benefits of the methodology for students' learning and professional development.

Participants

Twenty university students studying ECS at undergraduate and postgraduate level, three academics, and an administrator (of the ECRRR) were participants for the case study along with the lead researcher, who is also an academic member of staff. The diversity of membership allowed for collaboration between tutors, students and administrator and took into account the experiences and perceptions of different stakeholders (Richards, 2011); it also enabled the researcher to listen to the views of all, instead of a privileged few (Kidd and Kral, 2005).

Methods

Participants' views on the scope and purpose of ECRRR were collected and co-constructed via dialogic working and research group meetings (WGMs and RGMs) where everyone had an equal opportunity to participate. WGMs aimed at drawing upon participants' experiential, practical and theoretical knowledge of early childhood and utilising this knowledge to co-construct an agreed list of resource and research needs for the ECRRR. The RGMs focussed upon critical reflection, especially reflection upon participants' own collective decisions (taken in WGMs) which they further reviewed, critiqued and analysed for the needs and purposes of the ERCRRR. The intention, overall, was to democratise the whole process of research, with the student participants being able to share their views by using communication media of their choice, for example, in drawing, spider diagrams, verbal communication, written or typed text, and then use these ideas collectively to co-construct, deconstruct and reconstruct knowledge about ECS pedagogy. The students also filled out a final questionnaire to evaluate their participation in the project.

Findings

The overall findings from the project revealed that the students appreciated the dialogic and co-constructive nature of the project. Participants' agreements and disagreements whilst debating the resource and research needs of the ECRRR gave rise to co-construction, whereby students were able to negotiate, argue, reflect and agree on what was the cost, time, pedagogical, ecological and collaboration impacts of the listed resources and research needs of the ECRRR (see Kanyal, 2017). A combination of co-construction and critical reflection helped to create a participatory learning environment where the students were able to challenge any uncritical views and assumptions (Bovill et al., 2011), develop capacity to participate rationally and critically in group situations (Pant, 2008), avoid generation of false consensus and unequal participation (Veale, 2005) and, above all, due to the sharing of the control of the research process and analysis, felt empowered (Baum et al., 2006; Kanyal, 2017).

Conclusion

The overall aim of our work, such as that in these case studies, is to open up debate about forms of curriculum, pedagogy and assessment that can be both orderly and dynamic, and that pay attention to the subjective quality of children's, students' and educators' experiences. The inclusion of participatory learning, teaching and research offers prospects for experiential learning that place emphasis upon activity-based education where situations can be created for children and students to draw upon their previous knowledge as well as take inspiration from the environment that frames our overall lived experience. Integral to this are opportunities for reflection and action, consistent inclusion of which may demand a reconsideration of routine pedagogical and curriculum approaches. Changes, we argue, as learnt from these case studies, may be achieved by fulfilling three core conditions in our curriculum and assessment: firstly, by making relational learning associations between students and teacher, built upon more equal grounds; secondly and thirdly, by including elements of critical reflection and active learning in pedagogy and assessment (Freire and Macedo, 1995).

Knowledge construction, if solely left in the hands of market-driven initiatives, frames children's and students' experiences within a particular political and economic context, further accentuating consumerism as the dominant conceptual view of education. This restrictive view of education is arguably distant from its academic merit, pedagogical relevance and transformative and sustainable active global citizenship potential, as perceived by DEEEP. To make transformative education a sustainable initiative, we open up a debate to consider more participatory and collective forms of learning and assessment which, based on our experiences, hold potential for developing egalitarian and collegial ways of working together.

The inclusion of participatory approaches can help to stretch participants' learning from the personal to a relational and collective level. Participatory projects can therefore offer educative experiences that can make a difference to the lives and learning of individuals as well as the social and professional community where they live and work, and ultimately to wider society. The knowledge thus produced may enable the building of capacity amongst our children and graduates to offer more sustainable solutions to the long-term challenges facing society.

In short, we argue for meaningful and hopeful approaches that are judged by the opportunities on offer for the present and future growth of individuals and potential for community contributions and positive social change.

References

Baum, F., MacDougall, C. and Smith, D. (2006). Participatory action research. *Journal of Epidemiology and Community Health*, 60(10), pp. 854–857.

Bovill, C., Cook-Sather, A. and Felten, P. (2011). Students as co-creators of teaching approaches, course design and curricula: Implications for academic developers. *International Journal for Academic Development*, 16(2), pp. 133–145.

Brook, I. (2010). The importance of nature, green spaces and gardens in human well-being. *Ethics, Place and Environment*, 13, pp. 295–312.

Carey, P. (2013). Student engagement and the threat of consumerism: Testing assumptions. Available at: <http://researchonline.ljmu.ac.uk/1804/3/Carey%20student%20engagement%20the%20threat%20of%20consumerism%5B1%5D.pdf>

Davis, J. (2007). Climate change and its impact on young children. *Every Child*, 13(4), pp. 6–7.

Davis, J. (2008). What might education for sustainability look like in early childhood: A case for participatory, whole-of-settings approaches. In: Ingrid Pramling Samuelsson and Yoshie Kaga (eds.), *The Contribution of Early Childhood Education to a Sustainable Society*. Paris: UNESCO.

Department for Education (DfE). (2017). *Statutory Framework for the Early Years Foundation Stage*. Available at: <www.gov.uk/government/uploads/system/uploads/attachment_data/file/596629/EYFS_STATUTORY_FRAMEWORK_2017.pdf>

Dewey, J. (1903). Democracy in education. *The Elementary School Teacher*, 4(4), pp. 193–204.

Dewey, J. (1908). The bearings of pragmatism upon education. In: J. A. Boydston (ed.), *John Dewey: The Middle Works 1899–1924*, 4: 1907–1909, 178–191. Carbondale: Southern Illinois University Press.

Dewey, J. (1916/2007). *Democracy and Education*. Teddington, Middlesex: Echo Library.

Engdahl, I. (2015). Early childhood education for sustainable development: The OMEP world project. *International Journal of Early Childhood*, 47(3), pp. 347–366.

Freire, P. and Macedo, D. P. (1995). A dialogue: Culture, language, race. *Harvard Educational Review*, 65, pp. 377–402.

Fricke, H. J. and Gathercole, C. (2015). *Monitoring Education for Global Citizenship: A Contribution to Debate*. Brussels: DEEEP.

Friends of the Earth. (2017). *The Bee Cause*. Available at: <https://friendsoftheearth.uk/bees>. Accessed 10 October 2017.

Kanyal, M. (2014). Early childhood studies students' participation in the development of a learning space in a higher education institution. *Management in Education*, 28(4), pp. 149–155.

Kanyal, M. (2017). *Developing a shared pedagogical space for and with early childhood studies degree students: A participatory research project*. Ed.D. thesis. Anglia Ruskin University.

Kemmis, S. and McTaggart, R. (2007). Participatory action research: Communicative action and the public sphere. In: N. Denzin and Y. Lincoln (eds.), *Handbook of Qualitative Research*, 3rd edition, 271–329. Thousand Oaks, CA: Sage.

Kidd, S. A. and Kral, M. J. (2005). Practicing participatory action research. *Journal of Counselling Psychology*, 52(2), pp. 187–195.

Liu, Y. and Liu, F. (2008). Building a harmonious society and ECE for sustainable development. In: Ingrid Pramling Samuelsson and Yoshie Kaga (eds.), *The Contribution of ECE to a Sustainable Society*, 43–52. Paris: UNESCO.

Mackey, G. (2012). To know, to decide, to act: The young child's right to participate in action for the environment. *Environmental Education Research*, 18(4), pp. 473–484.

National Student Forum (NSF)—Annual Report. (2010). Available at: <www.gov.uk/government/uploads/system/uploads/attachment_data/file/31987/10-p83-national-student-forum-annual-report-2010.pdf>

Nussbaum, M. C. (2010). *Not for Profit: Why Democracy Needs the Humanities*. Oxford: Princeton University Press.

Pant, M. (2008). Participatory Research. Available at: <www.unesco.org/pv_obj_cache/pv_obj_id_8A4DA2D14C7705777AD77C0F25AF56E533F60100/filename/unit_08.pdf>. Accessed 8 October 2017.

Pramling Samuelsson, I. and Kaga, Y. (2008). *The Contribution of Early Childhood Education to a Sustainable Society*. Paris: UNESCO.

Richards, D. (2011). Leadership for learning in higher education: The student perspective. *Educational Management Administration and Leadership*, 40, pp. 84–108.

Rinaldi, C. (2006). *In Dialogue with Reggio Emilia: Listening, Researching and Learning*. London: Routledge Falmer.

Schumacher, E. F. (1973). *Small is Beautiful*. London: Blond and Briggs.

Seale, J., Gibson, S., Haynes, J. and Potter, A. (2015). Power and resistance: Reflections on the rhetoric and reality of using participatory methods to promote student voice and engagement in higher education. *Journal of Further and Higher Education*, 39(4), pp. 534–552.

Shore, C. (2008). Audit culture and illiberal governance universities and the politics of accountability. *Anthropological Theory*, 8(3), pp. 278–298.

Siraj-Blatchford, J., Smith, K. C. and Pramling Samuelsson, I. (2010). *Education for Sustainable Development in the Early Years*. Sweden: OMEP.

Starbuck, S. and Olthof, M. R. (2008). Involving families and community through gardening. *Young Children*, 63(5), pp. 74–79.

Sterling, S. (2001). *Sustainable Education: Re-visioning Learning and Change*. Schumacher Briefing No. 6. Totnes: Green Books for the Schumacher Society.

Sterling, S. (2011). Transformative learning and sustainability: Sketching the conceptual ground. *Learning and Teaching in Higher Education*, 5, pp. 17–33.

Sterling, S. (2012). *The Future Fit Framework: An Introductory Guide to Teaching and Learning for Sustainability in Higher Education*. York: The Higher Education Academy. Available at: <www.heacademy.ac.uk/knowledge-hub/future-fit-framework>

Taylor, P. and Fransman, J. (2004). *Learning and Teaching Participation: Exploring the Role of Higher Learning Institutions as Agents of Development and Social Change*. Brighton: Institute of Development Studies.

Veale, A. (2005). Creative Methodologies in Participatory Research with Children. In: S. Greene and D. Hogan (eds.), *Researching Children's Experience: Approaches and Methods*, 253–273. London, Sage.

11 Seeking to Unsettle Student Teachers' Notions of Curriculum

Making Sense of Imaginative Encounters in the Natural World

Helen Clarke and Sharon Witt

Introduction

This chapter seeks to unsettle undergraduates' notions of curriculum and experience and use imaginative and storied encounters with place to make sense of abstraction and inter-connectedness. Research completed alongside students in Initial Teacher Education (ITE) (primary science and geography specialists) and ten- to eleven-year-old children at a Hampshire Primary School in England illustrates that imagination is central to the process of becoming a teacher.

Taking a Courageous View with Education for Sustainability at the Heart

As teacher educators, faced with complex demands, it is all too easy to adopt habitual practices which meet the requirements of our many stakeholders. However, at the University of Winchester our underpinning vision of Rights Respecting Education (RRE) allows us to take a courageous view, where Education for Sustainability is at the heart of our Initial Teacher Education (ITE) programme. We aim to (re)focus our practice and (re)connect student teachers with meaningful learning in diverse contexts, including natural environments. We use an immersion approach to journey from different perspectives together, in reciprocal relationships, as we develop identities. These themes—Identity, Perspectives and Relationships—underpin our undergraduate and masters level teacher education programmes as our young professionals develop as respectful and confident curriculum makers. We know that rich experiences for our student teachers will in turn generate significant learning for the children they teach as student teachers and as future teachers in the primary phase.

Unfolding Curriculum Journeys

In the process of curriculum innovation we work in local landscapes as stimuli to unfolding ideas, and we find that "the act of moving may be as important as that of arriving" (Tilley, 1994, p. 31). As Education for Sustainable Development (ESD) moves 'from the edge to the centre' of our practice as teacher educators, we propose the metaphor of a 'vortex' as a means to represent this shift in thinking. A vortex has a spinning motion with a turbulent, vertical flow. Vortices can move, stretch, twist and interact in complex ways, and carry momentum and energy. We propose that curriculum making can be seen as a narrative of a journey, a "relational knowing" which "involves multisensory responses in a particular moment" and is produced in collaborations (Somerville, 2008, p. 212). We position ourselves with a firm belief in the power of eco-imagination to encourage new perspectives in learning, and to enrich relationships with the natural world. This position gives rise to "resonant moments" that guide our discussions, storied encounters, wonder and meaning making (Somerville, 2008, p. 216). In an emancipatory stance, which gives voice to the marginalised, we seek to listen to the 'other' and celebrate a diversity of perspectives as a *way of educating* (Biesta, 2010, p. 46). Our environmental encounters seek to disrupt dominant hegemonies which often see the educator in a position of authority possessing 'powerful knowledge' to transmit to learners, viewed as passive observers of the world. This emphasis on the face-to-face relationship between teachers, student teachers and the world is polyphonic (McDowell, 1994) as we take "a stance of *wondering* and *generating*" (Somerville, 2008, p. 217), firstly with our students in the context of local fieldwork, and then as the student teachers develop their practice alongside children.

Eco-Imaginative Fieldwork with Students in Initial Teacher Education

Our most recent fieldwork in the village of Selborne, Hampshire, prompted reflection on the centrality of imaginative encounters with nature in creative curriculum design. We aimed to maintain primary geography and science curriculum integrity, yet to unsettle students' notions of traditional subject boundaries through cross-curricular border crossing, where ideas of place, people and discipline emerged in an unpredictable mix of chaotic moments. Inspired by a "slow or eco-pedagogical" approach, we encouraged students to pause or "dwell in spaces for more than a fleeting moment", therefore enabling them to develop place attachments and make meaning within the landscapes they inhabit (Payne and Wattchow, 2009, p. 16). At Selborne we immersed the students in a range of activities. We followed in the footsteps of early naturalist Gilbert White (1720–1793) as we explored the chalk Hanger, beech woodland, meadows and river. We undertook activities, including sharing stories, making elf houses, positioning small-world characters and recording personal and professional reflections (see Figure 11.1). We worked on the premise that an "ecological imagination emerges out

Figure 11.1 Seeing the extraordinary

of students' participation with the world through activities and learning opportunities in which their bodies, emotions and imaginations are actively engaged" (Judson, 2010, p. 5) and would take us "to the new, the unusual and the extraordinary" (p. 4).

Imagination is central to the process of becoming a teacher as it enables student teachers "to see (and hear, and feel) beyond the visible world, the world as it is 'given' by experience" (Fettes, 2005, p. 3). Imagination also develops the "capacity to think of the possible rather than the actual" (Egan, 1992, p. 4). So, we engaged student teachers in activities where they might "look beyond things as they are" and "anticipate what might be seen through a new perspective or through another's eyes" (Greene, 1988, p. 49). As tutors of teacher education we modelled an attitude of contagious attentiveness (Matthews, 1992). When "we conceive of possibilities through imagination, we become emotionally engaged and connect value or significance to what we envision" (Judson, 2010, p. 4).

Students recorded their reflections on 'story stones' (Robertson, 2011). Responses included single words:

> *intrigue, peace, adventure, tranquillity, magical, isolation, serene, colourful, sleepy, stately, mystery, crisp, wonder, inspiring, informative, captivating, empathy, reflection, respect, solitude, spiritual moments, joy . . .*

. . . and phrases, fully formed, emergent or poetic:

It's more than a picture in front of your eyes
Looking closer at 'more than what's there'—there's more!
The golden Autumn colours singing in the trees
Watching the clouds floating by, can you take my spirit too?
I am just a shadow of the sun, waiting to fade as night falls
Bringing magic to an ordinary place . . .

The student teachers considered their identities as curriculum weavers, wanderers and makers who interlace values into their practice and who position themselves at the beating heart of the curriculum. They reflected on relationships with nature through stories of small-world 'others' and were alert to a "remarkable opening as an important experiential dimension of becoming aware of the ecological otherness of nature's places" (Payne, 2010, p. 295). Students suggested that the presence of miniature figures immediately created a relationship with landscape (see Figure 11.2).

Through a playful imaginative approach, we created experiences in the natural world that enabled students to uncover their sense of wonder and awe (Piersol, 2014, p. 19) and to make sense of abstraction and interconnectedness. The student teachers found many instances where an imaginative perspective illuminated the complexity of concepts too small

Figure 11.2 A miniature figure as a remarkable opening for ecological awareness

(for example, micro-worlds of photosynthesis and decomposition) or too vast (such as geological time) to experience for themselves. In this way they bridged the gap between experience and abstract contexts. Louv (2005, p. 117) suggests it "takes time—loose, unstructured dreamtime—to experience nature in a meaningful way", and so by inviting students into the presence of nature, we encouraged them to reflect on their relationship with the natural world (see Figure 11.3).

The student teachers' 'silent conversations' enabled them to engage in a continuous dialogue with Selborne as the place unfolded deep within them (Merleau-Ponty in Abram, 1997, p. 52). Students identified their relationship as: *interactive, observational, purposeful and respectful.* They recognised that relationships are dynamic and may vary with the seasons: *I love the changes nature goes through. I think I take the beauty of nature for granted.* Students expressed that relationships arise from listening. They mused on: *hearing what nature says, what nature knows, what nature does, what nature shows us.* They recognised that "landscape is loud with dialogues, with storylines that connect a place and its dwellers" (Spirn, 1998, p. 17).

Kaitlyn attributed opportunities for dialogue with nature as offering potential for making personal meaning:

> Small personal moments allow us to consolidate, organise and record our own thoughts . . . it is these 'in the moment' reflections that

Figure 11.3 Time and space for reflection

> I think could be the medium for children's 'eureka' experiences, when their thoughts and ideas begin to make sense.

Travelling with ideas around Selborne encouraged students as "meaning-makers to experientially and reflectively access and address their corporeality, intercorporeality, sensations, and perceptions of time, space and . . . place" (Payne and Wattchow, 2009, p. 30). In moving our students' ESD thinking from the edge to the centre of their awareness, we started from where they were, we roused their 'enthusiastic participation', and guided them "through increasingly sensitive activities and deep experiences to new, joy-filled awareness and understanding" (Cornell, 1989, p. 15).

ITE Students Apply Their Experience to Their Practice

The student teachers then applied this approach to their practice. A range of activities was shared with ten- to eleven-year-old children at a partner school. Their aim was to invite children to build "knowledge by acquaintance" with their school grounds (Bonnett, 2007, p. 714).

One group chose to use a story starter to introduce the idea of shrinking in size to view the natural world from a different perspective. John reflected on his role:

> We played the role of the facilitator rather than the imparter of knowledge which enabled a very positive relationship with the children, empowering them in their freedom of thought and direction of ideas.

Another group devised a creative activity which prompted the children to experience the world differently:

> Through the inclusion of mirrors, an alternative perspective of a location with which they were very familiar led to the development of higher-order thinking skills, making inferences of whose perspective they may be viewing through the mirror. Children's answers were varied, ranging from a bird to God, and this activity stimulated their excitement. One child commented "I'm on thin air. Wow, I'm flying".

The student teachers reflected on the implications of their experience:

> The children viewed learning through a different 'lens' or 'travelled with a different view'. The children were motivated in their learning. By immersing myself in the imaginative nature of learning and through transferring this to my own teaching, I now understand the benefits of this pedagogy and will continue to implement in my future practice.

Lara started with a picture book as a stimulus to a discussion of animal features and then she had the children design their own creature (see Figure 11.4) to live in a habitat in the school grounds:

> I hope that this experience has 'loosened the boundaries' on how the children view science. Personally, I re-gained an insight as to the purpose of this academic degree—to inspire children to be all that they can be.

Kaitlyn, inspired by beautiful grounds, encouraged children to take a look at trees in new ways:

> They used magnifying glasses to look closely at trees, they described what they saw. Most children were convinced they could see a face in the tree, and that the tree represented a person! They used mirrors to look up into the tree canopy. What does this look like? What could the branches represent? The children offered ideas such as 'an exploding blender', 'Einstein's hair', 'interlocking finger tips'.

Kaitlyn shed further light on her decisions:

> I feel that the essential attributes included adaptability, spontaneity and creativity. We encouraged the notion that you need to look at

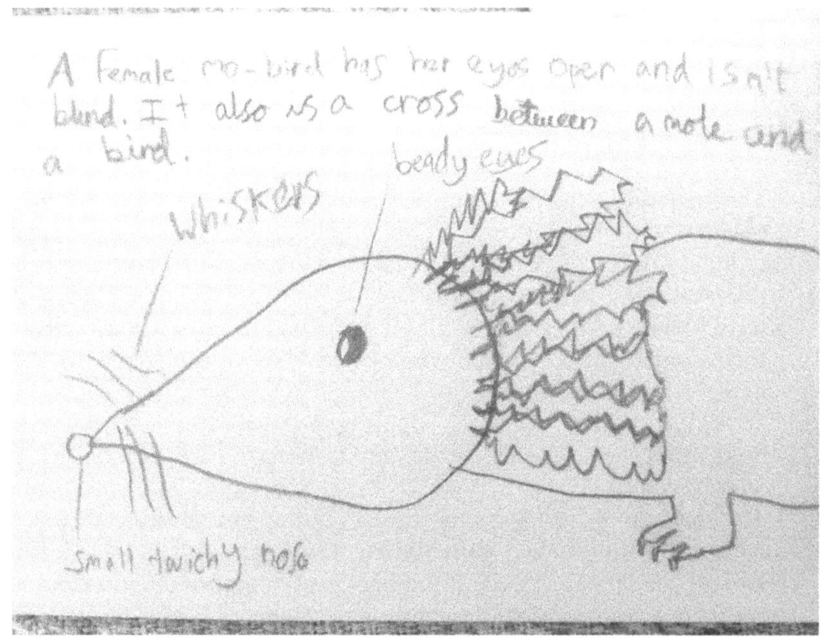

Figure 11.4 The Mo-Bird—loosening subject boundaries

something from many different angles and perspectives to unlock its true beauty and potential.

Annie's group took miniature figures on a small-world trail and used observation skills to overcome obstacles (Figure 11.5):

> We did not hold back . . . often lying down on the grass with the children to make careful observations. I have never known every single child to come up and want to talk us through all of their findings and that is a reflection on the enjoyment that they experienced.

Evie developed an activity around the theme of children as architects and place makers:

> The excitement level of the children that afternoon was tangible. Their work was imaginative and elicited their previous knowledge of materials within a creative context.

Robin's group expressed an expanded notion of den building:

> Den-building taught me there's more to nature than meets the eye.

Evaluation discussion included aspects of open, flexible, creative pedagogy, of complexity and transformation of practice. When asked in a

Figure 11.5 Making careful observations with miniature figures

focus group interview 'How do feel the experience in school has informed your practice?', responses included:

> I have more courage to take more risks, don't become set in your ways, go outside more, just get children to stop and look, invest in deep learning, use immersive tactics, and integrate imaginative techniques.

There was a realisation that:

> There's a proportional relationship between time, experience and depth of learning. Ecological imagination means looking at the environment differently.

When asked 'What possibilities does this approach offer to children?' responses included:

> It's a whole approach. It promotes progress but it is aimed at the child individually.
>
> It's a child centred approach—knowing your child, putting what they need to learn in their context.

Eco-Playfulness . . . Easing to the Centre of the Vortex

In a fast-paced curriculum, teachers are habituated with seemingly urgent concerns, and can lose sight of an underlying vision of education. "Of course we want to strive for excellence but if it comes at the expense of integrity, humour and creative insight, we are not really at our best—in truth we are diminished" (Crowell and Reid-Marr, 2013, p. 5 7). So what IS urgent? Love for nature is a powerful response that leads to a sense of care for the earth and "it seems urgent to expand the breadth, depth and orientation of how we make sense of the world; we limit our abilities to deal with ecological problems now and in the future if we do not consider how we may educate the ecological imagination" (Judson, 2010, p. 5).

John identifies play as an essential dimension of developing relationships with the natural world:

> I really like the idea of Ecological Imagination. Personally, I feel that this could link to the idea of Ecological Play, as through all of our reflections we noted a distinct importance between the relationship of nature and play. As tutors you allowed us the opportunity to be independent, imaginative and reflective learners during our time in nature which, in turn, allowed us even as adults to play and interact with nature in a variety of contexts and ways. Subsequently, for me, a key development was a pedagogical approach to teaching and learning with nature as a colleague.

The importance of play as a major activity in a child's relationship with nature is well recognised (Kalvaitis and Monhardt, 2012). A 'playful' interaction is a powerful approach to learning and underpins our belief in 'eco-playfulness'. Playfulness can be viewed as simplistic or unsophisticated, whereas in reality, as identified by Rose, it involves messiness and complexity.

> Real life is a completely interrelated journey with boundaries constantly being crossed and mixed.

Further, student colleagues acknowledged that playful innovation is not necessarily straightforward:

> I'm afraid I won't be able to do this in school.
> It's very easy to fall into the way a school does something.
> You don't want to rock the boat too much.

From the Edge to the Centre of the Curriculum Vortex

How might this complexity be represented? For our student teachers the experience was at the limits of their comfort zone. They were cast into a metaphorical vortex, where they experienced the turbulent flow of deep learning, in a spiral curriculum, and revisited ideas and practice from new perspectives. If we are to move ESD from the edge to the centre of the curriculum vortex, which enswirls the perspectives of learners, teachers, curriculum principles and disciplines, it is necessary to imagine new possibilities for curriculum making in a journey to the centre of a meaningful curriculum. We unsettled our students' notions and experience, and we used imagination to make sense of abstraction and inter-connectedness in our role as "agents of change" in teacher education (Reavey in Bilham, 2013, p. 196). Meaningful learning opportunities strengthen emotional bonds with the natural world (Bonnett, 2007) and adopting a 'futures perspective' (Hicks, 2012) develops mindfulness and attentiveness as essential ESD competences.

Conclusion

Our experiences suggest that storied encounters with nature inspire both student teachers and children to (re)imagine new relationships with places through elements of play, imaginative exploration and discovery. Sensory and immersive experiences invite eco-imaginations to take flight and promote deep and meaningful learning opportunities which strengthen emotional bonds with the natural world (Bonnett, 2007).

John mused:

> After thinking more about 'nature as a colleague', I like the idea of being equal. I personally don't like the idea of nature being portrayed

> as a resource. I think this takes away from its importance. When we take the time to go out into nature, when we treat it with respect, dignity and care, from my experience of Selborne and other trips it rewards us fantastically.

A playful eco-imaginative approach has a central role in ESD, as without imagination it may not be possible to open minds to future possibilities. These "*resonant moments*" have real impact (Somerville, 2008, p. 215). In chapter 6, our chapter in Part 1 of this volume, we use the metaphor of the vortex in the context of "Into the Vortex: Exploring Curriculum Making Possibilities that Challenge Children's Responses to Extreme Climate Events". Storied encounters with places can lead to relationships of respect, care and stewardship of the natural world, and are central to the experience of ITE students and their practice with children as a means to create a legacy of hopeful futures.

References

Abram, D. (1997). *The Spell of the Sensuous: Perception and Language in a More-Than-Human World*. New York: Vintage Books.

Biesta, G. J. J. (2010). A new logic of emancipation: The methodology of Jacques Rancière. *Educational Theory*, 60(1), pp. 39–59.

Bilham, T. (2013). *For the Love of Learning. Innovations from Outstanding University Teachers*. Basingstoke: Palgrave Macmillan.

Bonnett, M. (2007). Environmental education and the issue of nature. *Journal of Curriculum Studies*, 39(6), pp. 707–721.

Cornell, J. (1989). *Sharing Nature with Children II*. Nevada City: Dawn Publications.

Crowell, S. and Reid-Marr, D. (2013). *Emergent Teaching. A Path of Creativity, Significance and Transformation*. Plymouth: Rowman and Littlefield.

Egan, K. (1992). *Imagination in Teaching and Learning: The Middle School Years*. Chicago: University of Chicago Press.

Fettes, M. (2005). Imaginative transformation in teacher education. *Teaching Education*, 16(1), pp. 3–11.

Greene, M. (1988). What happened to imagination? In: K. Egan and D. Nadaner (eds.), *Imagination and Education*, 45–56. New York: Teachers College Press.

Hicks, D. (2012). The future only arrives when things look dangerous: Reflections on futures education in the UK. *Futures*, 44(1), pp. 4–13.

Judson, G. (2010). *A New Approach to Ecological Education. Engaging Students' Imaginations in Their World*. New York: Peter Lang.

Kalvaitis, D. and Monhardt, R. M. (2012). The architecture of children's relationships with nature: A phenomenographic investigation seen through drawings and written narratives of elementary students. *Environmental Education Research*, 18(2), pp. 209–227.

Louv, R. (2005). *Last Child in the Woods*. Chapel Hill, NC: Algonquin Books.

Matthews, J. R. (1992). Adult amateur experiences in entomology. In: J. Adams (ed.), *Inspect Potpourri: Adventures in Entomology*, 321–328. Gainesville, FL: Sandhill Crane Press.

McDowell, L. (1994). Polyphony and pedagogic authority. *Area*, 26(3), pp. 241–248.

Payne, P. G. (2010). Remarkable-tracking, experiential education of the ecological imagination. *Environmental Education Research*, 16(3–4), pp. 295–310.

Payne, P. G. and Wattchow, B. (2009). Phenomenological deconstruction, slow pedagogy, and the corporeal turn in wild environmental/outdoor education. *Canadian Journal of Environmental Education*, 14, pp. 15–32.

Piersol, L. (2014). Our hearts leap up. Awakening wonder in the classroom. In: K. Egan, A. Cant and G. Judson (eds.), *Wonder-full Education. The Centrality of Wonder in Teaching and Learning Across the Curriculum*, 1–21. London: Routledge.

Robertson, J. (2011). *Story Stones and Thinking Skills*. Available at: <http://creativestarlearning.co.uk/literacy-outdoors/story-stones-and-thinking-skills/>

Somerville, M. J. (2008). 'Waiting in the chaotic place of unknowing': Articulating postmodern emergence. *International Journal of Qualitative Studies in Education*, 21(3), pp. 209–220.

Spirn, A. W. (1998). *The Language of Landscape*. London: Yale University Press.

Tilley, C. (1994). *A Phenomenology of Landscape: Places, Paths and Monuments*. Oxford: Berg.

12 Reconceptualising Citizenship Education Towards the Global, the Political and the Critical

Challenges and Perspectives in a Province in Northern Italy

Sara Franch

Introduction

The notion of fostering citizenship, particularly in young people, is common both in education theory literature and in popular discourse. Schools are seen as key social institutions for the cultivation of citizens. On the one hand, citizenship is a governing principle of public education, and on the other, citizenship as a topic is given particular and explicit attention in schools through specific courses in citizenship education (Sears and Hughes, 1996). But, as Pashby (2011) underlines, "the project of cultivating citizens is recognised for certain inherent paradoxes at the same time that it is receiving a particular urgency within the global imperative" (2011, p. 430). So, while scholars are debating different pedagogical perspectives on citizenship education, many are also stressing the need to reconceptualise it in the context of a globalised world.

In this chapter I first outline the need for a citizenship education that is diverse, global, critical and political and argue that Global Citizenship Education (GCE), despite being complex and ambiguous, can be a new pedagogical framework that merges these four different perspectives. I then look at how GCE is conceptualised and practised in a province in Northern Italy. This analysis draws from a qualitative study, based on twenty-one intensive interviews with lower secondary school teachers, eight interviews with decision-makers and key informants, one focus group with nine teachers and a documentary review of provincial policies and curricular guidelines. In this province, GCE has a distinctive moral dimension. On the one hand, GCE is not an educational imperative but rather a 'moral optional' for willing and able teachers. And, on the other hand, it is essentially constructed as a new 'moral pedagogy', rather than a critical and political approach to citizenship education. I conclude the chapter stressing the role that teacher education can play to facilitate a more structural grounding of GCE in the curriculum. Teacher education can also be an important space to stimulate reflection on political and critical GCE approaches.

Diverse, Global, Critical and Political Citizenship Education

Historically, citizenship education was essentially about an individual's relation to the nation state, and its objectives were to "establish a shared identity and history among citizens-in-making and to foster patriotism and loyalty to the nation" (Pashby, 2008, p. 19). In the context of globalisation and multiculturalism, this interpretation of citizenship education began to be challenged (Tarozzi and Torres, 2016). Citizenship education began to be reconceptualised to make it relevant to the reality of multicultural societies that, in a globalised world, as Held and McGrew stress, are pushed and pulled in different directions, because globalisation "simultaneously engenders cooperation as well as conflict, integration as well as fragmentation, exclusion and inclusion, convergence and divergence, order and disorder" (Held and McGrew, 2003, p. 7).

Globalisation and multiculturalism challenge the idea of a citizenship education that is premised on a knowable and stable notion of 'national identity', as this "does not provide a context complex enough for students to integrate the various and overlapping geo-political perspectives that define their experiences and identities" (Pashby, 2008, p. 19). We are experiencing "a deterritorializing of citizenship practices and identities, and of discourses about loyalty and allegiance" (Sassen, 2002, p. 6). Therefore, today's political, economic and social contexts demand a notion of citizenship education that is both flexible and empowering, legitimises complex, overlapping and socially contextualised individual and group identities, and acknowledges different views and lifestyles (Pashby, 2008). Citizenship education should be about "learning to imagine the nation as a diverse and inclusive community" (Osler and Starkey, 2003, p. 245).

Globalisation, the growing sense of interdependency and interconnection and the emphasis on global justice to address inequities and inequalities demand that our understanding of citizenship shifts and expands towards the global (Pike, 2008; Torres, 2017). This call for an expansion of citizenship does not imply "dismantling the present construction of citizenship" (Pike, 2008, p. 48), but rather adding value to national citizenship (Torres, 2017). It means taking a pedagogical approach and a new perspective on citizenship education, so that while the state will continue to grant the constitutional rights and duties of citizenship, education should cultivate in students an "ethos of global citizenship" (Pike, 2008, p. 48). Peterson talks about the need for citizenship to be shaped by, and in turn shape, "a global imagination" (Peterson, 2016, p. 259). He stresses the importance of focussing citizenship education on a "globally oriented citizenship" that "is intimately intertwined with other forms of citizenship, whether local, regional or national, and that such forms of citizenship are mutually reinforcing" (p. 261).

Scholars drawing from postcolonial and critical theory challenge humanistic interpretations of a globally oriented citizenship education. Andreotti (2015) talks about the role of education in the "violent dissemination of a dominant modern/colonial global imaginary based on a single story of progress, development and human evolution that ascribes different value to cultures/countries" (Andreotti, 2015, p. 222). Within this global imaginary, the world is divided between cultures/countries (the West) that are perceived to be 'ahead', and cultures/countries (the rest of the world) perceived to be 'behind'. Andreotti's conceptualisation of "global citizenship education otherwise" emphasises "'unlearning' and 'learning to learn from below'" (Andreotti, 2006, p. 45) so that we can begin "to imagine otherwise" (Andreotti, 2015, p. 221).

Citizenship education, conceptualised as subjectification as proposed by Biesta (2014), adds an important political dimension to a reconceptualised citizenship education. Biesta does not see citizenship as the identification and taking up of a defined and existing social and political identity, but rather as dis-identification and subjectification, a process of becoming a democratic subject. In terms of civic learning, understanding citizenship as a positive identity will lead to "a socialization conception" of citizenship education, with an emphasis on acquiring the knowledge, skills and dispositions to become part of the existing socio-political order (p. 6). Seeing citizenship as a process of dis-identification demands "a subjectification conception" of citizenship education, which focuses on learning to engage in "the experiment of democracy" (p. 6).

In the context of today's globalised and unequal world, there is a need for a diverse, global, critical and political citizenship education. In the past two decades, the term Global Citizenship Education (GCE) emerged and rapidly became a highly debated pedagogical concept in the scholarly literature. Its inclusion in the Sustainable Development Goals (SDGs), adopted by world leaders in September 2015 at an historic UN Summit, means that it is one of the educational priorities of the twenty-first century. But can GCE be a new pedagogical framework that merges the diverse, the global, the critical and the political?

GCE is complex and ambiguous as "different agendas and theoretical frameworks . . . construct different meanings to the words *global, citizenship* and *education* that imply different curricula and intervention packages for education" (Andreotti and De Souza, 2012, p. 1). Drawing from Biesta's (2009) work on the purposes of education (qualification, socialisation, subjectification), Sant et al. (2018) built a typology that identifies three discourses within GCE. First, in *GCE as qualification*, the main focus is on facilitating the acquisition in students of global and intercultural competences that will help them compete for jobs in the global economy. Equally important in this discourse is building a pool of human resources with the competences that a country needs to position itself in the global market. Second, in *GCE as socialization*, the focus is on promoting certain values and identities to become 'better' citizens. The main emphasis is on fostering citizens that are committed to a world culture based on human rights, pacifist values and cohesiveness, and sustainable development. Third, in *GCE as subjectification*, three traditions can be identified: the liberal tradition encourages knowledge and competences that help students become critical and autonomous, the progressive tradition is about providing spaces for students to develop their own areas of interests, values and ideas about global citizenship, and the critical tradition sees education as counter-practice, i.e. education on non-dominant knowledges and values.

Despite this complexity, I believe that GCE is a useful concept to reimagine a diverse, global, critical and political citizenship education. It can support learners to be globally conscious citizens, i.e. citizens with a critical understanding of globalisation, aware of global inter-connectedness and the ways they and their nations are implicated in local and global problems, conscious of the role of humans for the future health of the planet, able to have a dialogical, complex and dynamic understanding of their identities, and capable of understanding and interacting responsibly with others while being self-critical of their own perspectives and positions (Pashby, 2011; Pike, 2008). From a critical postcolonial perspective, GCE can bring to the fore non-dominant knowledges and values, facilitate critical analysis of taken-for-granted concepts and universal values such as human rights, peace and sustainable development, and help learners "identify and disrupt global processes that perpetuate colonial legacies of violence" (Sant et al., 2018, p. 18). A political perspective demands that GCE is not reduced to a global socialisation that equips students with the knowledge, skills and dispositions to adapt and live successfully within the existing global socio-economic order. But rather it should provide spaces for students to be citizens and engage in democratic politics to realise social justice at the level and in a way appropriate to their age. In this perspective, students will not be directed towards predetermined types of action, such as fundraising or particular campaigns, but rather encouraged to experiment with informed, responsible and ethical action, arising from a critical engagement with global issues, difference, multiple perspectives, and addressing complexity and power relations (Andreotti, 2006).

Global Citizenship Education as a 'Moral Optional' Choice for 'Willing and Able Teachers'

In many countries, the language and practice of GCE is undoubtedly entering formal education. Considering the ambiguities and multiple meanings of global citizenship (Oxley and Morris, 2013), and the fact that calls for the integration of GCE convey an equally diverse range of agendas (Marshall, 2011), it cannot be expected that the integration of GCE in school curricula immediately reflects a critical and political perspective. Scholars use different pedagogical frameworks to study how GCE is understood and practised in schools (Blackmore, 2016; Bryan and Bracken, 2011; Gaudelli, 2016; Rapoport, 2015a, 2015b). These studies highlight that many challenges remain in terms of the structural integration of GCE in school practice or the adoption of political and critical GCE approaches. Drawing from a study of teachers in Indiana, Rapoport (2015b) in particular, identifies four key obstacles that inhibit the expansion of GCE in schools: (1) conceptual vagueness and ambiguity of the concept of global citizenship; (2) propensity to teach national or regional citizenship; (3) curricular insecurity of GCE and lack of disciplinary heritage; (4) lack of administrative and curricular pressure as an incentive to integrate GCE in schools.

A study I conducted in a province in Northern Italy to explore how GCE is conceptualised by teachers in a context of policy changes aimed at introducing GCE in the curriculum of local schools confirms some of the obstacles identified by Rapoport (2015b). Despite a modification of the provincial education law to include a reference to the importance of fostering in students the global dimension of their citizenship, and the presence of an EU-funded project aimed at integrating GCE in the curriculum, I found that in this province GCE occupies a marginal status within the provincial education policies and the formal curriculum. On the one hand, the educational priorities are the promotion of a trilingual school, where students are exposed to three languages, Italian, English and German, and a school system that facilitates knowledge of and links to the job market. On the other hand, the provincial curricular guidelines do not include a GCE curriculum or an explicit reference to the concept of global citizenship. What is mandatory is citizenship education, which, in the guidelines and the provincial priorities, foregrounds a civil rather than a civic understanding of citizenship at the school, the local and the national level. In sum, despite the fact that the provincial law refers to the global dimension of citizenship as one of the objectives of schooling, the provincial policies do not provide for schools and teachers an unequivocal definition of GCE or the global dimension of citizenship education, nor guidelines on its integration in the curriculum and the teaching practice. But does this mean that GCE is not practised in local schools?

My study highlights that teachers understand the importance of reconceptualising citizenship education in the global domain and are striving to shape their practice accordingly. During the interviews it became clear that many of the teachers were not familiar with the concept of global citizenship or GCE, and these terms were hardly used in their schools and in their classrooms. However, when prompted to discuss what aspects of their teaching practice could be captured by the concept of GCE, all the teachers were forthcoming with different experiences. As one of the teachers interviewed emphasised, "many things are done, but they are not always recognised . . . with this term". As noted also by Rapoport, "the absence of the term in teachers' vocabulary did not prevent them from teaching global citizenship-related themes" (2015a, p. 126).

Similarly to the research findings of Bryan and Bracken (2011) in post-primary schools in Ireland, my study shows that the responsibility for ensuring that students are provided with opportunities to explore the global dimension of their citizenship falls largely upon the shoulders of "willing and able teachers" (Bryan and Bracken, 2011, p. 14). These teachers are highly motivated and see GCE as a moral duty of all teachers of the twenty-first century. When prompted to reflect on GCE, many of the teachers stressed that a global citizenship outlook should be transversal and permeate all subjects, as we live in a globalised world that affects all aspects of our life. From this perspective, all subjects are needed to educate students to understand today's global world and live ethically. But in the schools studied, this is an aspiration, not the reality, as GCE is not yet a perspective that informs all subjects. It is not embedded in teachers' practice in a systematic manner, but rather remains a sporadic occurrence. In the schools studied, GCE therefore is not an educational imperative, but can be conceptualised as a 'moral optional' choice for 'willing and able teachers'. Three broad strategies are used by teachers in relation to GCE: (1) avoidance; (2) pioneering; (3) building communities of peers.

Avoidance

Avoidance is used by those teachers that follow a traditional curriculum and do not engage with global citizenship perspectives and issues. They refer to the curricular guidelines that, as previously stated, do not have a 'global citizenship breath'. Although the curricular guidelines are competency based, these teachers tend to follow a rigid syllabus of disciplinary topics, not prescribed by the guidelines, but rather grounded in tradition, i.e. what has always been taught in that subject. They choose and follow textbooks that lack or have a weak global citizenship perspective or they even skip the parts of the textbooks that deal with global citizenship perspectives and issues. Avoidance is reflected also in a traditional teaching style that is not based on active and participatory learning methods.

Pioneering

Pioneering characterises motivated and willing teachers who interpret and 'manoeuvre' the curriculum to provide students with opportunities to explore the global dimension of their citizenship. They imaginatively use the freedom and autonomy of teaching that the Italian Constitution grants them and draw on the fact that the curricular guidelines are broad and competency based. So, although the guidelines lack a 'global citizenship breath', they also do not prevent teachers from including a global citizenship perspective in their enacted curriculum out of personal commitment. Strategies used to bring a global perspective are: (1) designing specific GCE projects; (2) making choices about the curriculum; (3) responding to prompts arising in class.

A key modality mentioned by the teachers interviewed to integrate GCE in their practice is *designing or joining specific projects* on a GCE issue, or on topics with a more implicit global dimension. These projects are based on collaboration between teachers, often see the participation of external people (experts in GCE, or people that bring a particular testimony), and use student-centred active learning methods. They are generally considered as very valuable experiences because they give teachers a sense of working together towards a common objective, and provide students with the opportunity to engage with a topic from a multidisciplinary perspective. However, they are heavily dependent on the personal initiative and leadership of one teacher, engage a limited number of 'like-minded' teachers, involve only a few students (those of the teachers involved in the project), and are temporary, i.e. they last generally one academic year.

Another key modality to facilitate a global citizenship perspective is *making choices about the curriculum* which includes three basic strategies. The first strategy is to open up a particular curricular topic, that apparently may have little to do with GCE, such as the Fall of the Roman Empire or the Middle Ages, to the global dimension by finding connections to the present and to particular global citizenship issues. This allows teachers to introduce GCE indirectly, i.e. cover the content of the 'traditional curriculum', and therefore feel confident that what is expected is done, while at the same time providing a global citizenship perspective. The second strategy adopted is to freely choose to focus with a certain depth on a number of topics that teachers personally believe are conducive to stimulating a global citizenship perspective. This means being prepared to skip or address in a more basic way other curricular topics. A geography teacher, for example, chooses to deal marginally with physical geography, and to rather take a human geography perspective on issues such as globalisation, migration, global poverty or rights and denied rights. A science teacher works in depth on environmental education and sustainable development issues, while covering chemistry and physics in a more basic manner. The last and more radical strategy, but also less frequently found among the teachers interviewed, is to subvert the order of things. This means that, for instance in teaching history, the strictly chronological order of the history curriculum and most textbooks is abandoned in favour of a thematic approach that looks at the historical causes of current situations and 'explains the present through the past'. A history teacher stressed that she addresses globalisation in this manner. In sum, making choices about the curriculum is a key modality to integrate a global citizenship perspective in teaching practice and potentially ensures that GCE is taught in a holistic and comprehensive manner. However, it relies on teachers that have the experience and confidence to 'manoeuvre' the curriculum of their subjects to address global citizenship and 'defend' their choices. It may therefore be out of reach of newly qualified teachers.

Lastly, another key modality found to integrate a global citizenship perspective is *responding to prompts arising in class*. Comments, reflections or particular instances that happen in class encourage some teachers to prepare ad hoc lessons on a particular GCE topic. Alternatively, they lead teachers to address again a particular topic or issue because what happened in class reveals that the concepts had not sunk in. Teachers mentioned, in particular, racism and prejudices as a topic that they address over and over again whenever xenophobic or racist episodes occur in class or in society. When responding to prompts, teachers report that they often end up discussing topics and issues they had not planned to address. Responding to prompts arising in class demonstrates flexibility and capacity to adapt the lessons to what is relevant to students at a particular moment. It also demonstrates the ability to seize opportunities to address anew or refresh issues and concepts. However, if it is the only strategy used by teachers, it reinforces an approach to GCE as a sporadic occurrence, rather than an embedded and systematic practice. Moreover, whenever teachers seize the moment and address an unplanned issue, there is also the risk that it is done in a simplistic, superficial or inappropriate way. Indeed, many global citizenship issues are very controversial topics, and to address them with young learners requires conceptual and methodological tools to deal with them in an age-appropriate manner.

Building Communities of Peers

In the schools studied, pioneering teachers often feel quite isolated. Some tend to engage with GCE themes and topics mainly in the 'isolated' spaces of their classrooms and subjects. But other teachers do not resign themselves to this situation and strive to 'contaminate' colleagues by supporting the integration of a global citizenship perspective in the enacted curriculum of their school. They do this in a number of ways. Firstly, they use formal school structures, like the Interculture Commission (which facilitates the inclusion in school of foreign students), the Departments (which include all the teachers teaching the same subject across the school), and the Class Councils (which include the teachers teaching different subjects in the same class). In some schools, the Interculture Commission and the Humanities Department are indeed quite active promoters of GCE, but in the majority of cases they have not proven to be very effective: the Interculture Commission is primarily focussed on the integration of foreign students, and the Departments provide limited opportunities for pedagogical discussions and the development of shared educational projects. Secondly, teachers build informal communities of practice to plan together, and share practices and materials. Working closely with like-minded colleagues provides teachers with emotional and professional support. However, these communities are informal and often dependent on friendship bonds. Lastly, planning and managing special projects is, as we have seen, a key modality to integrate GCE in practice. It is also a way to build communities of peers, and often pioneering teachers, rather than proposing projects on explicit GCE issues, design projects on broad topics that are less threatening for 'conservative teachers' but where a global citizenship perspective can be included in a more implicit manner.

Global Citizenship Education as a New Moral Pedagogy

In the province studied, whose educational policy does not identify the global dimension of citizenship education as a priority nor provide support and guidance for its integration in school practice, GCE is reduced to a 'moral optional' for 'willing and able teachers'. This does not ensure a systematic and whole-school approach to GCE, nor facilitate the adoption of a political and critical perspective. GCE is not only a 'moral optional' but also a 'new moral pedagogy' with a marked qualification and socialisation connotation.

Applying the typology developed by Sant et al. (2018), my study highlights that GCE as qualification permeates the discourses of the provincial educational policies and plans. Within this perspective, a neo-liberal human capitalism discourse on GCE emerges as prevalent and gives priority to learning foreign languages (English), understanding the economic system and the job market, acquiring digital skills and intercultural communication skills, and demonstrating flexibility. GCE as socialisation with its emphasis on promoting civil virtues, legality and social cohesion is also present in the provincial educational discourse.

The perspectives of teachers are firmly located within a GCE as socialisation and a cosmopolitan human discourse that emphasises the moral and social development of students. The emphasis is on fostering understanding of rights and duties, legality and rule of law, human rights and sustainable development. Promoting a sense of belonging to a human community coupled with empathy and conflict-resolution are key socio-emotional skills, while ethical consumer attitudes and practices are the predominant form of action.

GCE as subjectification is marginal in the discourses that permeate policies and teachers' practice. In line with the liberal tradition, there is some emphasis on promoting critical thinking, but what is marginal is the progressive approach with its emphasis on critical literacy and social justice activism to transform political and economic structures of power and domination. The critical anti-colonialist perspective, which focuses on recognising and deconstructing the "dominant modern/colonial global imaginary" (Andreotti, 2015, p. 221), is virtually absent from both policies and practices.

In sum, in the province and schools studied, GCE is essentially a 'new moral pedagogy' that merges qualification with socialisation, reflects what is perceived to be a universal moral structure based on humanistic values, and does not incorporate a political and critical perspective.

Conclusion: The Role of Teacher Education for an Embedded Critical Global Citizenship Education

In a context where GCE is essentially a 'moral optional' and a 'new moral pedagogy', the role of teacher education is of paramount importance to facilitate a more structural grounding of GCE in the curriculum and stimulate reflection on the necessity for political and critical GCE approaches.

Teacher education is a key instrument to stimulate teachers' agency. Integrating GCE in initial teacher education programmes and providing in-service teachers with ample opportunities for professional development on GCE theories and practices can empower teachers to be GCE agents in their classrooms and schools. It can also contribute to building a community of practice that can push for policy change. In this respect, the provision of training on GCE to school managers is also fundamental. Unless GCE becomes an approach firmly embedded in educational policies, plans and curricular guidelines, it will be impossible to overcome its 'moral optionality'. But change of policies and curricular guidelines are more owned and therefore more likely to be translated into practice if the impetus for change comes from the bottom up, rather than the top down. Hence, the creation through teachers' education of networks of 'Global Schools' that will call for the integration of GCE in policies and curricular guidelines is fundamental.

Teacher education is also important as it can provide spaces where the multiple interpretations and approaches of GCE can be identified, discussed, debated. Such spaces are "not about 'unveiling' the 'truth' for the learners" (Andreotti, 2006, p. 49), telling them what GCE should be, what are best practices in GCE, and providing them with a ready-made GCE toolkit. But rather they should be spaces to discuss and reflect on the different theoretical frameworks, agendas and curricula that characterise GCE—spaces where teachers critically reflect on mainstream GCE discourses (neo-liberal human capitalism and cosmopolitan humanism) and are exposed to more critical and radical pedagogical frameworks based on GCE as subjectification (critical social justice activism, critical anti-colonialism). In this way teachers can become aware of the discourses and theoretical frames that give meaning to their practice, and begin to reflectively incorporate in their work more critical ones. In a context where teachers often look at teacher education as an opportunity to receive methodological tools and materials that they can readily apply in class with their students, it is important that spaces that critically reflect on GCE are constructed in ways that engage teachers in reflexive processes and that include also a sharing of critical GCE classroom activities that teachers can adapt and test with their students.

References

Andreotti, V. (2006). Soft versus critical global citizenship education. *Policy and Practice: A Development Education Review*, 3, pp. 40–51.

Andreotti, V. (2015). Global citizenship education otherwise: Pedagogical and theoretical insights. In: A. Abdi, L. Schultz and T. Pillay (eds.), *Decolonizing Global Citizenship* Education, 221–230. Rotterdam: Sense Publishers.

Andreotti de Oliveira, V. and De Souza, L. M. (2012). Introduction. (Towards) global citizenship education 'otherwise'. In: V. Andreotti de Oliveira and L. M. De Souza (eds.), *Postcolonial Perspectives on Global Citizenship Education*, 1–6. New York and London: Routledge.

Biesta, G. (2009). Good education in an age of measurement: On the need to reconnect with the question of purpose in education. *Educational Assessment, Evaluation and Accountability*, 21(1), pp. 33–46. Available at: <https://doi.org/10.1007/s11092-008-9064-9>

Biesta, G. (2014). Learning in public places: Civic learning for the twenty-first century. In: G. Biesta, M. De Bie and D. Wildemeersch (eds.), *Civic Learning, Democratic Citizenship and the Public Sphere*, 1–11. Dordrecht: Springer.

Blackmore, C. (2016). Towards a pedagogical framework for global citizenship education. *International Journal of Development Education and Global Learning*, 8(1), pp. 39–56.

Bryan, A. and Bracken, M. (2011). *Learning to Read the World? Teaching and Learning about Global Citizenship and International Development in Post-primary Schools*. Dublin: Irish Aid.

Gaudelli, W. (2016). *Global Citizenship Education. Everyday Transcendence*. New York and London: Routledge.

Held, D. and McGrew, A. (2003). The great globalization debate: An introduction. In: D. Held and A. McGrew (eds.), *The Global Transformations Reader: An Introduction to the Globalization Debate*, 2nd edition, 1–53. Cambridge: Polity Press.

Marshall, H. (2011). Instrumentalism, ideals and imaginaries: Theorising the contested space of global citizenship education in schools. *Globalisation, Societies and Education*, 9(3–4), pp. 411–426.

Osler, A. and Starkey, H. (2003). Learning for cosmopolitan citizenship: Theoretical debates and young people's experiences. *Educational Review*, 55(3), pp. 243–254.

Oxley, L., and Morris, P. (2013). Global citizenship: A typology for distinguishing its multiple conceptions. *British Journal of Educational Studies*, 61(3), pp. 301–325.

Pashby, K. (2008). Demands on and of citizenship and schooling: 'Belonging' and 'diversity' in the global imperative. In: M. O'Sullivan and K. Pashby (eds.),

Citizenship Education in the Era of Globalization. Canadian Perspectives, 301–325. Rotterdam: Sense Publishers.

Pashby, K. (2011). Cultivating global citizens: Planting new seeds or pruning the perennials? Looking for the citizen-subject in global citizenship education theory. *Globalisation, Societies and Education*, 9(3–4), pp. 427–442.

Peterson, A. (2016). Global justice and educating for globally oriented citizenship. In: A. Peterson, R. Hattam, M. Zembylas and J. Arthur (eds.), *The Palgrave International Handbook of Education for Citizenship and Social Justice*, 247–264. London: Palgrave Macmillan.

Pike, G. (2008). Citizenship education in a global context. In: M. O'Sullivan and K. Pashby (eds.), *Citizenship Education in the Era of Globalization. Canadian Perspectives*, 41–51. Rotterdam: Sense Publishers.

Rapoport, A. (2015a). Global citizenship education. Classroom teachers' perspectives and approaches. In: J. Harshman, T. Augustine and M. Merryfield (eds.), *Research in Global Citizenship Education*, 119–135. Charlotte, NC: Information Age Publishing Inc.

Rapoport, A. (2015b). Global aspects of citizenship education: Challenges and perspectives. In: B. M. Maguth and J. Hilburn (eds.), *The State of Global Education. Learning with the World and its People*, 27–40. New York and London: Routledge.

Sant, E., Davies, I., Pashby, K. and Shultz, L. (2018). *Global Citizenship Education: A Critical Introduction to Key Concepts and Debates*. London and New York: Bloomsbury Academic.

Sassen, S. (2002). The repositioning of citizenship: Emergent subjects and spaces for politics. *Berkeley Journal of Sociology*, 46, pp. 4–26.

Sears, A. M. and Hughes, A. S. (1996). Citizenship education and current educational reform. *Canadian Journal of Education/Revue Canadienne De l'Éducation*, 21(2), pp. 123–142.

Tarozzi, M. and Torres, C. A. (2016). *Global Citizenship Education and the Crisis of Multiculturalism*. London and New York: Bloomsbury Academic.

Torres, Carlos Alberto. (2017). *Theoretical and Empirical Foundations of Critical Global Citizenship Education*. New York and London: Routledge.

Part 3

Assessment

13 'Zero Is Where the Real Fun Starts'—Evaluation for Value(s) Co-Production

Katie Carr and Leander Bindewald

Introduction

In this chapter, we propose that the dominance of the discourse surrounding quantifiable measurable phenomena over qualitative, less tangible aspects of experience is simply a provisional, although ubiquitous, discursive artefact, a story no more necessary or truthful than any alternative view. The pedigree and increasing pervasiveness of this story can be traced to the ascent of the primacy of rational thinking, which assumes that knowledge is fixed and can be externally verified, that humans can 'know'—in an absolute sense—and consequently control, the material world around them, which in the Enlightenment period was closely associated with the scientific revolution. From the early eighteenth century, philosophy became increasingly dominated by scientific discourse, and its principles of reason and logic. Ethics were subject to the same rational treatment, with the emergence of the utilitarian principle guiding moral decisions: "the greatest happiness for the greatest numbers" (Hutcheson, 1726). The authority of the Church was challenged, in favour of attributing authority and legitimacy to government and individual liberty. Arguably, 'homo economicus'—the hypothetical portrayal at the foundation of modern economics of humans as rational self-maximising individuals, displaying predictable behaviour—was born, or at least conceived, during the Age of Enlightenment. Soon followed the Industrial Revolution, and even our modern education system mirrors the features and conditions then created to streamline and manage human resources within the ever-increasing pace of the commercial machine: "ringing bells, separate facilities, specialised into separate subjects . . . educat[ing] children in 'batches'" (Robinson, 2006). In the early twentieth century, the American industrial engineer Frederick Winslow Taylor published *Principles of Scientific Management*. 'Taylorism', as it became known, is a production efficiency methodology, which proposed to fragment tasks into the smallest possible measurable part, closely observe workers and measure their output in minute detail, and bestow reward or discipline accordingly.

There have, arguably, been many benefits of 'valuing what's measurable' and its associated conceptual landscape, which also included improved women's rights (Mary Wollstonecraft's *A Vindication of the Rights of Women* was published in 1791), protection of human rights through fairer judicial systems and widening access to educational opportunities. However, it is not difficult to also trace the origins of the social and environmental challenges of today—associated with our anthropocentric view of nature as a resource in service to our ever-increasing obsession with economic growth—in the various chapters and engrossing plot of this story. One need only scan the newspapers to find evidence that, in its extreme articulations, our obsession with quantification and measurability has long since become a burden, even for our educational system, on individual teachers and children. A recent article in *Der Spiegel*, entitled 'Release Our Kids—Grades Are Not Everything: What Really Matters in Life', laments the fact that schools have become highly stress-inducing systems, resulting in children moving from school to university already being burnt-out; the President of the German National Teachers Representation said, 'Grades have lost their indicative power (for future career/success), even if people still believe they do'. What matters, suggests the journalist, are 'Love, passion, curiosity' (Der Spiegel, 2016, p. 96).

In order to explore the ways in which this story, our current paradigm, has been created and reinforced, we here briefly introduce the concept and methodology of critical discourse analysis (CDA), which foregrounds language as being the prime site of the enactment and recreation of ideology, and as such suggests that it should be the focus of analysis for those seeking to understand power relations, domination and resistance.

The Importance of Words

> The limits of my language mean the limits of my world.
>
> Ludwig Wittgenstein

The study of language as a discipline originated in the early twentieth century, and early linguists took a generally scientific approach, much concerned with sorting through diversity, finding common structures and learning how to work with those. But gradually, and as a result of interdisciplinary cross-pollination from fields as diverse as epistemology, sociology and politics, a new powerful perspective emerged. Akin to how Newton's insights might have opened our eyes to the fact that the laws of physics apparently govern all of our existence, linguistics started to look at the interplay between language and social realities, and with the keyword of 'discourse', the boundaries of this previously niche field and its everyday relevance were thrown open. In the second half of the twentieth century the study of language and discourse became as fundamental to understanding our human world as mathematics was to the natural sciences.

Discourse in its narrower/colloquial sense refers to a particular form of communication, often implying an educated, specialist conversation, e.g. legal discourse is recognisable by its archaic technocratic nature. But to the linguist-sociologist, discourse has a much broader yet very specific meaning. It is understood as everything we do interpersonally, all that gives meaning to ourselves and our world(s). This includes texts of all kinds and genres, all spoken language, but also includes gestures, signage, pictures, film, etc. As such, discourse is the fabric into which the image of our world is woven—and without discourse we would not have any image of the world to look at. This 'social constructivist' approach is built upon the assumption that reality is not something we encounter and then describe as best we can, but, as far as human knowledge and its development is concerned, we make up, or construe, the world 'as we know it' through the act of communicating about it.

Communication is a social process, a collective endeavour. Whenever we express ourselves and say something about the world within or around us, we initiate 'discursive events' which create or reinforce (or, even, deconstruct) a particular world view. If words constitute not only world views but the world (at least all that we can know if it), a powerful tool seems to be at our disposal. But its uncritical use might amount to complicity in creating a world we would not want to sign up to. Here are just a few examples about how intricate yet relevant this process is:

- What does it convey about our collective compassion when people seeking help are described in the media as a crisis for us, with little regard to the crisis they are fleeing from? And what does it reveal about the state of our society when their arrival at our borders is thus, in our heads, turned into a "tidal wave"? (Burleigh, 2015).
- It seems we are willing to be 'hard-' or 'sweet-'talked into certain attitudes and assumptions by words nobody really understands. The phrase 'hard-working families' has become so familiar in political discourse that the use of these two words together serves to de-problematise each of them: what is a family anyway? Why should 'hard-working' become a common-sense synonym of 'worthy'?—a process called *collocation* in discourse studies (Fairclough, 2010).
- As a last example, what are the emotions, attitudes, perceptions of and assumptions about the world we live in that are conjured up when we describe our social processes and aspirations by applying words and imagery from economics? Phrases such as 'pay attention', 'homework', 'it pays off', 'the idea has currency' are economic metaphors that are so deeply embedded in discourse that they are difficult to spot. This phenomenon called 'econophonics' steeps every walk of

life with the neo-liberal sentiments of individualism, competition and inescapable austerity (Giacalone and Promislo, 2013).

These examples may seem extreme, arguably evoking forms of violence. But, whilst the process of the social construal of realities by communicating about them is seldom fast or dramatic, nothing is irrelevant. And the three cases presented also serve to illustrate one important element of contemporary discourse studies: the role of power. If we accept that the words we use matter, and that discourse is the site of the creation and reinforcement of our shared sense of reality, we also need to recognise that this is not a process in which everybody's contribution has equal weight. The amount of airtime that some people (or institutions) enjoy and the importance that others attribute to their words, varies greatly. And obviously, deliberately or naively, the advantage of determining the agenda by dominating the discourse can be used to fortify one's position and further one's own interests. Hence, discourse is never a neutral process and discourse analysis cannot simply be a description of what was said. It always requires a critical stance based on the values and objectives we as individuals or practitioners want to hold and manifest in this world. This values-driven attitude as a research programme is called 'Critical Discourse Analysis', or CDA. Paying attention to power and its determination within discourse means recognising that words not only do matter, they can actually kill.

How This Matters for Educators

There are innumerable possibilities for exploring the implications of a critical discourse lens for education practice, and a clear alignment with Education for Sustainable Development and Global Citizenship (ESD/GC). Individuals within this sector are 'practical critical theorists'. That is to say, global education is an approach based on principles of critical engagement, recognition of multiple perspectives, reflective practice and consciously 'holding a space' that enables equality and democratic participation, and that recognises the importance of co-creation of new forms of knowledge in order to challenge inequalities and support social justice. This includes engaging with the tension inherent in relying heavily on conditional grant funding for outcomes-oriented projects, and the implication of the Faustian bargain which has been struck, which "compromises [the movement's] radical roots and values base . . . within a donor-led agenda" (Troll and Skinner, 2013).

In terms of classroom practice, the current requirement for British schools to promote fundamental British values provides an illuminating example of the ways in which prevailing discourse gives clear indications of how power and societal conventions are replicated. 'British Values' is an example of collocation; the two terms being repeatedly used together serves to de-problematise both. And research carried out by the Common Cause Foundation (PIRC, 2011) has shown that values are a universally experienced socio-cultural phenomenon, a set of deeply held beliefs that influence, and are therefore evidenced in, our decisions and behaviours; they cannot be dictated or bestowed, but are co-created within a community, through the process of exchange amongst members, the communicative practices we here call discourse.

But beyond the explicit curriculum taught in school, CDA invites us to ask different questions about the ways in which discourse (language as well as other non-verbal 'texts') contributes to a whole wealth of lessons which children learn through the hidden curriculum. These may include:

- What do children learn about authority and power through teachers being always referred to as Mr or Miss/Mrs?
- Why does the term 'sustainability' no longer appear in the national curriculum?
- What does the term home*work* tell us about the implied purpose of education?
- What are the effects of learning being parcelled into discrete subjects?
- Despite often telling children that there is no right or wrong answer to a particular question, what is conveyed by the fact that their classroom walls are enthusiastically plastered with the right answers?
- What do fervent security measures at the school gates/reception tell children about the state of the world outside?
- What are we to make of the tension between the stated aims to build children's *self*-esteem, and the relentless barrage of external assessment that they are subject to?

It is not possible to 'teach' ESD/GC without giving children the tools to learn about things in a different way. Thus critical thinking, dialogic learning and child-led learning approaches become mechanisms for resisting or subverting the effects of dominant discourse, and moving away from an educational system which is evaluated purely on the basis of quantitative assessment.

How This Matters for Evaluation

When taking evaluation beyond a monitoring and management exercise by asking 'How do we know it's working?', critical discourse analysis offers various ways to engage with the question reflectively. In the first instance, it demands critical scrutiny of the original intention—or objective—of the activity under evaluation. How do we know that the aim of the activity was 'right' or 'useful', and is it described clearly enough to confidently measure progress against it? If those principal considerations are not taken seriously, the effort of evaluation would generate potentially interesting but ultimately irrelevant results. But beyond that, all elements of the question 'How do we know it's working?' need to carefully appraised as well.

For example, would any reply to 'how' be acceptable? Are there any unintended impacts of the evaluation approach itself which might contradict the initial objectives or values of that activity? And who are the 'we' that pose the question? Is it asked on behalf of the beneficiaries of the activity? And if yes, would they agree or even give consent to the evaluation efforts? Or is the 'we' those delivering the activity, being professionally interested in improving their own practice? Lastly, the 'we' could be another third party entity, funders for example, and their agenda is concerned with generating evidence of 'value for money', resulting in discoursive 'colonisation' of the delivery of activities by economic assumptions.

The ways in which critical discourse analysis may explore the idea of 'to know' has already ben illustrated. But particularly when it comes to measuring qualitative elements, our epistemology and heuristics—or what we think we can know and how we go about extending that knowledge—becomes a minefield of biases and fallacies. Ultimately, what can be said with scientific certainty might turn out to be so little that any effort expended proving it becomes misdirected. And if we allow ourselves to ascertain anything beyond that speck of certainty, one way or another we seem bound to commit one self-serving fallacy or another. With all these fundamentals considered, the first issue with the question 'How do we know it's working' might now look like the easiest part to answer: what is the 'it' we are trying to evaluate and what do we mean by 'it's working'? As ESD/GC does not primarily aim to deliver a specific knowledge content or some context-independent skills, but has its core and foundation in its values, any measure that conveys objectivity and quantifiability would seem to be at odds with ESD/GC intrinsically. And even if evaluation is an external requirement, a critical attitude is a necessary condition for sufficient clarity and transparency throughout the process, so that detrimental side-effects (akin to the 'hidden curriculum' referred to above) may be prevented.

The examples above represent a set of aspirational ideas, to which no simple guidance can be given other than a reminder of the importance of maintaining a critical stance. Nevertheless, we will suggest one talking point by looking at how the same questions have been addressed in another field, with specific reference to the role of discourse. In light of the above-mentioned econophonics, the nature of counting and the pervasiveness of money, an opportune example seemed to lie in the widespread but little known field of so-called 'community currencies'. Initiatives involved in this practice try to redesign the nature of money into something that is not in conflict with the objectives of convivial communities, social equality and environmental sustainability. Such initiatives range from informal grass-roots groups who use simple paper accounting or open source software applications for their transactions, up to commercial players who provide credit to businesses at no interest and with low transaction costs. From 2012 to 2015, the EU Interreg project Community Currencies in Action (CCIA) led by the New Economics Foundation in London convened six not-for-profit organisations, including several municipalities from the UK, France, the Netherlands and Belgium, to facilitate shared learning around their individual practices of community currencies, to develop shared tools and strategies and to consolidate the recognition of community currencies in the academic and policy arenas (CCIA, 2015). Part of the output of this project was the development of an evaluation framework to ascertain the impact of the different community currency models and practices.

Similar to ESD/GC, for this community of practice, even trying to adopt a holistic evaluation framework would have meant to enclose the practice of community currencies in a discourse that has its semantic and ideological roots in our current monetary regime and would thus hamper their efforts from the start. Even well-known evaluation approaches like the "Social Return on Investment" methodology still recognise value only in terms of proxy-pricing of intangible outcomes in their equivalent Pound Sterling value (Cabinet Office, 2009). In effect the 'it'—the activities and objectives of each community currency programme—is a unique intervention with a highly context-dependent set of stakeholders, objectives and legacies. Attempting to make sense of this diversity by seeking a common 'economic' denominator for all community currency practices would misrepresent what they stand for and aim to achieve locally.

In recognition of the dilemma that we here described as a merit of a critical discourse awareness, the evaluation framework proposed and tested by the CCIA consortium and described at length in their publication "No Small Change" (New Economics Foundation, 2013), did not focus on indicators and measurement options, as both would vary greatly for each case study, but supported the initiatives that are looking into evaluation to find answers to the question 'How do we know it's working?', the concrete outcomes sought and the often hidden assumptions that determine the interventions. Being mindful of the fact that evaluation itself is a discursive process is particularly relevant for values-driven interventions such as community currencies and ESD/GC. To this end, the framework described in 'No Small Change' focuses on the constellation and interaction of stakeholders, which constitutes the 'discursive community'. By employing a variation of the 'Theory of Change' methodology common to many evaluation approaches (see Anderson, 2009), it seeks to make the description of individual desired outcomes so concrete that deriving indicators for an ensuing evaluation can be easily achieved by external evaluators, researchers or the initiative's team itself. In so doing, the 'No Small Change' approach allows all stakeholders to continually reflect on what the purpose of the intervention is and what hidden assumptions and drivers determine the pursued activities.

The outcomes and indicators determined by all stakeholders of a given community currency will naturally be highly diverse across all the different initiatives, as will be the methodologies for data collection and analysis appropriate to them. However, providing a coherent and considered way to arrive at this diversity made more sense for this field of practice than the demands of observers, prospective partners and funders, and have been lauded and appraised by both the practitioners and researchers in the field (New Economics Foundation, 2015). In light of the conceptual insights from the previous sections we recommend a similar approach be considered for, or in lieu of, conventional evaluation methodologies for the diverse field of ESD/GC.

Conclusion

Max Weber used the term 'disenchantment' to describe the intellectual moves in modern society towards rationale, reason and scientific understanding, away from belief and imagination. Are there ways in which the ESD/GC movement can become consciously aware of the ways in which it is colluding in its own colonisation, and adopt discursive positions that challenge this story? What might education look and feel like if the discourse of economics and measurability was entirely absent? Weber described this as a "world [which] remains a great enchanted garden" (Weber, 1971, p. 270).

CDA can bring a fresh and illuminating perspective to help understand the ways in which we communicate with each other using language but also non-verbal 'texts'—as the prime site of co-creation of ideology.

There is potential for further exploration, both practical and academic, of the boundary between ESD/GC and the practices of community currencies. The inclusion of a critical education about economics, money/currency and exchange needs to be one of the core components of ESD/GC. There is already much finance education happening in schools, but it is aimed towards enabling children to become better consumers, good savers and effective pension planners. The principles of ESD/GC call for a more nuanced approach, supporting teachers to create materials and methodologies for a truly globally aware and sustainability-geared monetary, financial, economic curriculum. Economy is what we make of it, and it's about time we take it out of the hands of economists.

Our title 'Zero Is Where the Real Fun Starts' was borrowed from a short poem by the fourteenth century mystic poet Hafiz. Indeed there is only one more sentence to it: "There's too much counting. Everywhere else!" (Ladinsky, 1996, p. 47). There can be numerous interpretations of the verse, but it speaks to us of the fact that learning is the heart of life, and that the seemingly ubiquitous preoccupation with quantitative measurement, which has transformed schools even in the last ten years into data-driven units set in competition with each other, is at best missing the point, and at worst letting down the children in their stewardship. Not everything that matters can be counted, and not everything that is counted matters. Or, as the fox reminded the little prince: "It is only with the heart that one can see rightly; what is essential is invisible to the eye" (Saint-Exupéry, 1995, p. 23)—and to the *accountant*-evaluator, we may add: if what matters is love, curiosity (as proposed by the *Der Spiegel* journalist quoted earlier), personal development and critical literacy, then we need to transform ESD/GC evaluation approaches by starting with the values upon which they are based, consciously rejecting domination by quantification and monetary heuristics, and deconstructing the assumptions which shape our collective construal of what is *worth*while.

References

Anderson, A. A. (2009). *The Community Builder's Approach to Theory of Change—A Practical Guide to Theory Development.* Aspen Institute.

Burleigh, M. (2015). Forget the Greek crisis or Britain's referendum, this tidal wave of migrants could be the biggest threat to Europe since the war. *Daily Mail*, 26 June. Available at: <www.dailymail.co.uk/news/article-3141005/Tidal-wave-migrants-biggest-threat-Europe-war.html>

Cabinet Office. (2009). *A Guide to Social Return on Investment.* Available at: <www.socialvalueuk.org/resources/sroi-guide/>

CCIA. (2015). *People Powered Money—Designing, Developing and Delivering Community Currencies.* Available at: <http://communitycurrenciesinaction.eu/peoplepoweredmoney/>

Der Spiegel. (2016). Nr. 35. Spiegel Verlag.

Fairclough, N. (2010). *Critical Discourse Analysis: The Critical Study of Language.* 2nd edition. Harlow: Pearson.

Giacalone, R. A. and Promislo, M. D. (2013). Broken when entering: The stigmatization of goodness and business ethics education. *Academy of Management Learning & Education*, 12(1), pp. 86–101.

Hutcheson, F. (1726). *An Inquiry into the Original of our Ideas of Beauty and Virtue in Two Treatises, Treatise II, Section 3.* Edited by Wolfgang Leidhold. Indianapolis: Liberty Fund, 2004. Available at: <http://oll.libertyfund.org/titles/hutcheson-an-inquiry-into-the-original-of-our-ideas-of-beauty-and-virtue-1726–2004>

Ladinsky, D. (1996). *I Heard God Laughing: Poems of Hope and Joy—Renderings of Hafiz.* New York: Penguin Books.

New Economics Foundation and CCIA. (2013). *No Small Change—Evaluating the Success of Your Community Currency Project.* Available at: <http://communitycurrenciesinaction.eu/no-small-change/>

New Economics Foundation and CCIA. (2015). *Money with a Purpose—Community Currencies Achieving Social, Economic and Environmental Impact.* Available at: <http://communitycurrenciesinaction.eu/ccia-final-evaluation/>

Public Interest Research Centre (PIRC) (2011). *The Common Cause Handbook.* Available at: <http://publicinterest.org.uk/download/values/Common%20Cause%20Handbook.pdf>. Accessed 16 December 2018.

Robinson, K. (2006). *Ken Robinson: Changing Education Paradigms.* TED Talks. Available at: <www.ted.com/talks/ken_robinson_changing_education_paradigms>

Saint-Exupéry, A. de. (1995). *The Little Prince.* Translated by Irene Testot-Ferry. Ware: Wordsworth Classics.

Troll, T. and Skinner, A. (2013). Catalysing the 'shadow spaces': Challenging development discourse from within the DEEEP project. *Policy & Practice: A Development Education Review*, 17(Autumn), pp. 90–102. Available at: www.developmenteducationreview.com/issue/issue-17/catalysing-shadow-spaces-challenging-development-discourse-within-deeep-project. Accessed 16 December 2018.

Weber, M. (1971). *The Sociology of Religion.* Translated by Ephraim Fischoff. Boston: Beacon Press.

Wollstonecraft, M. (1791). *A Vindication of the Rights of Women.* Boston: Thomas and Andrews.

14 Rating Education for Sustainable Development in the Early Years

A Necessity or a Challenge?

Zoi Nikiforidou, Zoe Lavin-Miles and Paulette Luff

Introduction

In recent years there has been increasing interest in addressing Education for Sustainability and Global Citizenship (ESD/GC) in the early years of education. Policymakers, researchers and educationalists agree that the sooner children gain knowledge and develop values relating to ecology, economy and society, the more prepared they are as citizens of today working towards a sustainable future. As such, in educational contexts there has been an attempt to embed ESD in a more explicit way. The aim of this chapter is to contribute to the debate about the role and necessity of measuring ESD/GC in early childhood. In 2013 OMEP (World Organization for Early Childhood) proposed the Environmental Rating Scale for Sustainable Development in Early Childhood (ERS-SDEC) as an instrument for research or for curriculum assessment and development purposes for use in multiple contexts: in one classroom, across classrooms, or even across a whole local authority. Examples of cross-cultural ESD projects in England and Kenya are presented here. Two entirely different settings, Cranborne Pre-school in Dorset and Ng'ondu in Kenya, used the ERS-SDEC scale as a means to integrate ESD into their educational practices. The first project, named 'Matarajio' (Swahili for hope/expectations), highlighted two important Sustainable Development Goals (SDG): Goal 5 'Achieve gender equality and empower all women and girls' and Goal 15 'Sustainably manage forests, combat desertification, halt and reverse land degradation, halt biodiversity loss'. The second project, the W.A.S.H. UNICEF project, related to Goal 6: 'Ensure access to water and sanitation for all'. Findings and discussion show how children and staff engaged in experiential learning for ESD by unpicking and considering diverse aspects of the same themes and SDGs. The implications and future learning on monitoring and evaluating ESD in early childhood are assessed.

ESD/GC in Early Years

Education for Sustainable Development (ESD) provides a vision of education that seeks to balance human and economic well-being with socio-cultural traditions and respect for the environment. As a matter of fact, according to UNESCO (2014) 'there is now a growing international recognition of ESD as an integral element of quality education and a key enabler for sustainable development' (p. 9). ESD covers the three interdependent pillars of sustainability: environmental and ecological concerns, social and cultural implications and economic aspects (Brundtland, 1987), and over the last decade there has been increased interest in exploring why and how ESD could be enhanced more explicitly from early childhood (e.g. Pramling Samuelsson, 2011; Davis and Elliott, 2014; Davis, 2015). Setting values, attitudes and awareness from early in life sets the foundation of citizens who learn to care about a healthier, more equitable, more sustainable world. Indeed, investing in early childhood and building a sustainable society are strongly interconnected.

Early childhood education for sustainability has, traditionally, been related to environmental education. However, it is more than that, as it covers principles and practices related to ecology, economy and equity. ESD offers opportunities for transformative learning *in*, *about* and *for* the environment (Davis, 2009). This later aspect, underlined by Davis, indicates a strong sense of enabling children to become active agents in addressing sustainability issues. From this perspective, ESD should be about encouraging children to solve problems, to think and act, to be empowered in appreciating, familiarising themselves with, and if necessary making decisions on sustainability matters (Siraj-Blatchford et al., 2010). ESD has a humanistic approach. It encompasses an understanding of people, culture and diversity in "ways of being, relating, behaving, believing, and acting differently" (Pressoir, 2008, p. 60).

However, ESD has various iterations and meanings, and there is no one way to define or apply ESD in educational contexts. ESD might be interpreted or prioritised in different ways amongst diverse regional, national and international cultural contexts. Davis and Elliot (2014) state that ESD is a "co-evolution of social and biophysical systems played out in responsive and responsible relationships. The challenge is to translate these ideas into early childhood educational praxis" (p. 13). As such, there are barriers and fragmentation (UNESCO, 2009, p. 65) in implementing ESD in early childhood, and attention is directed towards harmonising these tensions by underlining the value of ESD.

One such attempt can be found in the initiative to develop rating scales or measurements of ESD in Early Childhood settings. Setting ESD/GC goals or indicators affords opportunities to ensure equity and parity in children's learning experiences; to see what is effective (what works) and what is not; to share good practice and perhaps apply it to different contexts; to make more explicit how aspects of ESD/GC can be embedded in the curriculum; and to set benchmarks which leaders, stakeholders, parents, learners and teachers can understand (Shaeffer, 2013) and, as such, to promote common understanding. Having a rating scale sets some common ground in exploring ESD among diverse early childhood settings.

Specifically, OMEP (International Organization of Early Childhood Education) developed in 2013 the ERS-SDEC (Environmental Rating Scale for Sustainable Development in Early Childhood). This scale is based on the same rating procedures as previous rating scales, namely: Early Childhood Environment Rating Scale-Revised (ECERS-R) (Harms et al., 1998) and -Extension (ECERS-E) (Sylva et al., 2003). It has a user handbook and is translated into nine languages. It can be used as a research tool but also as a self-assessment tool for practitioners (www.worldomep.org/wp-content/uploads/2013/12/ERS-SDEC_English.pdf).

Based on two-hour observations and data collection from other sources (i.e. interviews with staff-children-parents, documents-records-displays), it covers aspects related to (1) Social and Cultural Sustainability (Global Social Justice), (2) Economic Sustainability (Equality) and (3) Environmental Sustainability. The ERS-SDEC scale measures from 1 to 7 with 1 = inadequate, 3 = minimal 5 = good and 7 = excellent, and it applies to contexts and settings that host two-and-a-half- to seven-year-olds. It may be applied by individuals or groups of practitioners to audit their Education for Sustainable Development curriculum, and to help practitioners and preschool centre managers in setting curriculum development priorities. For example, under Social and Cultural Sustainability indicator 2, at an inadequate level (=1) would be: “1.2 No policy statement exists regarding the importance and value of social and cultural diversity in the setting”, whereas the same indicator at an excellent level (=7) would be: “7.2 Children explore and investigate unfamiliar social and cultural contexts”.

To this end, the aim of this chapter is to draw upon projects on ESD in UK and Kenya over three years. The purpose is to explore how similar thematic projects with the same SDGs are applied in diverse socio-cultural contexts. SDGs 5, 15 and 6 and the broader framework of ERS-SDEC are used here cross-culturally to provide insights on measuring ESD.

Application of ESD in Two Different Contexts: Dorset in England and Ng’ondu in Kenya

Cranborne Pre-School in Dorset, UK, and N’gondu Pre-School in Kenya were part of a partnership that was developed as a World OMEP pilot project in 2012. The UK/Kenya OMEP partnership has been promoting ESD projects between the two countries that empower the preschool child through a play-based approach. Two overarching projects are presented in relation to the UN SDGs (5, 15, 6) and environmental practices framing the ERS-SDEC. Specifically, the Matarijio project highlighted the work and life of a famous Nobel Peace Prize winner Wangari Maathai, who founded the Green Belt Movement (UN SDGs 5, 15), and the UNICEF W.A.S.H. project emphasised aspects of the water cycle (UN SDG 6). Both projects took place in the pre-schools in Dorset and Kenya and tackled aspects of the three core pillars of economic, cultural/social and environmental sustainability and the ERS-SDEC.

Goal 5: Achieve Gender Equality and Empower All Women and Girls (Matarijio Project)

The children at both Cranborne and N'gondu learnt about gender equality and empowerment through socio-dramatic play by the promotion of positive female role models. The UK children dressed up as doctors, firefighters and scientists and played in a set-up 'hospital', and this was replicated (using the same clothes) in Kenya. The children watched each other on videos and looked at photographs which helped them associate themselves with children from another part of the world, enabling them to become aware of children in another social/cultural context. These were repeated in the UK to other children in order to continue the learning cycle through the EYFS. These activities are linked to the ERS-SDEC indicators for Social and Cultural Sustainability (Global Social Justice):

> 7.1—The children share their ideas and knowledge of their own and others' cultures in group sharing times and are able to speak openly about diversity; 7.2—Children explore and investigate unfamiliar social and cultural contexts; and 5.3—Children participate in activities that cross stereotypical gender, racial, ethnic and tribal boundaries (e.g. providing diverse opportunities and materials for dramatic and social play).
>
> (OMEP, 2013a, p. 1)

Goal 15: Sustainably Manage Forests, Combat Desertification, Halt and Reverse Land Degradation, Halt Biodiversity Loss (Matarijio Project)

Continuing to highlight the work of Wangari Mathaai, who had a vision to plant a billion trees around the world, the teachers focused on arousing in the children environmental awareness and consciousness through a session called 'Doing the Best We Can', which was coined from the famous video from the movie 'Dirt' (see an extract at www.youtube.com/watch?v=-btl654R_pY). The session was a way to share with the children the implicit message that to make their world a better place for themselves and each other, every little thing they can do helps towards these goals. A woodland session was devised to introduce them to wood and natural products from woodlands as a way to interact and connect to products which could be seen as connected to themselves. These sessions brought across the message of worldwide deforestation in a sensitive and appropriate way for the age of the children, disregarding the often cited messages about early years children being too young for complex global topics. This part of the project is considered to match the ERS-SDEC indicators for Environmental Sustainability "3.2—Children's attention is explicitly drawn to the need to care for the environment of the setting and in the local community" and "5.2—The children are encouraged to identify a range of environmental protection issues and to suggest their own ideas for solving them"; and also indicator 5.4 under Economic Sustainability (Equality)—"The children's attention is specifically drawn to economic issues of concern to the local and international community" (OMEP, 2013a, pp. 2, 3).

Goal 6: Ensure Access to Water and Sanitation for All (UNICEF W.A.S.H. Project)

During 2015 and 2016, many sessions between UK partner pre-schools and Kenya pre-schools were devised in order to emphasise the 'rights respecting' work supporting the UNICEF Water, Sanitation and Hygiene (W.A.S.H.) programme in schools (www.unicef.org/wash/schools/), which was developed into World OMEP initiative W.A.S.H. from the Start (www.worldomep.org/en/wash-from-the-start/). At the start of 2015, Cranborne Pre-school planned activities for their children to understand hygiene and the importance of hand washing. This was done in conjunction with World Water Day. A session was done by Cranborne called 'Is it safe to drink?', where the children and their parents collected as many samples of water as they could find. They collected sea, toilet, tap, spring, river and puddle. They were asked to bring them in bottles and whether just by looking at them could they tell if they were 'safe to drink'. They made an association with the fact that toilet water looked exactly the same as tap water and that unsafe water was not always visible. They experimented with dissolving different products into the water, such as soil, flour, salt and sugar to see what happened. Could they tell what was in the water? The children were read stories such as *The Drop Goes Plop* by Sam Goodwin, about the journey of a water drop through the pipes and reservoirs before it reached our taps. They learned about the interaction of water resources and the hydrological cycle as a social construction and as part of human management, within the context of global awareness. To further highlight this, a 'tippy tap' was built in the playgrounds, which the children loved.

These tippy taps were brought in during sessions in 2016 in further projects by OMEP Kenya president Lilian Okal in her school Mount Kenya Academy and their UK partner Townsend Montessori. They highlighted the impact of water poverty in Kenya and the issues surrounding the lack of infrastructure. Differences of services and facilities for children between Kenya and the UK were highlighted. For example, as reported by Pramling Samuelsson and Siraj-Blatchford (2013), 122,000 under five-year-olds die each year and these deaths are caused mostly by lack of water, sanitation and hygiene, and 75% of children are unable to wash their hands with soap or ash after visiting the latrine and before eating. Moreover, for children in the UK it is hard to imagine that water is a scarce resource around the world, which is made scarcer by the lack of adequate infrastructure through the complexities of equitable political, social and economic discourse and the difficulties of landlocked countries' access to water through transboundary and local governance issues.

These messages are devised in such a way as to meet appropriate age-related curriculum goals and national targets. These activities connect to the ERS-SDEC rating Environmental Sustainability indicators 3.2 and 5.2 (see above) and also 7.2: "The children are encouraged to provide a variety of actions, including narrative accounts, to represent their efforts to solve environmental issues". They also link to Economic Sustainability indicators: "5.1—The children are encouraged to suggest ways in which costs can be reduced by conserving and/or recycling materials and resources such as paper, water and electricity in the setting, at home and beyond"; 5.4 (see above); and "7.2—The children are encouraged to provide a variety of actions, including narrative accounts, to represent their efforts to solve environmental issues; and indicate how the scales can be applied in diverse socio-cultural settings" (OMEP, 2013a, pp. 2, 3).

Discussion and Reflections

As the projects undertaken in England and Kenya show, the ERS-SDEC can be applied to evaluate provision for ESD. Where the activities above have been rated using a descriptor beginning with 3 (i.e. 3.2 for Environmental Sustainability), that represents a 'minimal' level and would apply to "the most common current preschool practice in environmental education around the world" (OMEP, 2013b, p. 1). Descriptors beginning with 5 (i.e. 5.3 for Social and Cultural Sustainability, 5.2 for Environmental Sustainability and 5.4 for Economic Sustainability) identify practices that can be considered 'good' examples of ESD in early childhood education. Finally, the items beginning with 7 (i.e. 7.1. and 7.2 for Social and Cultural Sustainability, 7.2 for Environmental Sustainability and 7.2 for Economic Sustainability) demonstrate 'excellence', where ESD has been taken the furthest in terms of understandings and actions. In the light of this, some advantages and challenges of the measurement of ESD in Early Childhood Education in general and of the ERS-SDEC tool are discussed briefly here.

Undoubtedly, a commitment to achieving the UN Sustainable Development Goals across the globe brings a greater need for recording progress, including provision for ESD in Early Childhood Education (Pramling Samuelsson, 2011; Davis, 2015). A tool such as the ERS-SDEC has potential for use in monitoring and auditing ESD activities, and the scales may provide a shared language (Shaeffer, 2013) for rating and celebrating ESD work in early childhood settings. This benefit of the scale can be seen in the bringing together of early years practitioners, in this case from England and from Kenya—and providing some common ground for the discussion and promotion of ESD. This has to be approached with caution, though, as it cannot be assumed that understandings are the same across diverse contexts. In the work with Kenya, the educator from the UK noticed that there were differences and tensions between intrinsic and instrumental values, particularly in relation to economic aspects of ESD. For example, when the educator in Kenya was talking to the children about the importance of elephant conservation, a priority was the attraction of elephants for tourists on safari holidays rather than for the sake of the survival and the increase of the elephant population itself. Whilst this anthropocentric view of the environment is unsurprising in a context where living standards for local communities may be dependent upon tourism, it is at odds with the respect for ecology and for animal rights and freedoms that may be part of ESD in other settings. The ERS-SDEC items are therefore just a starting point for dialogue and learning for the promotion of ESD in two diverse places.

Conclusion

The three-page ERS-SDEC tool, with up to five elements for each of the three aspects of sustainability, is designed to be user-friendly (OMEP, 2013a, 2013b). It can become a valuable tool for professional development. It can draw practitioners' attention to specific areas of practice and provide a basis for dialogue and reflection that may lead to advances in provision. As with similar tools, this positive approach can become a way of overcoming cultural diversity and setting a common ground for discussion on matters of ESD in early childhood. However, these rating scales should be approached with caution too; it might be the case that they are used for surveillance or rigid assessment, within a culture of managerialism. In the latter case, work is often carried to increase scores on the scales with a consequent loss of commitment to the values that underpin the tool itself.

In England, where 'sustainability' and 'sustainable development' are not yet part of the everyday vocabulary of practitioners, the ERS-SDEC can provide a useful means of defining these topics and can offer insights into the areas that might be covered by ESD. Nevertheless, whilst this is beneficial, a ready-made scale presented by external experts that is perceived as something to be understood and learned may diminish practitioners' confidence to develop their own understandings of, and commitments to, ESD. In conclusion, therefore, we argue that the ERS-SDEC may assist in the task of defining and applying ESD in Early Childhood

Education but work must continue to support practitioners to develop their own critical awareness of the potential and scope of ESD in differing regional, national and international cultural contexts.

References

Brundtland, G. (ed.). (1987). *Our Common Future: The World Commission on Environment and Development*. Oxford: Oxford University Press.

Davis, J. M. (2009). Revealing the research 'hole' of early childhood education for sustainability: A preliminary survey of the literature. *Environmental Education Research*, 15(2), pp. 227–241.

Davis, J. M. (ed.). (2015). *Young Children and the Environment: Early Education for Sustainability*. 2nd edition. Melbourne: Cambridge University Press.

Davis, J. M. and Elliott, S. (2014). *Research in Early Childhood Sustainability: International Perspectives and Provocations*. London: Routledge.

Harms, T., Clifford, M. and Cryer, D. (1998). *Early Childhood Environment Rating Scale, Revised Edition (ECERS-R)*. Vermont: Teachers College Press.

OMEP. (World Organization for Early Childhood) (2013a). *Environmental Rating Scale for Sustainable Development in Early Childhood*. Available at: <www.worldomep.org/en/esd-scale-for-teachers/>

OMEP (World Organization for Early Childhood). (2013b). *Guidance for the Use of the OMEP Environmental Rating Scale for Sustainable Development in Early Childhood (ERS-SDEC)*. Available at: <www.worldomep.org/wp-content/uploads/2013/12/Guidance-Final.pdf>

Pramling Samuelsson, I. (2011). Why we should begin early with ESD: The role of early childhood education. *International Journal of Early Childhood*, 43(2), pp. 103–118.

Pramling Samuelsson, I. and Siraj-Blatchford, J. (2013). *Education for Sustainable Development in Early Childhood Care and Education: A UNESCO Background Paper*. Unpublished.

Pressoir, E. (2008). Preconditions for young children's learning and practice for sustainable development. In: Pramling Samuellson, I. and Kaga, Y (eds.), *The Contribution of Early Childhood Education to a Sustainable Society*, 57–62. Paris: UNESCO.

Shaeffer, S. (2013). Early childhood development in the post-2015 development agenda. *NORRAG News*, 49, pp. 77–79.

Siraj-Blatchford, J., Smith, K. C. and Pramling Samuelsson, I. (2010). *Education for Sustainable Development in the Early Years*. Gothenburg: World Organization for Early Childhood Education.

Sylva, K., Siraj-Blatchford, I. and Taggart, B. (2003). *Assessing quality in the early years: Early Childhood Environment Rating Scale-Extension (ECERS-E): Four Curricular Subscales*. Stoke-on Trent: Trentham Books.

UNESCO. (2009). *Review of Contexts and Structures for ESD* (by A. E. J. Wals). Paris: UNESCO.

UNESCO. (2014). *UNESCO Roadmap for Implementing the Global Action Programme on Education for Sustainable Development*. Paris: UNESCO.

15 Results, Results, Results

Seeking Spaces for Learning in a European Global Learning and STEM Project

Angela Daly and Julie Brown

Introduction

There is a growing interest in the monitoring and evaluation of Education for Sustainable Development and Global Citizenship (ESD/GC). Development education practitioners highlight tensions between the demands of monitoring and evaluation for reporting purposes and opportunities for learning about practice within funded global learning education projects (Bond, 2012; Fricke, Gathercole with Skinner, 2015). This chapter presents a post-project reflection on the monitoring, evaluation and learning (MEL) processes of a three-year European Commission (EC) funded project involving non-state actors in formal education systems on development education and global learning in Science, Technology, Engineering and Mathematics (STEM) curricula. The Make the Link project focussed on development of engaging materials and professional development for teachers. The authors provide an overview of what was involved in developing a monitoring and evaluation framework that aimed to capture progress against results as defined by the project's EC logical framework, as well as learning about experiences of global learning and STEM from partners across four country contexts. This reflection contributes to discussion on the theme: how can ESD/GC monitoring, evaluation and research engage meaningfully with practice and vice-versa?

The Project

The Technology Challenging Poverty: Make the Link project focussed on embedding global learning in European STEM curricula through the development of engaging STEM materials and professional development for teachers. Practical Action was the lead organisation for the project and worked alongside six project partners: Engineers Without Borders (UK); Tomorrow's Engineers (UK); Sheffield Hallam University's Centre for Science Education—CSE (UK); Centre for the Advancement of Research and Development in Educational Technology—CARDET (Cyprus); Oxfam

Italia (Italy); and Fundacja Centrum Edukacji Obywatelskiej—Centre for Citizenship Education CEO (Poland).

The aims of the Technology Challenging Poverty: Make the Link Project were to:

- Raise awareness and understanding among young people of development issues, the interdependent world and their own roles, responsibilities and lifestyles in relation to a globalised society;
- Integrate development issues and global learning methodologies into the science and technology curricula in policy and practice in four European Union (EU) countries (UK, Poland, Italy and Cyprus).

The main activity to achieve these aims was to develop teaching resources linked to STEM curricula focussed on students aged nine to fourteen years. Teaching resources were provided as free online resources, hosted on individual partner websites in the four participating countries. A curriculum mapping processes ensured that educational materials were relevant and reflected the different curricula of each of the countries involved (Practical Action, 2013). Resources include the following:

- Beat the Flood is a STEM challenge where students use their science skills to design, build and test a model of a flood-proof house. Students examined global contexts where flooding had occurred in Bangladesh, Italy and England and considered consequences for families and their needs in developing future flood-proof homes. (http://practicalaction.org/beattheflood)
- Plastics Challenge is a new STEM challenge that focuses on the reuse and recycling of plastics. The resources were developed and field-tested by a secondary teacher and her group of Year 10 'Plastic Chemists' before being made available. (http://practicalaction.org/plastics-challenge)
- Make the Link resources are a comprehensive set of materials made up of four units of work, each with six lessons. Materials include PowerPoint slides, notes for teachers and student task worksheets. Topics covered include water, climate change, energy and food, reflecting key themes in STEM curricula. Developed with the Centre for Science Learning, videos were provided by Practical Action on authentic global contexts on topics discussed. (http://practicalaction.org/make-the-link)
- Power for the World is an activity where students learn about inequalities of energy access and then design, make and test a wind turbine. These resources were developed and used in UK classrooms by Engineers Without Borders (UK) and further developed in Oxfam Italia in continuing professional development workshops with primary teachers. (www.ewb-uk.org/our-initiatives/inspiring-

change-in-engineering-education/outreach-programme/power-for-everyone-everywhere)

Methodology

Before the Make the Link project began, the authors attended a BOND workshop to consider approaches to monitoring evaluation and learning (MEL) in practice, and in the context of the upcoming EC funded project. BOND is a UK-based Non-Governmental Organisation (NGO) that supports development organisations on a range of topics including MEL and programme design (see www.bond.org.uk). In particular, we discussed how to integrate a results-based logical framework with a range of mixed methods to track progress against results as well as to gather evidence of good practice. Methodological challenges arose in planning how best to monitor progress, how to evaluate impact and how to identify opportunities for project learning as part of the external evaluation of the project. We wanted to avoid dualist thinking around qualitative versus quantitative data and to move to a point of identifying what it was that we wanted to know to inform and develop practice and what we wanted to know to ensure accountability and reporting to funders.

Research from the NGO sector identifies several challenges in reporting requirements that are useful for ESD/GC practitioners to consider when designing monitoring and evaluation processes for projects. The EC reporting frameworks utilise four key themes to measure success and to define results: relevance, efficiency, effectiveness and sustainability. These themes suggest there is a connection between valuing results as outputs and results as an ongoing learning process during and beyond the project. The NGO research highlights how similar themes contain potential challenges for practice. The effectiveness agenda, by which NGOs are required to demonstrate their effectiveness, efficiency and impact, requires good monitoring and evaluation systems to capture change within the constraints of a time-bound project or programme (Bond, 2012). The Improve It Framework (Bond, 2008) supports NGOs by providing a resource that links domains of change measured over time with appropriate data collection tools to assess and communicate outcomes of project activities. The accessibility agenda, whereby NGOs need to be answerable for good use of public funds, suggests that monitoring and evaluation is part of accountability as well as of good project management (O'Donnell, 2016). Many monitoring and evaluation reports remain on the shelf, whereas results made public in accessible and useful ways facilitate greater accountability and promote wider learning about the work of development organisations in the public domain. This is linked to a further challenge of 'lost learning' though limited dissemination of evaluation findings (Cooke, 2015). ESD/GC practitioners in particular may be highly reflective and able to capture useful knowledge in innovative MEL approaches. However, there may be insufficient funds for in-depth research and evaluation beyond results-based and financial reporting. For many development organisations, there are rarely time and financial resources for sharing learning beyond reporting to funders (Cooke, 2015). Therefore, seeking broader opportunities for dissemination and developing skills in public engagement with research may not be a priority. Finally, short project timeframes may militate against the capture of longer-term impact and change over time, with particular difficulties in attributing effects and impacts within the complexities of social development programmes (Fricke, Gathercole with Skinner, 2015).

Findings

A MEL framework for Make the Link was designed to mirror and build on the EC logical framework of the project which listed intended activities and anticipated results (Daly and Brown, 2013). The results outlined in the project's EC logical framework were ambitious, as noted below.

Result 1: A set of teaching resources complementing the Science and Technology curricula accessed by 13,000 teachers.
Result 2: 1,600 teachers inspired and empowered to integrate development education into their teaching through training.
Result 3: 200 key influencers in education actively engaged in encouraging teachers to integrate project materials into their teaching.

The MEL framework provided evidence that Make the Link Project exceeded its ambitious results and objectives. Methods used and a reflection on findings are outlined below.

Webstats

Use of webstats was incorporated into the project monitoring design. Google Analytics captured downloads of Make the Link educational resources across partner websites and differentiated between the countries where materials were accessed from. Information was input into a shared data set by each partner. The project had significant reach with 18,200 teachers downloading quality materials that combine global learning methodologies with development contexts for STEM learning. An unexpected finding was that a small number of teachers from other EU countries not involved in the project have accessed online materials, indicating their suitability for teachers more widely. In addition, 1,368 teachers engaged in professional development. Six months after this training, 93% of teachers said they were likely to incorporate global learning in their planning. Incorporating webstats as a monitoring tool provides longer-term evidence that resources are relevant and dissemination is continuing post-project.

Case Studies of Impacts on Teachers and Students

Three-monthly partner reports provided detailed information on activities, numbers of teachers and students in schools reached, qualitative reflections on progress against objectives, short case studies of practice including photographs of educational activity, teacher and student reflections, and findings from teacher questionnaires following any training delivered. A mid-term review of the project used a case study approach to analyse outcomes and effects resulting from the project's implementation and strategies (EC, 2005). A final review brought partners together for a participatory evaluation workshop (Chambers, 2002). The project had positive impacts on teachers and their students. It is estimated 1,026,000 students aged seven to nineteen engaged in the project through teachers' access to materials. Feedback from students was not easy to obtain; however, valuable student feedback was received via engaged teachers, through small scale observations and focus groups. Rich qualitative evidence of students' understanding of the relevance of STEM in tackling global issues and their interest in global debates on development issues was found. Students expressed their feelings of empathy, attentiveness to inclusive design, and, an unexpected outcome, their interest in STEM careers, as noted by these students:

> I've learnt that bamboo isn't very absorbent—so we have used it to make our house. You never know when the weather will change. The climate is changing due to global warming. A flood proof house would help because if there was extreme weather, this would stand it. I have built my house so that all people can use it. It has a ramp so anyone in a wheelchair can get up to safety if the water comes over.
>
> (Primary students)

> Today has been amazing. I really want to do this when I am older.
>
> (Secondary student)

Teachers and students were involved from the outset in developing quality resources. A youth panel worked with teachers to design and test materials and to identify global STEM contexts that they thought would be engaging for students. Practical Action's authentic materials from real world development contexts were used to augment and connect global issues to STEM content as explained by one of the partners:

> It really works in our schools and it helps to have high quality videos, scenarios and resources from development. We have gone on

> to develop our own materials based on real stories from across the globe.
>
> (Partner)

Engagement in Dissemination Activities

A 'key influencer log' was compiled detailing engagement with global learning practitioners, teachers and STEM stakeholders. The project engaged with over 300 key influencers at local, national and European levels through innovative use of social media, writing material for over thirty-five education materials and dissemination at networks and conferences. The extent to which teachers were peer influencers was an unexpected finding. Teachers created a multiplier effect by sharing resources via locally organised 'Teach Meets', social media groups, and involvement in subject associations and networks. A teacher with a lead role in supporting newly qualified teachers commented on the importance of engaging with new materials and continuing to learn as a mentor:

> It's given me a context to talk about an experiment with different fuels. As a teacher who is trying to inspire others, it has certainly changed my approach.
>
> (Secondary teacher)

Reporting to and Hearing From the EC

The EC funding strand required annual and final narrative and financial reports. These contained selections of qualitative and quantitative data provided by partners and case studies of good practice, and recommendations and actions arising from the mid-term and final review. In addition, a Results Only Monitoring (ROM) visit was carried out on selected projects by the EC. The ROM Visit for Make the Link was held between 13 September and 5 October 2015, and EC auditors met with partners and stakeholders across the project. The ROM report was received by the lead partner on 3 January 2016 and comprised a five-page report using a traffic light system to evaluate the project. Make the Link achieved 'green' for good/very good in each of the themes of relevance, efficiency, effectiveness and sustainability. As the project ended on 31 January 2016, the report came too late to consider comments, and many of the recommendations had already been made in the mid-term review. The EC also held a post-project lead partners' meeting in March 2016 to reflect on experiences arising out of the funded projects under the EC action 'Non-State Actors and Local Authorities in Development: Global Learning in formal education system 2013–2015'.

Discussion

This reflection has enabled us to identify spaces for learning in the project's MEL processes that helps address the challenges for development education organisations in demonstrating effectiveness, accountability, accessibility and sustainability. We offer some suggestions for project evaluation in development education and ESD/GC based on our experiences.

Firstly, we suggest collaboration of partners in the development of MEL as an initial and ongoing part of the project. The overall management of the project was supported by a robust but flexible MEL framework and methods. Internal and external technical expertise were drawn upon, including technical support on social media, webstats and project management from Practical Action; external monitoring and evaluation workshops provided by BOND; and the expertise of a researcher with experience of qualitative, quantitative and participatory research methods. This enabled collection of data in a variety of ways and demonstrated efficiency and effectiveness in MEL processes (Bond, 2012; EC, 2005).

Opportunities for partners to reflect on MEL included face-to-face kick-off and mid-project meetings intended to support the production of monitoring tools, and dissemination plans to ensure deadlines and reporting expectations were realistic, achievable and meaningful. Recommendations from the mid-term review helped partners to feel more connected: themed Skype calls were introduced in the second year to share aspects of interesting learning such as teachers as influencers, e-learning modules and working with networks of teachers. Limited funds meant thinking creatively about the final review (Cooke, 2015). It comprised a participatory evaluation workshop and a seminar in Liverpool where ideas and achievements were shared locally with other global education stakeholders. Partners defined aspects of MEL to take forward to new areas of their individual and collective work. In two subsequent projects, a research strand is integral to the project plan, demonstrating how longer-term learning can be integrated into practice (Fricke, Gathercole with Skinner, 2015).

Secondly, we suggest developing a meaningful team approach to support collective project learning. Partners contributed to the achievements of the Make the Link project and benefited from the rich experiences from working in a 'European team'. The participatory methods in the mid-term and final reviews included workshops and Skype seminars, and co-development of case studies supported this sense of connectedness (Daly and Rogers, 2016). These spaces for joint project evaluation revealed areas of highly reflective learning among partners that enabled thoughtful yet critical perspectives on the role of development organisations, the contested nature of development contexts in STEM resources, and the diversity and relevance of global learning in training educators across European countries. The relevance of making the link between STEM, global learning methodologies and a concern with ESD/GC was captured by one of the partners:

> That's part of the tension, to bring the rich context of global development and global issues, and at the same time cover the science required in a conceptually sensible way.
>
> (Partner)

Thirdly, we suggest being open to opportunities to build capacity in MEL and sharing findings as the project progresses. All partners grew in confidence in engaging with the wider ESD/GC practitioner and research community. The blend of traditional reporting and use of findings to communicate with a variety of interested groups enabled partners to demonstrate the value of global learning and development education to wider public audiences (O'Donnell, 2016). This included attending and winning an award at the European Scientix conference (Scientix, 2014), delivering an academic research chapter at the European Science Education Research Conference (Daly and Brown, 2015), publishing in the Association of Science Education publications, *Primary Science and Education in Science* (Seeley, 2014; Cox, 2014) and discussing our reflections on MEL processes with ESD/GC educators at the TEESNet conference (Daly and Brown, 2016).

Finally, we would be braver about asking for support and feedback from EC funders. This may promote adequately resourced MEL, research and dissemination work. Learning about the project and learning about MEL processes has not been lost (Cooke, 2015). Based on our experience, we value the link between research and monitoring and evaluation practice for deeper learning about global learning and STEM. We have sought to design into future programmes adequate resources for a more central role for project learning that includes mixed evaluation methods, research including more participatory action research, and public engagement with findings.

Conclusion

In conclusion, the project achieved its intended results regarding involving non-state development actors in providing resources for STEM curricula in the UK, Poland, Cyprus and Italy. We also learned a great deal by focussing on good monitoring and evaluation systems from the start and throughout the life of the project. We conclude that monitoring, evaluation *and* learning is important to all stakeholders, but each must consider what 'useful knowledge' is for their purposes. By combining the requirements of the EC logical framework with our own MEL framework of mixed methods, we were able to make a connection between results and outcomes for teachers and students, and were able to capture rich data and unexpected outcomes. Spaces for learning were both planned for and serendipitous. As the project developed, we became sufficiently confident to take advantage of opportunities that were not in the overall project plan to engage in wider opportunities to sharing learning. This points to a more central role for participatory learning spaces as an integral element of future global learning projects. This methodological reflection has informed our future developments in approaches to researching what is valuable in global learning and STEM practice.

References

Bond. (2008). *'Improve It' Framework*. London: Bond.

Bond. (2012). *Assessing Effectiveness in Education: Thematic Paper for Consultation*. London: Bond.

Chambers, R. (2002). *Participatory Workshops: A Sourcebook of 21 Ideas and Activities*. London: Earthscan.

Cooke, M. (2015). *Making Evaluations Work Harder for International Development*. London: CSLP/Bond.

Cox, J. (2014). 'Beat the Flood'. Redmoor Academy and Practical Action engaging students in STEM. *Education in Science*, 255.

Daly, A. and Brown, J. (2013). *Make the Link Monitoring, Evaluation and Learning Framework*. Liverpool: Angela Daly Research/Practical Action.

Daly, A. and Brown, J. (2016). Results, Results, Results: Seeking Spaces for Learning in a Global Learning and STEM Project. Presentation at the Teacher Education for Equity and Sustainability Network (TEESNet) Ninth Annual Conference at Liverpool Hope University.

Daly, A. and Brown, J. (2015). Global learning meets science and technology: Teaching technology justice in European classrooms. In: *Science Education Research: Engaging Learners for a Sustainable Future, e-proceedings of the European Science Education Research Conference*, Helsinki, 31 August–4 September, Part 8, pp. 1143–1450.

Daly, A. and Rogers, L. (2016). *Technology Challenging Poverty, Make the Link: Final Review of the EC Funded Project 'Non-State Actors and Local Authorities in Development: Global Learning in the Formal Education Systems in UK, Poland, Cyprus and Italy 2013–2016'*. Angela Daly, LJMU/Practical Action.

European Commission. (2005). *EuropeAid Evaluation Guidelines*. Paris: European Commission.

Fricke, H-J. and Gathercole, C. (2015). *Monitoring Education for Global Citizenship: A Contribution to Debate*. DEEP/Concord.

O'Donnell, M. (2016). *Publishing Results to IATI: Will It Improve Learning and Accountability? A Discussion Paper*. London: Bond.

Practical Action. (2013). *Global Learning in the Science National Curricula*. Available at: <http://practicalaction.org/globallearninginscience>

Scientix. (2014). *3rd Round of the Scientix Resource Awards Announced*. Make the Link. Available at: www.scientix.eu/news/news-all/news-detail?articleId=274674

Seeley, C. (2014). Using science and much more to 'Beat the Flood', *Primary Science*, 132.

16 Evaluating an International Approach Within Teacher Education to the Refugee Crisis

Chris Keelan, Jacqueline Neve and David Vernon

Introduction

This chapter investigates an international approach within teacher education to the refugee crisis. The study was undertaken by teacher educators at Liverpool Hope University (LHU) and the University of Cologne, alongside teachers and student teachers as well as colleagues working with refugees beyond the classroom environment. Five student teachers from LHU took part in the project as part of the Wider Perspectives programme, a compulsory, assessed module of their teacher education course looking at global educational issues. After providing an initial overview of key aspects of the project, this chapter will reflect upon: the connections between the student teachers' teacher education and their wider experiences; the impact of the project on the student teacher confidence, ability and motivation to teach; the value of international experience in enabling student teachers to engage with global issues; and the impact of the project on the teacher education curriculum and whether this might be adapted in light of the project's findings. We will seek to demonstrate that the project had a significant impact on all of the above and reflect upon ways in which the issues raised by the project may be carried forward and pursued in subsequent iterations of this work.

Background and Project Overview

This project was a two-phase international study of best practices in teaching and working with refugee children in Liverpool (phase 1) and Cologne (phase 2) as part of the Liverpool Hope University Wider Perspectives programme. In reflecting upon practices in refugee education in the two countries, a fundamental aim was to consider the extent to which student teachers are able to make connections between course content and their experiences beyond the university: in their role as young teachers in UK schools, as interested observers in German schools and as active agents in shaping societal change in modern Britain. Another key aim was to demonstrate the impact of the project on student teachers in terms of their confidence, knowledge and motivation to teach. Knowledge should be seen here as "not at all neutral or static, but a fluid, constantly changing phenomenon, shaped in the ideological, political and economic spheres of society" (Jackson and Conteh, 2008, pp. 265–280).

We also sought to consider how the student teachers' experiences gained over the course of the project might lead to adjustments to the future course content for the Wider Perspectives programme and for the undergraduate teacher education programme in general to enable more student teachers to benefit from the insights gained on this project. An overarching aim was to consider the extent to which the student teachers were able to develop an understanding of global issues by working at a local level and to explore the value of international experience in engaging student teachers with global issues. We sought to explore whether a combination of local and international experience might help towards providing a model of best practice for engaging student teachers with global issues.

The project sought to provide an educational response to the refugee crisis. The approach was in keeping with the belief that "exposure to issues of social injustice in a global context, such as child poverty, climate change, Fairtrade and the plight of refugees, alongside a period of community engagement, can impact upon who the future educator is as a person" (Bamber and Bullivant, 2016, p. 126). In 2016 there were 38,500 new asylum applications in the UK and 722,400 in Germany and in 2017 an estimated 33,500 in the UK and 198,300 in Germany. In UK primary schools, 21.2% of children are exposed to a language known or believed to be other than English in their home. This is an increase of 0.6 percentage points since January 2017, and the figure has been steadily rising since 2006. In secondary schools, 16.6% of young people are exposed to a non-English language in their home. This rate has also steadily increased over the last ten years and by 0.4 percentage points since January 2017. The 2015 PISA study found that 61% of fifteen-year-old students tested in Germany spoke German at home. Beginning teachers in both countries will continue to need skills in working with children who speak English and German as additional languages, as well as the knowledge and skills required to support children with an array of complex issues related to the refugee crisis.

The project enabled the student teachers to work with refugee children in a Liverpool primary school before travelling to Cologne to see how teachers work and interact with refugee students in both primary and secondary settings. The student teachers were subsequently invited to reflect upon the impact of the project from a number of perspectives: (1) local and global perspectives—how they viewed the refugee crisis, having engaged with the issue at a local level and to what extent their perspective evolved after the international experience; (2) knowledge and skills impact—what the student teachers learned about how the refugee crisis has impacted upon both refugees and the general population in Liverpool and what they discovered about the issue from an international perspective; what pastoral and pedagogical (language teaching) skills the student teachers acquired from their local and international project experience; (3) affective and attitudinal development—the extent to which the two phases of the project inspired the student teachers to tackle the issues of the refugee crisis in the classroom and the extent to which the project reinforced their decision to become teachers. The student teachers were able to consider these perspectives in their final presentation, which forms a compulsory part of the Wider Perspectives programme.

Making Connections between the Students' Teacher Training Course and Their Wider Experiences

This section will reflect upon the extent to which student teachers are able to make connections between course content and their experiences beyond the university. In the first phase of the project, the student teachers attended a primary school in the Liverpool area to meet teaching staff, support staff and young people to learn how the school organises the induction and subsequent educational development and pastoral care of its refugee children. The student teachers worked with three Year 6 children, who have come to the UK from Syria within the last two years, and a classmate who acted as their 'buddy'. The three refugee children had experienced traumatic events in their home country. In their interactions with these children, the student teachers were able to rely on the support of the children's class teacher but also to draw on prior learning from some of the key areas of the Wider Perspectives teaching module, including: Philosophy for Children training, a teaching approach which promotes critical, caring and collaborative learning; the Rights and Responsibilities theme, which encourages teachers to address wider issues connecting the local and global experience of children's lives; Working with Diversity, exploring how life in modern Britain impacts upon the lives of children and how young teachers might respond; their experience of Character Education and Personal, Social and Health Education (PSHE).

In her impact statement one student teacher, Katelin, makes explicit links between her university sessions and her experience on the project, reflecting on how meeting the refugee children and listening to their stories brought her prior training to life: "Through this project I have also been able to see the significance of discussing social, moral and global issues within the classroom through programmes such as Spiritual, Moral, Social and Cultural Development (SMSC)/PHSE and Philosophy for Children". Another student teacher, Megan, experienced an affirmation of her university-based Philosophy for Children training in the school-based practice: "The school talked to us about the relevant agendas that have helped them, they praised the use of P4C and showed us the social, emotional and moral progression the refugee children have had from using it". Within the group of student teachers as a whole, there was nonetheless a sense of palpable shock at the reality of the refugee experience and at the reserves of resilience—a key quality targeted in Character Education programmes—evidenced by the children. The matter of fact way in which the children spoke of their homes being bombed and their subsequent displacement and the profound effect this had on the student teachers would suggest that still greater engagement with such projects might better prepare young student teachers to engage with difficult global issues in their classrooms.

The student teachers felt that they had learned an important lesson from the children about resilience. The research on the experiences of young refugee children offered an opportunity for the student teachers to reflect on their own current and future practice, which is in keeping with the assertion that action research "engenders powerful learning for participants through combining research through reflection on practice" (Somekh, 2006, p. 9).

The student teachers also articulated the view that their training had, to some extent, prepared them for their discussions with refugee children but that still more engagement with the issue prior to the project would have been beneficial. Experienced teachers in Cologne also related hearing very distressing accounts of events in Syria from the children in their schools, having had little or no training on how to respond in these situations.

The student teachers undergo training on how to teach young people with English as Additional Language (EAL), focussing on the importance of a thorough school induction programme, EAL pedagogy and assessment. However, another student teacher, Gemma, highlighted the need for more university and school-based inputs on EAL pedagogy: "Prior to this project, I already had an insight into EAL learning due to Modern Foreign Languages being my specialism, but I had very little practical experience of delivering such teaching. I had some understanding of what was expected when teaching refugee children but was unsure of the direct approaches to use, especially to accommodate the emotional aspect". At the Liverpool primary school, the student teachers were able to see how the school assesses and meets the diverse language needs of its refugee children; how it forges positive relationships with parents and guardians; how it provides the children with a safe space to discuss pre-migration, trans-migration and post-migration aspects of the refugee experience (Hamilton and Moore, 2004); and how the whole-school ethos supports the children in adapting to their new surroundings as quickly as possible. However, due to time constraints, the student teachers were not able to observe this good EAL teaching in school, and the university-based EAL coordinator has expressed the desirability of inviting schools to bring

EAL children into university with their experienced EAL teacher so that student teachers can observe outstanding practice at first hand.

Impact on Student Teacher Confidence, Ability and Motivation to Teach

With regard to confidence, the opportunity to hear the children's testimonies, to question them about their experiences and to engage with their teachers made the students feel better placed to address sensitive issues in their own classrooms in the future. Beyond the classroom, the student teachers also visited Liverpool World Centre, a local Development Education Centre, to gain a broader perspective on refugees in the city. Merseyside Police facilitated a meeting with a victim of hate crime. These broader experiences left the student teachers feeling more able and motivated to provide factual counter-narratives to the more contentious explanations of events their students sometimes hear in the volatile atmosphere engendered by the ongoing Brexit debate. Conversations with colleagues and children in Cologne about the challenges faced by refugees mirrored the experiences related by teachers and young people in Liverpool, emphasising the global nature of the issues. This served to remind the student teachers of the vital importance of their pastoral role as a primary teacher and to reinforce their own motivation to make a difference. This is of particular importance given Morrison's contention that learning about global issues may be a significant factor in retaining teachers, particularly amongst those recently qualified. It provides a compelling incentive to incorporate this perspective, especially when the number of entrants to the profession in the UK is falling and those leaving is at an all-time high (Morrison, 2015).

The student teachers saw value in ensuring that the children, both in Liverpool and Cologne, were collaborative partners in the project, so that the Liverpool-based children were empowered to tell their own stories and the Cologne-based children assumed the role of teacher in sharing their Arabic skills with the student teachers. This is in keeping with the view that the research relationship should be neither research 'on', nor research 'for' the young people, but research 'with' the young people, which is the only kind of relationship which can lead to empowerment (Cameron et al., 1992).

In terms of language pedagogy, the student teachers were able to observe a very experienced and committed practitioner in action in a Cologne secondary school (phase 2). The student teachers remarked on the refreshingly low-tech approach to vocabulary building and felt confident and motivated to replicate these ideas in their own classrooms: "A change the trip has had on me is that I am going to try not to overthink and complicate my lessons by using fancy resources when teaching; sometimes the most simple resources are the most effective" (Kathryn).

Likewise, Gemma highlighted how the trip to Germany bolstered her confidence to teach, reinforcing her enthusiasm to teach language in particular:

> This project as a whole, and especially the trip to Germany, has had a great impact on me by confirming how much I am passionate about language learning and how I have now a better understanding of the wider educational issue of refugees. I feel more confident for the future to be able to work with EAL and refugee children and have a better understanding of how to support those children within my classroom.

Impact on Teacher Education Curriculum

How might the student teachers' experience in this project impact upon future iterations of the Wider Perspectives programme and on the teacher training at Liverpool Hope in general? In the future, and despite the current uncertainty over Brexit, colleagues in both Liverpool and Cologne remain determined to facilitate similar projects. There is also the possibility of broadening the refugee project to include other European countries. Still, the number of student teachers participating in the project is relatively small and we might consider how to broaden its reach, perhaps by exploiting multi-media (e.g. Skype) to facilitate dialogue about the refugee crisis across national boundaries. In Cologne the student teachers learned about the work of Prompt!, an organisation which trains student teachers to work with refugee children both in and out of school. However, time constraints meant that they were not able to work directly with their German counterparts involved in this programme. Again, a Skype exchange between British and German students might help to deepen our student teachers' understanding of international approaches to this issue. There has also been some discussion around incorporating a refugee strand into the wider EAL programme at undergraduate level. We might also provide opportunities for project participants to pass on their newly acquired expertise to their peers and to upcoming students intending to take part in Wider Perspectives projects.

The Value of International Experience in Enabling Student Teachers to Engage With Global Issues

Barr (2005) proposes that structured opportunities such as international exchanges and linking programmes are particularly successful in changing attitudes amongst teacher educators and their students to global education. Whereas Bamber and Bullivant (2016, p. 127) assert that "a genuine worldwide horizon must be grounded in a concern for the local as much as the global and *does not demand international experience*" (our italics).

Certainly, the student teachers commented on the rich opportunities for engaging with global issues at a local level. Gemma spoke passionately of the impact of her experience at the local primary school: "We learnt so much in such a short space of time from the school and the refugee children themselves. It was great to see the whole-school approach that the school had to a welcoming and inclusive atmosphere. Whilst we were there, we met four refugee boys who openly told us their story. This was an eye-opening experience and was very moving to see how calm they were with sharing their experiences". Gemma also felt that the opportunity to engage with local agencies outside the classroom was beneficial in deepening her knowledge and understanding of the issues: "The visit to World Centre then impacted on my own understanding of refugees. Prior to this project, I had a basic understanding of what a refugee was and was not fully aware of the distinction between a refugee or asylum seeker. I wasn't aware of the extent of the application process and the required documentation that is needed to complete the application. It was interesting to see how this, and other organisations support refugees, asylum-seekers and the destitute in Liverpool".

Gemma also considered that the time spent in Cologne helped her to reflect upon the contrast in learning environments, a somewhat different approach to pedagogy and the adjustments she might make to her own teaching as a result: "I found the English and German schools to be noticeably different. I was aware of the difference in the structure of a school day but to experience it first hand was interesting and quite eye-opening as a teacher. There is a much more relaxed approach to school life, assessment and way of teaching in general. This was a different environment to the one we are used to in Liverpool. We saw many strategies which were simple but effective for language learning and how easily adaptable they were to any class. We saw the approaches that the teachers used when working with the refugee children which impacted how we needed to adapt our style of teaching when doing the short inputs during our trip".

Similarly, Kathryn felt that the Cologne visit was instrumental in helping her to reflect on her own practice: "For me the trip to Cologne was crucial to completely understand and compare the refugee situation in the United Kingdom and Germany. Going forward from the trip, I have a better understanding of how to teach refugee children and different teaching strategies I could use in the classroom". Perhaps in moving away from a familiar local teaching environment and looking at different approaches in an international context, student teachers are more able to reflect on their own practice. In reflecting upon the language learner's interactions with home and target culture, Kramsch (1993) considers the need to identify a 'third space': "At the intersection of multiple native and target cultures, the major task of language learners is to define for themselves what this 'third place' that they have engaged in seeking will look like, whether they are conscious of it or not" (p. 233). This notion of the need for a 'third space' may equally apply to the student teachers investigating their responses to the refugee crisis on a local and international level.

Katelin found herself surprised by the impact her input had on refugee children in such a short period of time and was reminded of the broader role of a teacher in promoting children's development: "Before going on the trip, I did not expect to have any significant impact on the children's learning as I would only be there working with the children for two days. However, when reflecting it was clear to see that we were able to have a huge influence on those children. They didn't only come away from the sessions with more language, but the children were also able to grow in confidence with our help. Before visiting the children, we were told that the children were highly sensitive, and many had additional needs, and by the time we left on Tuesday the children were able to present a 10 minute lesson to the rest of the class in their home language. This reiterated the fact that teachers are no longer there to educate the children to pass tests but to educate and support the whole child".

Maeve identified how first-hand experience boosted her confidence to teach children with EAL: "We probably could have found information online about it, but experiencing it for yourself and being able to ask the relevant questions is something that you can't really achieve online and it's an experience that will stay with us especially when we have our own classes, which are likely to include EAL learners and possibly refugees". The students' overall impressions of the experience were perhaps most powerfully encapsulated by Katelin, whose concluding words indicate a highly developed sense of empathy:

> The project as a whole has helped me become a well-rounded teacher as I am now more aware of the additional needs that could arise in children in our future classrooms and what support needs to be put in place to allow these children to settle in and progress as quickly as possible. It has also given us an insight into the struggles of refugees which allow us to have greater understanding of the children and their needs as well as the struggles their families might be facing. Meeting the children from the Liverpool was a reminder that refugees are not just numbers that you hear about in the media, but real people, all with their own journey and with their own story to tell. The stories that the children told were harrowing and it resonated with me that these children have been through some extraordinary things in their lives and it is our job to ensure that they are supported.

In actively listening to what the children had to say, the student teachers demonstrated an interest in and respect for the wealth of knowledge and unique identities before them and reflected upon their own identities as teachers. The student teachers' encounters with the young people in both Liverpool and Cologne enabled them to fulfil the requirement that in order to access the diverse funds of knowledge in their classrooms, teachers need to become researchers of their own students, of their own practices and of themselves (González et al., 2005).

Conclusion and Next Steps

With regard to impact on the student teachers in terms of *making connections between the teacher training course and wider experiences*, the student teachers made explicit reference to aspects of the course that took on greater meaning or 'came to life' as a result of the project. This is true for instance, of the Philosophy for Children strand of their training course, which they saw in action at the Liverpool-based primary school in phase one; the Rights and Responsibilities themes, which the student teachers saw as very relevant to their work with refugee children; as well as issues explored in the PSHE and Character Education and Working with Diversity topics. The project helped the student teachers to see the Wider Perspectives programme as highly relevant to their overall training and instrumental in developing a broader view of education and promoting a real enthusiasm for teaching and a determination to be successful.

The *impact on student teacher confidence, ability and motivation to teach* emerged as a crucial theme in the project given the ongoing problems identified in teacher recruitment and retention in both the UK and Germany. The student teachers felt that the project gave them a clearer sense of the purpose of education, including the moral purpose, and a stronger sense of their role. The student teachers highlighted all of these aspects as heightening their motivation to enter the teaching profession. One student offered the opinion that the group had worked so hard on the project because the project content was intrinsically motivating.

In reflecting upon the *possible impact of the project on the Wider Perspectives programme* and the broader teacher training curriculum, student teachers noted that "their training had, to some extent, prepared them for their discussions with refugee children but that still more engagement with the issue prior to the project would have been beneficial". The issue of what constitutes sufficient preparation for dealing with sensitive issues was also highlighted by more experienced teachers in Cologne and raises a question about how to devote more time to preparation for this within the Wider Perspectives programme. One option might be to focus more on relevant approaches and methods, including the Philosophy for Children inputs highlighted by the student teachers, for exploring sensitive and controversial issues within their training. One of the most inspiring aspects of the project was the opportunity it provided for the student teachers to witness student voice in action, suggesting this aspect of the project should be emphasised in future iterations of the programme.

The project's role in articulating the *value of international experience in enabling the student teachers to engage with global issues* is linked to the confidence aspect and to the student teacher perception that they were now equipped with the skills, knowledge and understanding to tackle these issues within their own practice with sensitivity. The student teachers felt that the experience as a whole challenged their prior values and beliefs and, in one case, even left a student teacher feeling more 'politicised'. The impact of local experience, both in the primary school and through engaging with wider organisations, seems to have been significant. This supports the contention that fostering a global outlook is not necessarily dependent on international experience, although the international aspect does seem to have played a role in reinforcing and developing some of the ideas explored at first at a local level. In discussions with German colleagues, the student teachers were able to reflect upon two approaches to the refugee crisis that were very different. In 2016, the German government adopted an approach to the refugee crisis that was, initially at least, very open and welcoming. This meant that there were considerably more refugee children in Cologne schools. In contrast, the approach adopted by the British government has been criticised in some quarters as fuelling an anti-immigrant discourse. The student teachers were also able to reflect upon the British values approach as it is perceived in Germany: colleagues there recognised the underlying aim of promoting tolerance but expressed bewilderment about values they saw as universal values being described as specifically British. Such reflections are important given the expectation that teachers promote British values in their interactions with children in schools.

At both local and international levels, good collaboration between university, schools and wider agencies leads to the most beneficial experience for the student teachers. Local and international projects can result in changing dispositions towards the role of education in addressing global issues by providing the student teachers with the opportunity to compare different approaches. However, fostering such change is a long-term process and it may be helpful to revisit these issues with the student teachers at a later date.

Britain and Germany, and indeed Europe as a whole, continue to face significant challenges relating to the ongoing refugee crisis and these will be reflected in schools in Liverpool and Cologne. For this reason, we will repeat the project with a new cohort of students to test some of the conclusions reached in its first iteration and to see if we can modify the project to deepen our understanding of the issues. In the Liverpool phase of the project, the intention is to repeat the student voice opportunity with refugee children, but also to focus more deeply on pedagogy, with the student teachers observing the class teacher working closely with EAL children. Beyond the classroom, we also intend to visit the Liverpool World Centre again to learn about the broader issues affecting families with a refugee background. We have also recently established links with Liverpool City Council colleagues who have a particular brief of sensitising council employees to the specific needs and challenges facing refugee families, and we intend to invite them into the university to share their expertise with the student teachers working on the project. In Cologne, we plan to visit both primary and secondary schools again, but also to learn more about broader approaches to supporting refugees in the wider community with research into university-linked organisations such as Prompt!, which trains students to provide language tuition and other forms of support to refugee families. We intend to review whether international experience is required to engage student teachers with global issues or whether the same effect can be achieved at a local level. We will sharpen our focus on what the two cities can learn from each other and how this impacts on the knowledge and skills of our student teachers, their confidence and motivation to teach our children about global issues, and their broader commitment to enter the profession in the challenging times ahead.

References

Bamber, P. and Bullivant, A. (2016). Partnership and teacher formation for global social justice. In: *Teacher Education in Challenging Times*, 126–136. Routledge, London.

Barr, I. (2005). *In the Situation of Others. The Final Evaluation Report on the Department for International Development's Initiative on Embedding the Global Dimension in Initial Teacher Education in the UK 2001–2005*. Unpublished report.

Cameron, D., Frazer, E., Harvey, P., Rampton, M. B. H. and Richardson, K. (1992). *Researching Language: Issues of Power and Method*. Routledge: London.

González, N., Moll, L. C. and Amanti, C. (2005). *Funds of Knowledge: Theorizing Practices in Households, Communities, and Classrooms*. Mahwah, NJ: Lawrence Erlbaum Associates.

Hamilton, R. and Moore, D. (2004). *Educational Interventions for Refugee Children*. Routledge: New York.

Jackson, A. and Conteh., J. (2008). Different ways of seeing: A socio-cultural approach to global education through art. *Education 3–13*, 36(3), pp. 265–280.

Kramsch, C. (1993). *Context and Culture in Language Teaching*. Oxford: Oxford University Press.

Morrison, N. (2015). Number of Teachers Quitting the Classroom Reaches 10 Year High. *TES*, 30 January. Available at: <https://news.tes.co.uk/b/news/2015/01/29/number-of-teachers-quitting-the-classroom-reaches-10-year-high.aspx>. Accessed 15 October 2015.

Somekh, B. (2006). *Action Research: A Methodology for Change and Development*. New York: Open University Press.

17 Measuring Teachers' Impact on Young Peoples' Attitudes and Actions as Global Citizens

Barbara Lowe and Liz Allum

Introduction

This chapter reports upon a European Union (EU) funded project that aimed to improve the quality of global citizenship education (GCE) taking place in schools across five countries and to increase the number of teachers actively engaging with GCE through creating and testing methodologies for measuring impact on attitudes and values. The project builds upon over ten years of work by Reading International Solidarity Centre (RISC), a UK Development Education Centre (DEC), supporting teachers to identify which of their teaching interventions have the greatest positive impact on young peoples' attitudes and actions.

The EU project was led by RISC with important roles taken by key European partners: People in Need in the Czech Republic, and the Milan Simecka Foundation in Slovakia. This work involved other DECs across London and the South-East of England including Brighton Peace and Environment Centre, 18 Hours, Centre for Global Awareness, World Education Group, EDJI, Humanities Education Centre, and Commonwork. Other participating Civil Society Organisations included Galway One World Centre in Ireland, People in Need in Ethiopia, alongside twenty-one teacher training institutions in UK, Czech Republic, Slovakia, Ireland and Ethiopia.

The Project Aims

The project began with RISC working alongside a group of six 'Global Schools' that had committed to achieving and sustaining whole school change through embedding GCE. This involved audit activities, joint curriculum planning, development of a training programme, identification of good practice and appropriate resources to enhance GCE in each setting.

RISC, as the external provider, assumed the role of 'critical friend' (Critchley and Unwin, 2008). In return, schools committed themselves to prioritising GCE in their school policies and plans for schools' improvement, participating fully in the training programme, promoting the initiative throughout the school community, and developing and disseminating good practice in the delivery of GCE.

The 'Global Schools' initiative required the development of a methodology addressing three key questions (QCA, 2007):

1. What are you trying to achieve?
2. How will you organise learning?
3. How well are you achieving your aims?

Given GCE may increase knowledge without changing attitudes (i.e. increasing understanding of diversity, a more balanced view of people and places, and awareness of how we can make a difference), it was necessary to devise a method of evaluating the impact of GCE (Lowe, 2008) upon attitudes.

The methodology deployed here was first developed by RISC with funding from the UK Department for International Development and published as *How do we know it's working? A toolkit for measuring attitudinal change from early years to KS5* (Allum et al., 2008). It has proved to be a popular and invaluable tool in enabling teachers to assess the impact of their teaching on young peoples' GC attitudes and actions (Bamber et al., 2013). When used alongside its sister publication, *Are we nearly there? A self-evaluation framework for Global Citizenship* (Allum et al., 2010), it supports schools in achieving and sustaining whole-school change. A senior advisor for a large local education authority in England commented: "*It responds to the challenge of measuring what is valuable, rather than valuing what is measurable*".

The EU project explored here developed the methodology further to ensure its applicability to a range of curricula and contexts across the five countries participating in this project. This drew upon the expertise of hundreds of teachers, who created and trialled new activities to evaluate GCE in their classrooms. The case studies in this chapter describe the process of teachers using a series of activities to audit young peoples' attitudes towards human rights, diversity, interdependence, sustainability, peace and conflict. These key concepts of GCE appear in multiple guidance documents on Global Learning and GCE, most recently updated in Oxfam's *Education for Global Citizenship: a guide for schools* (Oxfam, 2015). The case studies illustrate how evaluating students' attitudes in relation to these key concepts can inform the development of GCE learning objectives for future teaching. The chapter describes how revisiting audit activities following teaching interventions influences teachers' future plans in relation to GCE.

The Role of Attitudes in GCE

> *While motivation is explored in teacher training, the shaping and tracking of [young peoples'] attitudes is often overlooked. [Young people] may*

> *be motivated to act in a certain way, without a teacher understanding or questioning the attitudes underlying their behaviour. Exploring how [young people] think about the world around them enables teachers to develop their understanding of [young peoples'] attitudes and the impact their teaching has as these attitudes develop.*
>
> Allum, Lowe and Robinson (2015)

Where GCE is delivered in schools the aim is often to improve knowledge, skills, values and attitudes. Knowledge, whilst often the focus of initiatives such as the recent Global Learning Programme across the UK (Huckle, 2017), cannot be delivered in isolation from values and attitudes. Arguably, as Oxfam's *Guidance for Global Citizenship* (2015) recognises, teaching skills and attitudes are part of the way in which knowledge is delivered. However, there is little that supports teachers in measuring impact on attitudes and values. In UK schools, success is often measured by the numbers of lessons taught that contain any qualifying global content, or numbers of teachers engaged in a project, rather than on the attitudinal or behaviour change amongst young people (Pibilova, 2016). This chapter provides a response to concerns that global learning research and evaluation of global education interventions tend "*to focus upon short-term, observable outcomes rather than longer-term changes in behaviour, attitude, and practice*" (Bamber et al., 2013, p. 5).

Rather than short-term learning outcomes, the methodology deployed here assesses the impact on behaviour by considering actions alongside values and attitudes. As Bliss (2005) notes, challenging and shaping values are inherently linked, and therefore the teaching of particular values is also an integrated process "*often requiring 'mindset changes' in moving students beyond thinking and feeling to acting*". Values and attitudes therefore play a significant role in translating the aspirations of GCE to practice yet to date have not been a focus for research and evaluation in this field (Storrs, 2010; Bamber et al., 2013). The challenges of measuring values and attitudinal change is well documented; for instance, "*similar attitudes can be based on different values, the same value can be at the basis of different attitudes. Apparently similar actions can also be associated with different values and attitudes*" (Allum et al., 2008, p. 6). RISC's methodology engages with the "hard-to-grasp" objects of knowledge usually unmonitored, but more it "*engages the very complex inter-relations existing between values, attitudes and action*" (Royant, 2017, p. 154). Indeed, "*what we do know is that attitudes inform our behaviour and the broader and more balanced our information is, the more flexible and open our attitudes and views tend to be*" (Allum et al., 2015, p. 9).

A recurring educational debate considers whether teachers should intentionally influence young peoples' attitudes or instead remain 'neutral' in the classroom. This debate surfaced in this EU project regarding controversial or political issues, with concerns raised that external agencies were indoctrinating, setting a potentially unknown 'agenda'. This is summarised in a 'Mid-Term Evaluation report' of the project:

> *[Civil Society Organisations] thought that they should have impact on [young peoples'] knowledge, skills and attitudes/values. According to the project partners, some teachers shared this opinion, while others were less comfortable with this idea. Especially student teachers in the UK and the Czech Republic reportedly preferred to be 'neutral'.*
> (Pibilova, 2016, p. 9)

As part of the evaluation process, participants at Milan Simecka Foundation's national education conference were therefore asked: should teachers only measure attitudes or aim to actively influence them? Three responses from different teachers further illuminate this issue:

> *School is not a sterile environment and [young people] are directly or indirectly influenced by the behaviour of teachers, presentation of their own attitudes and opinions. It is not possible to separate 'measuring' from 'affecting' and 'changing'.*
>
> Changing attitudes of [young people] is an indispensable part of the education process. It is and will be happening no matter what methods teachers apply. It is thus important they know how to work with attitudes and values of [young people]. And measuring them is the first step.
>
> It is controversial and disputable but by measuring only, teachers would take the role of statisticians. I take this project as a big challenge which opens up a public discussion on the role of schools.

We would argue that these responses highlight the need to openly continue this discussion. GCE is never value-neutral or apolitical. Furthermore, "*practitioners must be completely transparent and acknowledge that they are working to promote particular values*" (Bamber, 2016, p. 186). The final independent impact evaluation (Pibilova, 2016) found that most teachers, civil society organisations and tutors in initial teaching training institutions were in agreement that educators should have a clear impact on young peoples' attitudes as well as knowledge. Interestingly, student teachers were again more hesitant to agree, many believing that teachers should instead remain 'neutral' in the classroom. It is therefore not surprising that evidence suggests (Royant, 2017) tutors in initial teaching training institutions value the role of an external agency advocating GCE with their student teachers, as undertaken as part of this particular project:

> *[RISC] challenges beginning teachers to re-examine their prejudices, to make visible their unconscious bias, to raise questions about equity, about poverty, about the way the planet and the world work, or not. And take the trainee teachers to places both literally and metaphorically that need to be explored because young people in their classrooms need to be engaged in those questions as well.*
>
> (Royant, 2017, p. 148)

The Project

At the outset of the project, a review of the pilot *How do we know it's working?* toolkit (Allum et al., 2008) indicated that while some of the activities exploring stereotypes of Africa and those identifying similarities and differences between children in a photograph were virtually unchanged in each partner country, others had a much more localised appeal. For instance, *Who will have which job?*, an activity that asks participants to match children with a range of jobs, exploring stereotypes around race, gender and disability, was popular in the UK but considered too controversial by respondents in the Czech Republic, so adaptations were made and variations created and trialled.

Each of the participating organisations in the United Kingdom, Czech Republic, Slovakia, Ireland and Ethiopia established a teachers' working group to create, discuss and trial new activities; these working groups met termly and were formed of teachers from nursery, primary and secondary schools from each context. Ideas and findings were shared through a single online forum used across the project.

In parallel to this activity in schools, opportunities were identified to embed the audit methodology within initial teacher training. While opportunities for student teachers to trial the activities on their school experience were limited, due to the time constraints of university-based teacher training, there were some student teachers on school-based training programmes that had greater capacity to trial activities and provide feedback, with their regular access to students.

Through this process, more than forty new audit activities were developed, at least five for each of the GCE key concepts: human rights, diversity, interdependence, sustainability, peace and conflict. This chapter will now detail case studies of four audit activities used across the project. Each of these activities is designed to be used as a baseline, and with minor amendments, repeated after the end of a curriculum intervention—ideally six to twelve months later to assess impact, as per the process illustrated in Figure 17.1. The case studies include examples of the data collected in particular instances, to help illuminate the methodology undertaken.

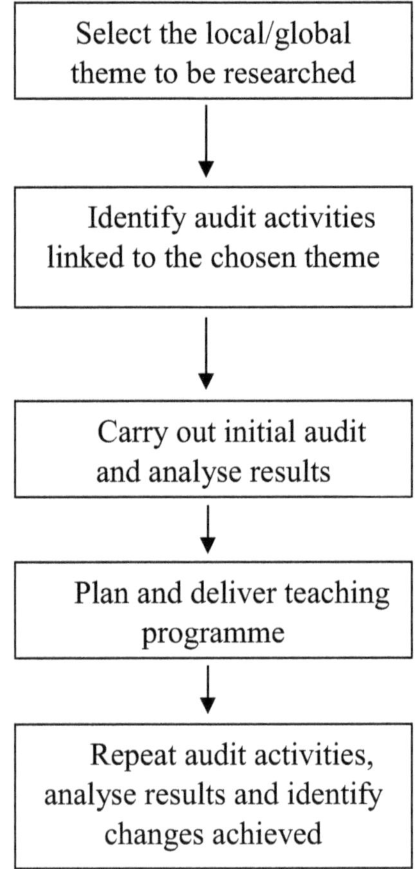

Figure 17.1 Recommended process for evaluation leading to change

Case Study 1: What Makes a Good Community?

The aim of the activity is to find out:

- what children consider to be important for the life of a community;
- the extent to which they take into account the needs of others;
- their awareness of the impact of their choices on people and the environment, locally and globally;
- their understanding of the importance of participation and action.

The children are asked to 'Imagine a new town is going to be built nearby, and the people building it want to know what *you* think it should be like'. They are shown captioned photos grouped by theme, e.g. Housing, Schools or Trade, one theme at a time, three photos per theme. Within each theme they vote for what they would prioritise in the new town.

A straightforward comparison is made of the number of times each image is prioritised within each theme in the baseline audit and in the follow-up. The children's voice, justifications and discussions are also noted which enables comparison of their understanding and insight into their attitudes.

The theme of 'Housing' offers young people choices of 'expensive houses', 'houses everyone can afford' and 'a hostel for the homeless' (see Figure 17.2). In a peri-urban school serving an affluent area in South-East England, a group of year 4 students, aged eight to nine, were found to prioritise homeless shelters over affordable homes and expensive homes. This reflected the pattern of responses across years 2, 4 and 5 in this school with 'expensive houses' receiving 2 votes, 'houses everyone can afford' 53 votes, and 'a hostel for the homeless' 70 votes.

Student voice: "*Houses everyone can afford and a shelter for the homeless—both really*" (year 2).

The theme of 'Schools' offers young people choices of 'a school which welcomes everyone', 'a school with good results', and 'a school with the best resources'. These year 2 students rank schools which welcome everyone above good results and the best resources (see Figure 17.3). This reflects the responses from all 3 year groups in this school, with 'a school which welcomes everyone' receiving 117 votes, 'a school with good results' 19 votes, and 'a school with the best resources' 18 votes.

Student voice: "*If poor people don't have a house and no money the child could go there and do well*" (age nine).

Student voice: "*It's more important to welcome everyone like with disabilities—it's more fair*" (age eight).

Student voice: "*Welcomes everyone because otherwise no one would want to come to the school, more friendly, important to welcome people who are black*" (age nine).

The theme of 'Trade (food and shopping)' offers young people choices of 'local shops', 'big supermarkets' and 'growing your own food' (Figure 17.4). In this student responses were more evenly distributed with 'big supermarkets' receiving 35 votes, 'local shops' receiving 15 votes, and 'growing your own food' 26 votes.

Student voice: "*Supermarkets because there's more to choose from, more fair trade*" (age seven).

Student voice: "*Supermarkets have lots of food, they never run out*" (age seven).

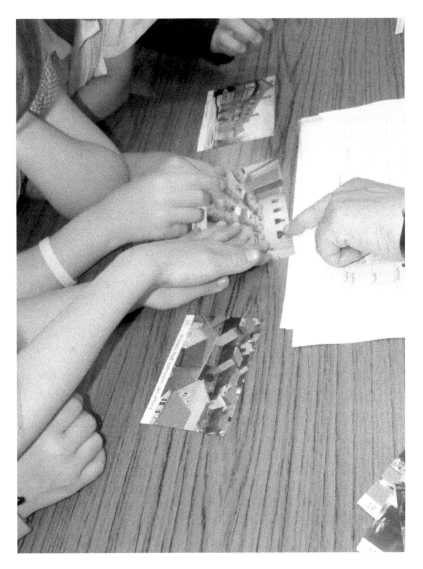

Figure 17.2 Young people explore choices of homes

Student voice: "*You can't grow bananas (here)—or dinners—or spaghetti*" (age seven).

Teachers reviewed responses from these and the remaining themes: transport, healthcare, law and order, democracy (participation), places to go (leisure), energy and waste.

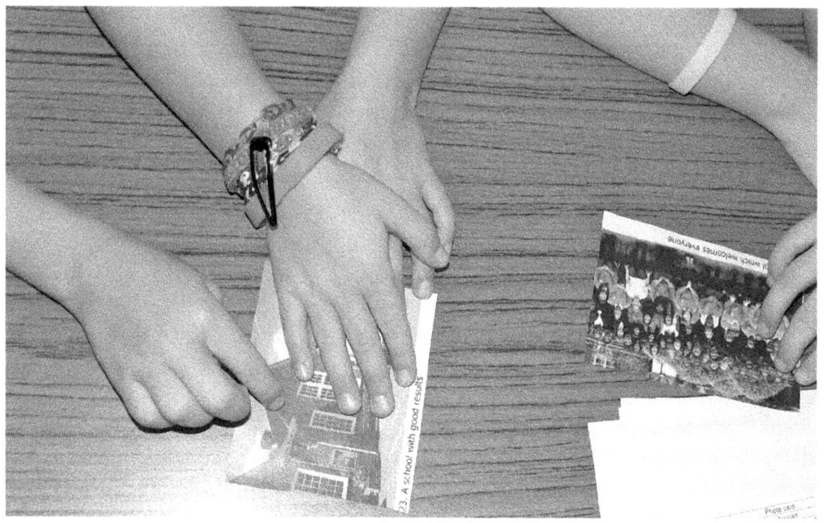

Figure 17.3 Young people explore choices of schools

Figure 17.4 Young people explore choices of trade

Having undertaken this audit in this one particular school, school leaders felt happy that when students were considering schools, homes and transport, they reflected the school's ethos and values of respect, resilience and responsibility; however, the data they collected helped them to decide they needed to create opportunities to develop students' ability to think critically about food production, consumption and waste and its impact on producers, communities and environments.

Case Study 2: How Can I Make the World a Better Place?

The aim of this activity is to explore attitudes and values towards taking action, and whether students are able to see a range of causes and therefore potential solutions to local and global issues. This case study discusses the results of the activity when used by an infant and junior school (students aged five to eleven) who wanted to ensure they were having an impact on students' belief that they could make a difference in the world.

Students were asked 'What can I do to make the world a better place?', and they recorded their ideas on blank paper. Comments are classified into one of four categories: local sustainability, local social justice, global sustainability and global social justice. These categories are not exhaustive, but are intended to give a broad overview. For instance, the following actions were categorised as follows:

- Stop dropping litter in the playground = sustainability + local
- Stop climate change = sustainability + global
- Be kind to your neighbour = social justice + local
- Buy fair trade = social justice + global

Whilst some comments are hard to categorise, especially with very young children, staff decided on criteria and remained consistent in applying it. Student responses can be very broad and open-ended, making it more challenging for teachers to analyse the data.

The data provided below follows the youngest students, who were audited twice, initially when in year 1, aged five to six, and then a year later when in year 2, aged six to seven. The comments below are grouped in topics, rather than verbatim.

The teachers reflected that there was little evidence of students' awareness of actions they might take that would have a global impact and that their responses were heavily focussed on charitable giving. As one teacher commented:

> *We felt this showed the [students] had a good awareness of some of the ways they can act sustainably, and this reflects some of the schools' priorities. However we were disappointed that they had so few ideas about social justice, locally and globally. So we looked for*

Local Sustainability	*Local Social Justice*	*Global Sustainability*	*Global Social Justice*
Pick up litter x12 Be kind to animals and pets x8 Recycle your rubbish x7 Clean up your local area x4 Plant more trees x4 Grow your own food x3 Walk instead of driving x2	Help people x10 Be kind/ friendly x9	Don't kill wild animals x3 Save electricity x3	Give to charity x16
Total: 40	Total: 19	Total: 6	Total: 16

Figure 17.5 Data showing baseline responses from students aged five to six

> *opportunities throughout the year to raise [students'] awareness of injustice and provide them with opportunities to make a difference to people's lives, beyond (but not excluding) raising money for charities.*

Using the Send My Friend to School campaign and focussing on lack of access to education as a cause and consequence of poverty, teachers worked to empower children with knowledge of actions that were possible and to engage them in political processes (Figure 17.6). They invited their local MP to attend a school assembly, and infant school children prepared questions about child poverty and access to education, and about the government's plan for action.

A school-wide set of objectives was agreed, focussing on taking action, celebrating diversity, exploring trade justice and representing different families. This was decided upon by the whole staff, in response to training that highlighted the problems with a charity mentality, sense of pity and a focus on giving aid when talking about Africa and Asia in particular. Staff, with adequate support and space to reflect and discuss, were able to identify the impact that traditional fundraising can have on stereotypes and prejudice. As Simpson (2017) points out, addressing the real causes and consequences of poverty and injustice enables learners to see opportunities for action without reinforcing negative stereotypes.

The follow-up data shows a significant increase in quantity and variety of responses (Figure 17.7). Staff were pleased to observe an increase in students' awareness of homelessness and poverty, and their references to

Figure 17.6 Young people engage in the Send My Friend to School campaign

Local Sustainability	*Local Social Justice*	*Global Sustainability*	*Global Social Justice*
Pick up litter x5 Recycle your rubbish x4 Walk instead of driving x3	Less crime x7 Homes for everyone x3 Share resources equally x2	Don't kill wild animals x10 Save electricity x6	Education for all children x7 Share food more equally around the world x7 Better healthcare x6 Clean water x5 Reduce poverty x5 Fairtrade x1
Total: 12	Total: 12	Total: 16	Total: 31

Figure 17.7 Data showing follow-up responses from students aged six to seven

the right to water, healthcare and education. The students demonstrated a change in their understanding of poverty as a form of injustice, rather than just a lack of money or resources. Most notably, however, was the shift within the global social justice category, highlighting a dramatic change in students' awareness of interdependence and their ability to affect change locally and globally. Their responses have moved from a heavy focus on donating money to charity as the only possible action they can participate in, to an awareness of a range of solutions and needs in addressing a complex situation, as outlined by Simpson in this volume.

Case Study 3: What Would Make the Most Difference?

The aim of the activity is to encourage young people to consider the consequences of their actions and become motivated by injustice to take action. It does this by assessing the extent to which students understand their potential power as consumers and as agents for change, individually or as part of a bigger group. In groups, students are shown a photo of Kenyan flower growers and are asked to rank, in a diamond 9, a series of action statements according to which they believe would make most difference to this situation. They are also asked to indicate, by adding a sticker after their diamond 9 has been constructed, which actions they are most likely to do/have done (Figure 17.8).

Only buy Fairtrade flowers	Flowers shouldn't be flown thousands of miles when pollution from planes damages the environment. So only buy locally grown flowers	Pesticides from flower farms poison the growers and contaminate their water supply – campaign for organic flowers
Convince other people to take action too – tell people at school and at home about the problems in the flower trade	Stop buying flowers	Flowers shouldn't be grown on land where food for local people could be grown. Write to flower companies asking them to stop taking land for growing flowers
What one person buys won't change anything – one person can't make a difference so it's pointless doing anything	People in countries like Kenya, need work. The flower industry provides jobs – so choose imported flowers	Talk to your local shop about stocking Fairtrade flowers

Figure 17.8 The nine action statements

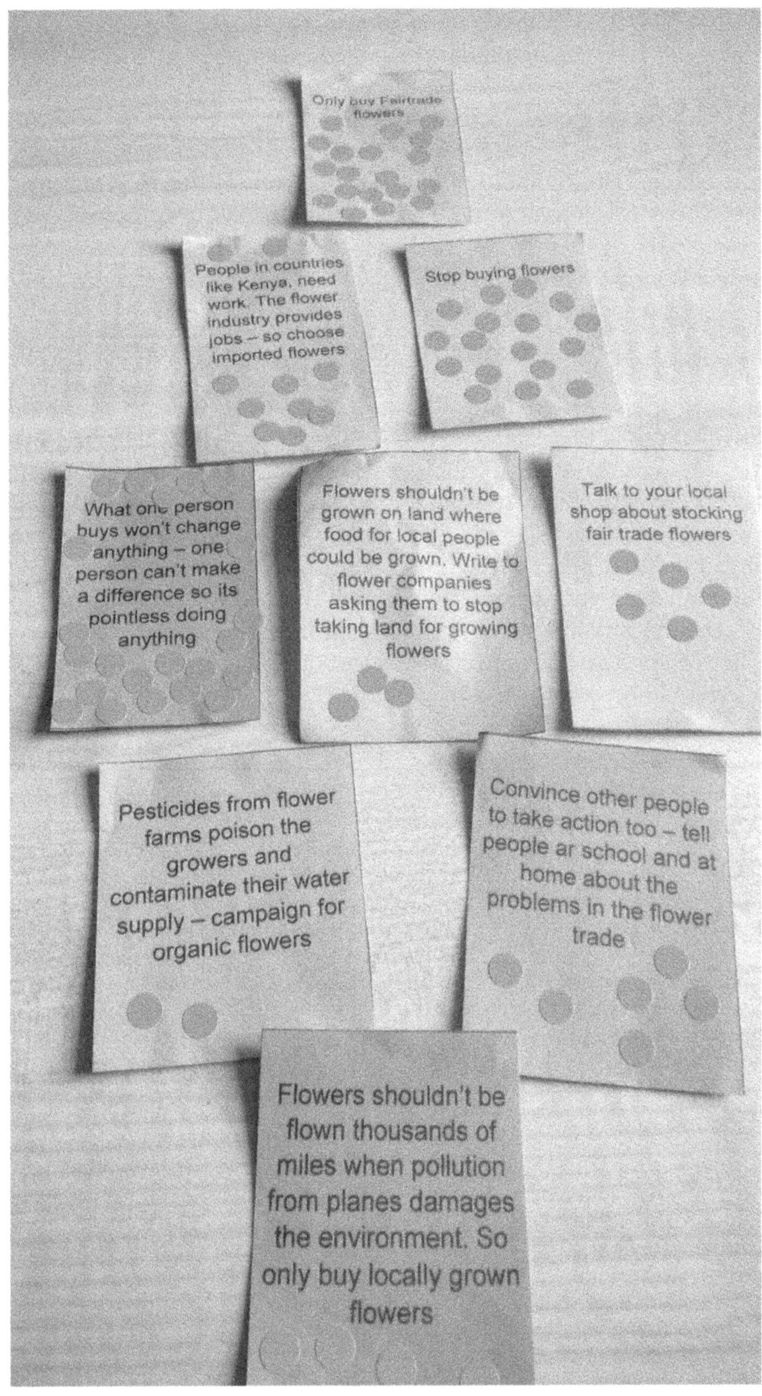

Figure 17.9 Young people use stickers to demonstrate which action they would be most likely to do, or which they have done

The action statement placed at the top of the diamond is given a score of 9, the two in the row below each score 7, the 3 in the middle row each score 5, the cards in the fourth row each score 3, and the card at the bottom of the diamond scores 1.

In a peri-urban secondary school serving a mixed community in West Berkshire, England, Year 8 students, aged twelve to thirteen, ranked buying fair trade flowers highest (scoring 63), with concern and action about the impact on Kenyan food production (14) and on pollution of the Kenyan water supply (15) lowest. When the teachers undertook the analysis they identified that students were "*were more inclined to value actions they could relate to. Most didn't really understand what campaigning was and how they might be involved*".

The teachers involved felt that young peoples' superficial understanding of fair trade should be challenged, their understanding of social justice should be deepened and, critically, that action for change should be explored. As a consequence, as part of their Geography study of globalisation, students researched flower production in Kenya, Colombia and Nicaragua, and campaigners and activists around the world (Figure 17.9). The follow-up activity two weeks later was analysed by the students themselves and compared with the baseline results.

The young people observed that the action statement, "*What one person buys won't change anything—one person can't make a difference so it's pointless doing anything*", had in most cases moved from the top to the bottom part of the diamond, with students agreeing that through working together it is possible to bring about change. The young people also observed that the action statement "*Convince other people to take action too—tell people at school and at home about the problem in the flower trade*" had risen from the bottom to the top part of the diamond. This move was substantiated by the students' decision to organise an assembly before Mothers' Day to raise awareness and suggest alternatives to imported flowers. Another group set-up a petition to the main flower companies, asking them to abide by the Ethical Trading Initiative base code of workers' rights.

The activity enabled students to reflect on their own learning and how it impacted on their attitudes and actions as global citizens. As one participating teacher commented, "*empowering students to reflect on their own learning, how it impacted on their attitudes and what they would or wouldn't be prepared to do was interesting and an area we would aim to develop further*".

Case Study 4: 'Developed' or 'Developing'?

The aim of this final case study is to discover students' preconceptions about the characteristics of developed and developing countries, their understanding of (global) interdependence of the developing and developed world, and their similarities. This discussion draws upon data when this activity was undertaken with fifty-seven student teachers at Hawassa College of Teacher Education in Ethiopia, when it was built into an existing Advanced Civics and Ethical Education course.

The student teachers were asked: Are these features of developed countries, developing countries or both?:

> *use of family planning; supply of electricity; provision of health care service; long distance to school; mothers' employment; unemployment; industrialised economy; homelessness; big cities.*

Following the baseline audit, the intervening programme of study was intended to raise student teachers' awareness of the "*harsh living conditions of people in various parts of the world (not only in developing countries) and understand that the world is not developed and developing, but a single world, the one we are living in*" (Abebe et al., 2014, p. 5). The evaluation concluded that these global citizenship activities exposed stereotypes regarding developing countries, such as the "*conception of developed nations as a paradise for all its inhabitants whereas in the developing nations there is no such thing to mention as a good prospect for betterment and change for good*" (ibid., p. 11). However, the report also found that "*after attending lessons on the topics during the intervention activity, they [participants] changed their minds and came to understand that both developed and developing countries share the positive as well as the negative aspects of the nine issues at hand*" (ibid., p. 11). (See Figure 17.10.)

	These points are features of	*No of respondents (out of 9 groups)*	
		Initial audit	*Final audit*
Unemployment	Developed countries	9	
	Developing countries		9
	Both countries		
Mothers employment outside the home	Developed countries	9	2
	Developing countries		7
	Both countries		
Big cities	Developed countries	9	3
	Developing countries		6
	Both countries		
Industrialised economy	Developed countries	9	3
	Developing countries		6
	Both countries		

Figure 17.10 Responses to characteristics associated with 'developed' or 'developing' countries

Discussion: Impact on Teachers

We asked project participants across the five countries involved about the impact of using this methodology, and found that for many, the focus on measuring attitudes had provided support, insights, inspiration and led to increased confidence to teach GCE:

> *I think I changed the attitudes of [students]. At the same time I took the risk that my own attitudes changed as well. And the change really happened. My [students], me and relations between us have changed. That is why I value this project.*
>
> (Teacher in vocational school in Slovakia)

> *Measuring attitudes and their change had an impact on my teaching. I know better how to define the goals of each lesson and I think more about the characters of my [students].*
>
> (Teacher in primary school in Slovakia)

A significant shift in teachers' and student teachers' perceptions of the importance of attitudinal teaching and the possibility of measuring attitudinal change took place where significant training was involved. For instance, a teacher educator in the Czech Republic concluded, "*Student teachers ask why [do we need] to measure children's attitudes if we see them the whole day [in first 4 grades]. But this is not [right]—I am often surprised [at the findings] too*".

A small number of factors were identified by project participants across all partner countries as significant in challenging their perceptions of the barriers to teaching and measuring GCE. These included the support provided by external agencies such as DECs and other Civil Society Organisations and face-to-face peer support. Project participants greatly valued the opportunity to see the impact on their own students through trialling activities. Schools who used measuring tools to impact on curriculum development, school policies and ethos saw the most significant and lasting changes in student attitudes. This substantiates evidence (Bourn and Hunt, 2011) that barriers to successful GCE delivery and the measuring of impact are often a lack of confidence and a focus on short-term objectives and knowledge in GCE.

An independent impact evaluation at the end of the project (Pibilova, 2016) echoed this observation, finding that most participating teachers, GCE providers and tutors of initial teacher training interviewed were in agreement that educators should have a clear impact on students' attitudes as well as knowledge. Pibilova's (2016) evaluation found that "*while the concept of attitude was often found difficult to grasp by teachers, concrete values, attitudes and behaviours related to social or environmental issues are easy for teachers to build on*". As highlighted earlier, student teachers in particular continued to be more hesitant to agree, believing instead that teachers should remain 'neutral' in the classroom. Indeed, "*specifically in Slovakia, the need to impact students' attitudes was found incidental among teachers*" (Pibilova, 2016, p. 14). The connection between teachers' levels of experience and confidence and their likelihood to implement measuring attitudinal change activities is clearly reflected in her findings.

Conclusion

The impact of the project as a whole has been to create a widely tested set of practical tools for the observation of impact of GCE in schools across five European countries. Changes to GCE activities was most discernible where teachers used data from the methodology to improve curriculum planning with the full support of school leaders. Schools where young people were already familiar with interactive and participatory learning methods fared better at implementing the measuring change activities, but all faced some challenges in recording data and finding time to reassess. A number of strategies were used by schools to encourage 'whole school' approaches that include the collection of multiple data sets. For instance, peers have been involved in collecting data and recording observations, contributing their own thoughts and stimulating wider debates, groups of parents have been recruited and trained to supervise activities, and having observed how students respond to the activities, have become themselves energetic advocates for GCE, both within the school and outside at the school gates.

The strength of this form of GCE evaluation is teachers' active engagement in research: for example, where teachers triangulate chosen activities to improve the consistency of results. For instance, triangulation can involve

> *asking the same sort of question in three different ways—if you are interested in attitudes towards poverty in Africa, you might want to use the activities* What would you see in a country in Africa? Why are people hungry? *or* Who will have which job? *all of which explore attitudes on the same issue, but from different perspectives.*
>
> (Allum, Lowe and Robinson, 2015, p. 10)

Subsequent focus group interviews with teachers (Royant, 2017) evidenced how this methodology developed teachers' reflexivity and their understanding of professionalism. For example, what students say during these activities

> *inform[s] teachers about what they need to do to develop children's and young people's understanding. Re-doing activities inform*

> *educators about the ways in which their interventions have been successful and the ways in which they have not been successful. It constitutes a qualitative evaluation of the ways in which [young peoples'] attitudes have shifted towards being more inclusive, or less inclusive.*
> (Royant, 2017, p. 154)

Importantly, the RISC model of evaluation exemplified in this chapter takes account of the fact that changes brought about by GCE interventions can be very subtle. For example, they can relate to the ease with which students use language to talk about a theme or to their willingness to express themselves (Allum, Lowe and Robinson, 2008, p. 61). Moreover, in contrast with mainstream audit and evaluation methodologies, "*the extent to which young people are able to challenge the activity itself*" (Allum, Lowe and Robinson, 2008, p. 103) can constitute a 'best result'.

References

Allum, E., Lowe, B. and Robinson, L. (2008). *How Do We Know It's Working? A Toolkit for Measuring Attitudinal Change*. Reading: RISC.

Allum, E., Lowe, B. and Robinson, L. (2010). *Are We Nearly There? A Self-Evaluation Framework for Global Citizenship*. Reading: RISC.

Allum, E., Lowe, B. and Robinson, L. (2015). *How Do We Know It's Working? Book 2, Tracking Changes in Pupils' Attitudes*. Reading: RISC.

Abebe, G., Abera, B., Asregid, D. and Teshome, N. (2014). *The World I Live In: A Report on Global Citizenship Activities Carried Out at Hawassa College of Teacher Education*. Unpublished, Hawassa CTE.

Bamber, P. (2016). *Transformative Education through International Service-Learning: Realising an Ethical Ecology of Learning*. London: Routledge.

Bamber, P., Bullivant, A. and Stead, D. (2013). Measuring attitudes towards global learning among future educators in England. *International Journal of Development Education and Global Learning*, 5(3), pp. 5–27.

Bliss, S. (2005). Australian global education values for a sustainable world. *Social Educator*, 23(2), pp. 26–38.

Bourn, D. and Hunt F. (2011). *Global Dimension in Secondary Schools*. DERC Research Paper No. 1. London: Institute of Education.

Critchley, M. and Unwin, R. (2008). *Whole School Development and the Global Dimension: Capturing Models of Practice Across the UK*. Sheffield: DECSY.

Huckle, J. (2017). Becoming critical: A challenge for the global learning programme? *International Journal of Development Education and Global Learning*, 8(3), pp. 63–84.

Lowe, B. (2008). Embedding global citizenship in primary and secondary schools: Developing a methodology for measuring attitudinal change. *International Journal of Development Education and Global Learning*, 1(1), pp. 59–64.

Oxfam. (2015). *Education for Global Citizenship: A Guide for Schools*. Oxford: Oxfam.

Pibilova, I. (2016). *Quality or Quantity: Final Evaluation Report*. Unpublished, Prague.

QCA. (2007). *The Global Dimension in Action: A Curriculum Planning Guide for Schools* London: QCA.

Royant, L. (2017). *Global Citizenship Education: A case study of the UK-based non-governmental organisation, Reading International Solidarity Centre*. Ph.D. thesis. University of Reading, Reading.

Simpson, J. (2017). 'Learning to unlearn' the charity mentality within schools. *Policy & Practice: A Development Education Review*, 25(Autumn), pp. 88–108. Available at: <www.developmenteducationreview.com/issue/issue-25/%E2%80%98learning-unlearn%E2%80%99-charity-mentality-within-schools>. Accessed 16 December 2018.

Storrs, G. (2010). Evaluation in development education: Crossing borders. *Policy & Practice: A Development Education Review*, 11(Autumn), pp. 7–21. Available at: <www.developmenteducationreview.com/issue/issue-11/evaluation-development-education-crossing-borders>. Accessed 16 December 2018.

Universities Participating in the Project

UK: Brighton University, Cambridge University, Canterbury Christ Church University, Chichester University, Cumbria University, London South Bank University, Oxford University, Oxford Brookes University, Reading University, Winchester University

Czech Republic: Charles University, Hradec Kralove University

Slovakia: Comenius University, Matej Bel University, Zvolen Technical University

Ireland: Church of Ireland College, Froebel College, Marina College, Mary Immaculate College, St Patrick's College

Ethiopia: Hawassa College

Conclusion

Empathy, Adaptability, Moderation and Sharing

Victoria W. Thoresen

Introduction

As the diverse chapters in this book indicate, Education for Sustainable Development and Global Citizenship (ESD/GC) is a means of implementing a global mission statement, the Sustainable Development 2030 Agenda. It is an effort, particularly as regard teacher education, to promote holistic, transformative, values-based learning. The authors of this compilation have provided us with useful observations about the role of education in nurturing peace, tolerance, justice and prosperity for all. These observations gain increased relevance when viewed against the backdrop of knowledge development and social change.

Learning processes are fluid and organic. They consist of the transferal of social norms, beliefs and experiences and of the exchange of understanding via dialogue. Transformative learning is dependent on the presence of critical thinking, caring collaboration and moments of creativity that convert past knowledge into constructive, new insights. The framework within which knowledge grows and social change occurs is that of a constantly evolving global community where systems are increasingly interdependent.

Awareness of the basic principles underlying the values upon which ESD/GC is based is essential when assessing teacher Education for Sustainable Development and Global Citizenship. Equally important is recognition of the complex role time and context play in determining both the contents and the practices of ESD/GC. Acknowledgement of roles and expectations is needed when evaluating teacher-learner interaction. Examination of each of these aspects contributes to further identifying what has been successful, what has created uncompromising tensions, and what may have been absent so far from ESD/GC.

Values: Fundamental Principles

The United Nations *Global Environmental Outlook 5* report (UNEP, 2012) emphasised the urgent need for a new narrative that examines more basic root causes and investigates the processes motivating behaviour change. The deeper causes and processes which influence behaviour are intimately connected to how people understand the basic principles—both material and non-material—directing the forces of existence. As Stephen Scoffham states in his chapter on 'In Search of Core Values', "values provide us with a sense of direction and help us to make choices".

Historian Arnold Toynbee (1961) claimed that changes in civilisation were due to humans' responses to their social and physical environment and are, therefore, an expression of human understanding of the principles underlying existence. Pitirim Sorokin (1967) built upon Toynbee's ideas by developing a theory of immanent change in which the dominate cultures were 'ideational' (value-driven, spiritually focussed) rather than 'sensate' (favouring empirical evidence and a practical, materialistic way of life). Ideational cultures arose from 'internal forces' resulting from the integration of peoples' understanding of principles and values in everyday situations. Social movements, whether they took the visage of resistance or revolution, or were of limited reformative nature, have always had an ideological foundation regardless of the material manifestations of the ideology. Cries of 'Liberté' were accompanied with 'Give us bread!' Demands for equality were the motivating force behind pleas to 'Free the slaves!' Value-driven internal forces are seen by many to be as powerful, if not more powerful, than external ones. Material culture is a physical reflection of one's principles and spiritual beliefs (Miller, 1995). The way people sing and dance, eat, build houses, dispose of waste, establish relationships, wage wars or build civilisations—all these and more indicate in a million ways what is deemed right or wrong, just or unjust, honourable or dishonourable, achievable or impossible, sustainable or extravagant, compassionate or hedonistic. Purpose and meaningfulness are recognised as major determinants of lifestyles and central drivers of behaviour and behaviour change.

Purpose and meaningfulness are contingent upon society's understanding of how the universe functions. With the increased recognition of the complexity and interdependency of systems, insights have emerged concerning the principles determining both material and non-material dimensions of existence. Some of the fundamental principles underlying the values of sustainable development can be briefly described as follows:

- *Connectivity and cohesion:* This principle refers to a power of attraction which holds atoms together, which keeps plants and animals as distinct beings, and which causes societies to cooperate rather than immediately kill each other off. When the power of connectivity and cohesion is lacking, disintegration occurs, and the mineral or plant or animal or human civilisation as we know it collapses. This power of attraction has been called many things: love, the life force, solidarity, etc. Without connectivity and cohesion, coexistence and collaboration do not exist. Some social scientists see the growth of empathy as related to connectivity and cohesion in the social world (Rifkin, 2009).

- *Transference and transmutation:* This principle refers to the processes of change and augmentative power of growth. There are universal processes of change and growth: minerals are absorbed into the life of a plant; a plant loses its life into that of an animal; an animal becomes a part of humans when it is eaten. Seen in terms of existing natural and social systems, one can recognise these transformations as having to do with growth, adaptation and evolution. In a social context, this leads to social learning processes which develop collective knowledge and action.
- *Finiteness:* This principle refers to the recognition of mortality and the existence of immortality. There are limits to growth, resource abundance/scarcity, planetary boundaries, life and death, and civilisations that exist and some that become extinct. Acknowledging and accepting the finiteness of resources, of time and space, contributes to our ability to manage the use of resources and to expand our understanding of moderation and sharing.

Empathy, adaptability, moderation and sharing are values that have acquired new meaning in light of these fundamental principles. They are not the equivalent of traditional concepts of the 'charity-mindset' that Jen Simpson refers to in her chapter in this book. Nor do they spring from an inflexible set of preconceived ideas. These values provide a framework for critical, reflective, even 'disruptive' learning practices that involve all participants, even the marginalised, in a constant re-evaluation of the state of the world and their individual role in contributing to change. These values supplement the common concepts of ESD/GC that deal with conservation, stewardship, resource management and equality. They are central elements in teacher training as they provide teachers with a foundation upon which to build learning processes.

Stephen Scoffham emphasises in his chapter that it is essential to give explicit visibility to the values on which ESD/GC rest. Alison Clark questions in her chapter, "How Do Teachers Engage with School Values and Ethos?", arguing that there is a critical need for inclusion of what she refers to as a 'values cycle', e.g. space in which the learner can reflect on the values in their lives and continually try to improve their actions in relation to them. In keeping with their conclusions, let us look more closely at why empathy, adaptability, moderation and sharing are vital to teacher training for ESD/GC.

Empathy is a source of global cohesion. Jean-Jacques Rousseau (1762/1907) stated that empathy springs from compassion and is a natural feeling, which, by moderating the violence of love of self in each individual, contributes to the preservation of the whole species. Some researchers, such as Jeremy Rifkin, claim that certain qualities, such as empathy, are inherent to human civilisation and that globalisation has served as a catalyst which has contributed to the development of empathy and its increased role in the modern world. Human civilisation, when examined from a historical meta-perspective, can be said to have evolved over centuries from small self-contained units to a large system of interdependent groups. The condition of one's family members has, throughout centuries, been paramount to most people. Their family has been there, beside them, in the same room. They could see their tears, hear their sighs and feel their pain. Today we see the tears, hear the sighs and feel the pain of people across the globe. The intimacy of globalisation and modern telecommunications has expanded the threshold of our awareness of how others exist. The expansion of collective identification has changed the meaning of solidarity, trustworthiness and empathy.

Empathy and social awareness are primarily aspects of individual behavioural development, and scientists disagree as to whether similar stages of development exist in relation to groups as large as nation states. From Adam Smith onwards, many voices claim that the loyalties and responsibilities of a government to its citizens demand a prioritising of initiatives and potential 'tradeoffs' in favour of the country's own well-being. However, never before has the large majority of people in the world been embedded in the complexly interconnected infrastructures and interactions of modern society. Never before has money, food, products and information moved across the globe twenty-four hours a day. Never before have so many travellers, workers—even germs—been transported from one corner of the planet to the other. Never before have so many people lived beyond the constrictions of fighting for survival. And never before has humanity faced such extensive destruction of the environment and the consequences this has on their very existence. These new conditions have expanded the individual's realm of contact and experience and have also contributed to the development of empathy as a significant element determining behaviour.

Jeremy Rifkin claims that empathy becomes the thread that weaves an increasingly differentiated and individualised population into an integrated social tapestry, allowing the social organism to function as a whole.

Adaptation springs from collective social learning. The 'augmentative power of growth' occurs when learning provides insights and alternatives. The drastic consequences of climate change, the rapid spread of environmental damage, the expansion of social illnesses, and the instability of governance and financial systems all point to the immediate need for intensified collaboration in order to deal with the overload of information, managing the many, often rapidly changing, messages received and thus create useable, relevant knowledge.

Social learning theories, be they those of Lev Vygotsky, Albert Bandura or others, usually focus on contextual, reciprocal aspects of an individual's learning process. 'Social learning' can also encompass the collective learning processes of groups and societies. These processes are contextual and reciprocal, and involve 'stakeholders' and 'minorities' in the learning processes. Collective social learning, as presented by Garry Jacobs and Harlan Cleveland (1999), refers to frank, open consultation where intellectual rigour and creativity are valued but where the voices of experience and indigenous knowledge are also heard, appreciated and taken into consideration:

> The outcome of this learning process is the organization of physical skills, social systems, and information, which are then utilized to improve the efficiency and effectiveness of human activities. It is a cyclical process in which people are continuously learning from past experiences and then applying that learning in new activities. This learning process culminates in a higher level of mental effort to extract the essence and common principles or ideas from society's organized physical experiences, social interactions and accumulated information and to synthesize them as conceptual knowledge.
>
> (Jacobs and Cleveland, 1999)

Moderation and sharing are necessary ways of managing resources. Finiteness and limits to growth are concepts which are not new. But advertisers continue to maintain that excessive consumption is every individual's right, and the majority of nations continue to measure growth in purely economic terms. The material and financial flows from industrialised countries in the North to the Global South continue to be unbalanced and disproportionate. The unequal distribution of wealth and use of resources increases. Producers claim it is due to consumer demand; consumers claim it is due to their rights as purchasers with money; governments claim it is due to their origins and national boundaries; media claims that marketing luxury is their only means of survival. Yet we have exceeded the finite carrying capacity of the earth and know that a majority of people still do not have their basic needs fulfilled.

Curriculum: Time and Place

Katie Carr and Leander Bindewald, in their chapter "'Zero Is Where the Fun Starts'—Evaluation for Values Co-production", confront us with a brief description of the historical evolution of processes of analysis. They point out that what is considered valuable can, and often does, vary over time. Religions, philosophies, social structures, politics and economics influence not only what is deemed measurable, but also what the content of curricula is and how it is taught.

Attempts at describing 'the' content of ESD/GC have been made over several decades. However, a universally accepted consensus as to what should be taught and how evades us still, and rightly so. Just as the definitions of sustainable development and global citizenship evolve, the content and pedagogy of ESD/GC are also continually evolving. Compelling and closely interrelated processes have forced individuals, as well as governments, to rethink how they live their lives and manage their communities. Awareness has grown of the many negative impacts that existing production processes and consumption patterns have on the environment. Large groups of people are being forced to deal with the serious consequences of climate change. Lifestyle-related illnesses, such as diabetes, obesity and addictions, are steadily increasing around the world. Increased travel, expanded use of social media and steadily intensifying immigration issues are among the many changes societies around the globe are facing. The debates about cultural heritage, well-being and development have brought to the foreground concerns about identity, universal equity and the very goal of development.

For many years, development was understood by many to mean economic advancement and access to the mass consumption of the global middle class. Despite the focus given to indicators such as health, literacy, shelter, environmental degradation, etc. by, among others, the Human Development Index, development was continued to be defined as economic progress almost regardless of the social or ecological toll such progress might take. The Millennium Development Goals (MDGs) of 2000–2015 embedded the concept that economic growth would lead to prosperity. The Goals were intended to raise the 'non-developed' countries from the quagmire they were in and help them have lives like those of the 'developed' countries. The Goals did manage to change the lives of millions across the globe, reducing child mortality, improving pre-natal health, providing education, promoting gender equality and combatting HIV/AIDS and malaria. Along the way, research emerged showing that increases in human development were not always dependent on economic wealth and that many 'developed' countries had increasing social, economic and environmental problems while some 'underdeveloped' countries were, in fact, successfully addressing these same problems. Global citizenship, once something few took seriously, became, during the time of the MDGs, an accepted topic of discussion, moving out of the shadows of doubt and realm of utopia.

As 2015 approached, the international community tried collectively to define the future it wanted. The Sustainable Development 2030 Agenda emerged from a long and convoluted, though uniquely democratic, negotiation process over several years. Parallel to the Sustainable Development Goal (SDG) process were the international efforts to deal with climate change. New definitions of development, prosperity, growth and well-being were agreed upon. Development was no longer seen as only having to do with wealth and Gross National Product. Sustainability was no longer solely limited to environmental issues. Global citizenship was no longer considered to only be a matter of human rights. More holistic, life-cycle approaches were focussed on in relation to planning and production, approaches that included social, economic and environmental dimensions. Poverty was identified as the greatest global challenge and its eradication an indispensable requirement for sustainable development. The 2030 Agenda called on all countries and all stakeholders, acting in collaborative partnership, to implement the SDGs.

Carr and Bindewald remind us in their chapter that "discourse is the fabric into which the image of our world is woven". Discourse sheds light on what is considered important to learn at a specific time and place. In light of the discourses that led up to and followed the adoption of the SDGs, specific issues have gained space in the ESD/GC curricula. Some disparate examples of these are the displacement of populations and the challenges of migration; the causes and effects of plastic pollution in the oceans; and corporate social responsibility, transparency and accountability.

Are teachers, then, expected to keep abreast of all the ongoing international debates in order to ensure that pertinent topics are reflected in the ESD/GC curricula? Angela Daly and Julie Brown, in their chapter "Results, Results, Results: Seeking Spaces for Learning in a European Global Learning and STEM Project", present a project that aims to increase the actuality and relevance of the STEM curricula in the project countries. This project developed resources that were highly contemporary, dealing with issues facing communities today. The need for updated, locally relevant learning resources is evident. Even the growth of the vocabulary of sustainable development can at times be daunting to a school teacher who is not abreast of recent changes. An example of this is the growth of the 'de' concepts, such as de-growth, de-coupling, de-materialising, etc.

The HEADSUP project, described in chapter 8 by Karen Pashby and Louise Sund, also demands that teachers continually stay up-to-date not only on the details of current events but also on the political profiles of countries, corporations and non-government organisations around the world. While this is an admirable expectation, it often proves difficult in practice, given the many obligations teachers must fulfil each day. Thus, it is important that the teachers who implement the HEADSUP methodology encourage the learners themselves to explore the context and background of the issues under consideration. Doing so is in itself an exercise in critical thinking, as online search motors often have inbuilt biases and available information may often come from prejudiced sources.

Several of the other authors in this compilation, such as Mallika Kanyal, Paulette Luff and Opeyemi Osadiya in their chapter "Advocating for Democratic, Participatory Approaches to Learning and Research for Sustainability in Early Childhood", contend that relational, active learning and critical reflection are the core conditions for ESD/GC. The implication is that content is secondary to methodology, assuming the learning process is contextual, experiential and participatory. While it is evident that participatory, critical, experiential learning increases the contextual dimension of learning, bringing 'home' abstract topics and making them personally relevant, pedagogy without content is like dancing without music. In this age of access to immediate information via digital channels, teachers are no longer fountains of facts; nor are they any longer expected to be completely familiar with all the rapid changes that occur around the world. Nonetheless, if ESD/GC is to have weighty impact, there should be a balance between updated content and relevant methodology.

Assessment: Facilitation and Progress

Maintaining a balance between content and methodology when facilitating learning is not an easy task, as several of the contributions in this book explain. Teaching in culturally diverse classrooms has its pitfalls and possibilities; creating participatory spaces is often challenging; and stimulating critical thinking, particularly in young children, is difficult. UNESCO states in "*Rethinking Education-Towards a Common Good?*":

> The changes in the world today are characterized by new levels of complexity and contradiction. These changes generate tensions for which education is expected to prepare individuals and communities by giving them the capability to adapt and to respond.
>
> (UNESCO, 2015, p. 9)

Zoi Nikiforidou, Zoe Lavin-Miles and Paulette Luff, in their chapter 'Bat Conservation in the Foundation Stage', write of the importance of enabling environments for the ESD/GC learning experience. They emphasise the value of assisting young children to identify and question issues at hand. This approach, which echoes Lev Vygotsky's theory of zones of proximal development, is an integral aspect of transformative learning. There are, however, other complementary elements of transformative learning that must not be overlooked. Two important elements are the fostering of caring collaboration and the promotion of creativity. These two are often labelled affective, as opposed to purely cognitive elements, and, thus, are not always considered important. Fortunately, Alison Clark, in her chapter "How Do Teachers Engage with School Values and Ethos?" clearly states that her research indicated that "for a curriculum to be made meaningful it needs to move from the cognitive to the affective".

Jack Mezirow (2000) built on Thomas Kuhn's (1962) theory of paradigm shifts and contended that transformational learning involves the expansion of cognitive consciousness based on altering deep set perspectives and world views. In response to Mezirow's approach, Larry Daloz (2012) highlighted the intuitive and psycho-social elements of transformative learning. Caring falls into the category of psycho-social elements and is used to mean feeling interest or concern, expressing compassion. Creativity in the transformative learning context is *defined* as the tendency to generate or recognise ideas, alternatives or possibilities that may be useful in solving problems, communicating with others, or entertaining oneself or others (Franken, 1982).

Learners, particularly those in early childhood, can easily identify with and appreciate a caring attitude exhibited by the teacher. Most of the time they have experienced caring concern in their homes. Caring collaboration is a means of indicating to the learner that the teacher is genuinely engaged in the learning process, not only in transferring curriculum content. Many early childhood educators have mastered the art of caring collaboration, kindly assisting the youngster along the path of increased insight into how the universe functions. By doing so, they cast off the cloak of authority and power and join the learner in a collective process. Rosalind Duke, in her chapter "Restorative Practice: Modelling Key Skills of Peace and Global Citizenship", maintains that restorative practices are not only useful in conflict resolution but also as a way of establishing an atmosphere of openness and respect. "[T]he shift from denouncing difference to being willing to listen and explore that difference is essential", Duke continues. Listening and exploring together are vital aspects of caring collaboration.

Several of the chapters in this compilation deal with assessment of ESD/GC. Both content and methodology are examined. While the Make the Link Project described in Angela Daly's and Julie Brown's chapter fosters systems thinking and connectivity, few of the cases presented in the book highlight creativity or consider how expressions of creativity can be assessed. The absence of a focus on creativity in ESD/GC is common. Evaluation of ESD/GC is most often carried out as a review of topics dealt with. Occasionally, as in the case of the OMEP ECERS-R Rating Scale, evaluation is based on the subjective interpretation of the individual making the assessment. Nonetheless, creativity has been perceived in diverse learning theories as a desirable outcome of learning. In some theories, such as Engestrøm's expansive learning theory (Engestrøm, 1987), creativity is seen as a means to an end, a path along which learning occurs. In light of traditional transformational learning, creativity appears to have a double role. The recognition of new ideas arises from the alteration of perceptions. The generation of alternatives or new solutions brings the elements of imagination and empowerment into play. Both are important in relation to ESD/GC.

Transformational learning is about individual change, new insights, altered behaviour. Katie Carr and Leander Bindewald ask, in their chapter in this book, whether critical discourse analysis can effectively contribute to, among other things, assessing individual progress. Their answer points to how such evaluation stimulates a continual reflective and discursive process. Assuming that knowledge about sustainable development and global citizenship is constantly evolving, and given that the present international community is constantly undergoing social change, assessment that focuses on progress in relation to transformational learning looks at an essential part of ESD/GC.

Another vital aspect for assessment of ESD/GC is interdisciplinarity. "Educators have to create a learning ecology that helps people make connections, create networks and gestalt switch", suggests Arjen Wals (2010), an internationally renowned ESD educator. Zoi Nikiforidou, Zoe Lavin-Miles and Paulette Luff clearly describe how the Bat Conservation Project is connected to various areas of learning and development. The integrated approach they present reflects a natural interdisciplinarity and assists teachers and learners in making connections between illnesses, urban development, cultural biases and the loss of biodiversity. The HEADSUP project methodology in chapter 8 also provides a useful interdisciplinary approach to ESD/GC themes.

Conclusion

ESD/GC is a field in constant flux in a global community in continual evolution. This compilation provides valuable perspectives on teacher education for ESD/GC. The contributions have pointed out the need for identifying values such as compassionate connectedness based on empathy, adaptability, moderation and sharing. They have suggested relevant methodologies and considered the strengths and weaknesses of various assessment models. But, questions remain. Are we sufficiently aware of the underlying principles connected to issues and dilemmas of ESD/GC? How does ESD/GC stimulate significant transformation of both the learner's inner life and external conditions? How can ESD/GC better help learners acquire an understanding of power structures, complex systems and intricate processes while strengthening insight into interconnections? How can ESD/GC assist learners in recognising the short-term and long-term consequences of their personal choices? These and other questions still need to be dealt with in greater depth in order to further improve teacher education for ESD/GC.

While we are searching for answers, it is essential that we recognise that understanding changes and grows. What was once thought to be right may not always be so. In order for learners to function in a world of constant change, it is important that ESD/GC contributes to an even greater extent to the development of empathy, adaptability, moderation and sharing.

References

Daloz, L. A. (2012). *Mentor: Guiding the Journey of Adult Learners*. 2nd edition. San Francisco, CA: Jossey Bass/Wiley.

Engestrøm, Y. (2010 [1987]). Studies of expansive learning: Foundations, findings and future challenges. *Educational Research Review*, 5(1), pp. 1–24.
Franken, R. E. (1982). *Human Motivation*. 3rd edition. Monterey, CA: Brooks/Cole.
Jacobs, Garry and Cleveland, Harlan. (1999). *Social Development Theory*. Available at: <www.motherservice.org/Essays/SocialDevTheory.htm>
Kuhn, T. (1962). *The Structure of Scientific Revolutions*. Chicago, IL: University of Chicago Press.
Mezirow, J. (2000). *Learning as Transformation: Critical Perspectives on a Theory in Progress*. San Francisco, CA: Jossey Bass.
Miller, D. (1995). *Acknowledging Consumption*. London: Routledge.
Rifkin, J. (2009). *The Empathic Civilization*. New York: Penguin Group Publishers.
Rousseau, J. J. (1762). *Emile; or, Treatise on Education*. Translated by W. H. Wayne. New York: Appleton and Co., 1907.
Sorokin, P. (1967). Causal-Functional and Logico-Meaningful Integration. In: N. J. Demerath and R. A. Peterson (eds.), *System, Change and Conflict*, 99–113. New York: Free Press.
Toynbee, A. J. (1961). *A Study of History*. Oxford: Oxford University Press.
UNEP. (2012). Environment for the Future we Want. *Global Environment Outlook 5*. Malta: Progress Press.
UNESCO. (2015). *Rethinking Education: Towards a global common good?* Paris: UNESCO.
Wals, A. E. J. (2010). *Message in a Bottle: Learning Our Way Out of Unsustainability*. Inaugural Lecture, 27 May, Wageningen University, The Netherlands. Available at: <http://library.wur.nl/WebQuery/wurpubs/fulltext/157118>

Index

For Product Safety Concerns and Information please contact our EU representative GPSR@taylorandfrancis.com
Taylor & Francis Verlag GmbH, Kaufingerstraße 24, 80331 München, Germany

www.ingramcontent.com/pod-product-compliance
Ingram Content Group UK Ltd.
Pitfield, Milton Keynes, MK11 3LW, UK
UKHW020939180425
457613UK00019B/464

* 9 7 8 0 3 6 7 7 2 7 4 3 7 *